THE ART OF OSCAR WILDE

THE ART OF

OSCAR WILDE

EPIFANIO SAN JUAN, JR.

PRINCETON, NEW JERSEY

PRINCETON UNIVERSITY PRESS

1967

FOR DELIA

Contents

Acknowledgments

I wish to thank Professor Jerome H. Buckley for his constructive criticism of the original manuscript and Professor Douglas Bush for various improvements. Professor Howard Mumford Jones gave helpful and warm encouragement. I am grateful to Professors William Van O'Connor, Brom Weber, Robert Wiggins, Celeste Wright, and my other colleagues at Davis for their generosity and trust.

I am indebted to the Rockefeller Foundation, and to Dr. Boyd Compton in particular, for support of my research at Harvard University (1963-65); to the Committee on Research, University of California, Davis, for a faculty grant which made possible the revision of the manuscript.

My wife Delia Aguilar-San Juan has sustained me throughout the writing of this book, and to her I owe a gratitude beyond words.

E. S. J. JR.

Davis, California
March 1966

THE ART OF OSCAR WILDE

Introduction

With the appearance of the first substantial collection of Wilde's letters, superbly edited by Rupert Hart-Davis, students of Wilde's writings now possess an assuredly reliable body of facts on which a reassessment of his work can be based. Almost all the critical evaluations of his achievement, except for highly specialized papers on sources and influences, vitiate themselves in accepting biased popular judgments of the writer's personality. Dubious speculations on motives behind the poems or plays have served as implicit assumptions of criticism to the extent that we scarcely know why Wilde still occupies a position of some importance in literary and intellectual history. Can the works sustain and justify a persevering scrutiny? Can any reader still derive pleasure from the "imitative" poems, for example.

The literary fashion today goes for astringent wit, irony, paradox, and subtle understatement. Wilde's "baroque" exercises, his melodramatic and extravagant posings, easily arouse censure for emptiness and vulgarity. From one point of view, his attitudinizings are often sentimentally dishonest. Is Wilde's aestheticism as objectionable now, after so many revolutions in taste, as when Max Nordau, in 1895, condemned it as criminal and degenerate?[1] What would be a valid criterion for Wilde's writings which would not jeopardize them by intruding preconceptions of the author's character?

Sir Arthur Quiller-Couch, recalling his Victorian youth, indicates one type of reaction: "The aesthetic business was in decline. Oscar Wilde had gone down. . . . Never, either then or later in London, did I meet with anyone who held Wilde to be a writer of importance. The legend of his influence in the nineties, though one has watched it growing, is

[1] *Degeneration* (2nd edn.; New York, 1895), pp. 319-22.

to men of my age a purely incredible myth."[2] Yeats, on the other hand, memorialized Wilde's passionate and masterful personality, his love of ritual and style, and the masculine energy displayed by the poet of *The Ballad of Reading Gaol*. Yeats thought that Wilde, "a man of action, a born dramatist, finding himself overshadowed by old famous men he could not attack, for he was of their time and shared its admirations, tricked and clowned to draw attention to himself."[3] Just as Yeats emphasized Wilde's mask, the complex interplay of gesture and wit, Joyce equally celebrated Wilde as a "court jester to the English," calling attention to his "keenness, generosity, and a sexless intellect."[4]

In recent years Wilde's stature has undergone novel if not radical alteration. W. H. Auden is one of the contemporary men of letters who has discerned in Wilde's character the lineaments of pre-existentialist man: a "phony prophet but serious playboy," he typifies the modern "alienated soul."[5] The rehabilitation of Wilde's public image, pursuing the changes in cultural norms and ideological temper of the times, reflects the infinitely suggestive quality of his work. And though the interpretations by Auden or Roditi may at times prove arbitrary and too "far out," they nonetheless perform the important service of ushering us into a state of alert and articulate discrimination, no longer subject to the spell of hackneyed, generalized opinions. With the growing interest in Wilde—Auden and Richard Ellmann have devoted long serious commentaries to his personality and his literary achievement—the reader is encouraged to

[2] "Books and Other Friends," *Fifty Years; A Composite Picture of the Period 1882-1932 by 27 Contributors to the Times*, ed., G. M. Trevelyan (New York, 1932), p. 47.

[3] "Introduction," *The Oxford Book of Modern Verse* (New York, 1936), p. vii.

[4] *The Critical Writings of James Joyce*, eds., Ellsworth Mason and Richard Ellmann (London, 1959), pp. 202, 205.

[5] "A Playboy of the Western World: St. Oscar, the Homintern Martyr," *Partisan Review*, XVII (April 1950), 394.

examine the writings in order to determine their significance
in the light of contemporary literary appreciation. It would
appear on a revaluation of the works that Wilde's continu-
ing vitality and cogency lie nowhere else but in the moral
discriminations which he exercised on his subject. And this
trait is itself a reflection of the artist's position in his milieu.
Stuart Sherman was fundamentally correct when he stated
that Wilde's "art is inseparable from his morality."[6]

Of the nature of this "morality," there have been conflicting notions. Counted as one of the "perplexed prophets,"
Wilde is said to have possessed a heightened social consciousness which coincided with the time-spirit of the
eighties and nineties.[7] Like the reformers and the utopians,
Morris and Shaw among them, he wanted to redeem society
not so much by purifying the individual—as Carlyle and
Arnold hoped to do—but by altering the social structure, the
atmosphere of mental and physical activity in English culture. One reviewer dilates on the message of "The Young
King" to the exploited working class.[8] But of course Wilde
was not so deadly serious as the socialist commentators now
presume him to be, least of all in his fairy tales. Even that
enthusiastic "testament," *The Soul of Man Under Socialism*,
which is more an exercise in irony than a religious tract, presents ideas by indirection. It has more meanings than the
simple advocacy of "socialism." The understanding of its
implications depends on a grasp of the formal verbal techniques and the logic of the imagination which Wilde brought
to bear on the exposition of abstract thought.

How then can one accurately express the quality of
Wilde's achievement so as to convey its enduring pro-
vocativeness? To Archibald Henderson, Wilde's value lies

[6] *Critical Woodcuts* (New York, 1926), p. 198.
[7] Gaylord C. Le Roy, *Perplexed Prophets* (Philadelphia, 1953),
p. 154.
[8] Alick West, *The Mountain and the Sunlight* (London, 1958),
p. 134.

mainly in "the palliative charm of his personality," in "the orchidaceous modernity and brilliant exoticism" of his art.[9] Auden was impressed by Wilde as a performer, "a verbal musician of the first order," who dramatized his thoughts in a series of vivid improvisations inevitably climaxed by a "nightmare Pantomime Transformation scene" when Wilde was convicted for sexual aberration and sentenced to hard labor.[10]

The course of Wilde's life may be said to approximate the movement of Greek tragedy. But its tragic hero is not Prometheus but the dandy who embodies the force of revelation. For while the dandy affirms life as "a supreme mode of fiction," he continually destroys those fictions he creates. This attractive type in the works—the villains of the plays, Lord Arthur Savile, the Canterville ghost, Lord Henry in *Dorian Gray*—ultimately derives its virile strength from the absurdities and incongruities of life.

Wilde's skill for serious joking and for "romantic pantomime" signifies the necessity for the adoption of poses or masks. He recognized the value of Browning's technique, in *The Ring and the Book*, of varying viewpoints to elucidate an ambiguous truth. In "The Truth of Masks," in "Pen, Pencil and Poison," in his stories and fairy tales, Wilde dramatized the conflict of interests, of prismatic glimpses of reality arising from man's necessarily limited understanding. Whether by sarcastic understatement or arresting hyperbole, he tried to encompass as many aspects of a situation as he could. He exploited the dialogue in *Intentions* in full awareness of its correspondence with an outlook which, unable to invoke any absolute sanction, consistently relied on personal certitudes. Using the dialogue as a scheme for comparing ideas, he was able to illuminate from as many sides as

[9] *European Dramatists* (Cincinnati, 1913), p. 257.
[10] "An Improbable Life," *The New Yorker* (March 9, 1963), 171.

possible the complexity of a given subject. Wilde's showman-
ship, in rhetorical or symbolic trappings, took the measure of
the milieu in a clown's funny and bluntly honest way.

The Wildean dandy, all-knowing and impeccably con-
scientious, performs the function of nineteenth-century
England which, in G. M. Young's words, is "to disengage
the disinterested intelligence, to release it from the entangle-
ments of party and sect—one might almost add, of sex—
and to set it operating over the whole range of human life
and circumstance."[11] This is also the sovereign ideal behind
the meditations and sermons of the Victorian prophet:
Arnold, Ruskin, Newman, Carlyle, and others.

One example of the disinterested intelligence in action
may be perceived in Wilde's definition of art as a kind of
"lying." Art, precisely because it is indefinite and infinitely
suggestive, is a "lie." The "liar's" purpose is artistic: "to
charm, to delight, to give pleasure." The dandy, whose credo
is "Truth is entirely and absolutely a matter of style," is
the exemplary "liar." "Lying for its own sake," or "the telling
of beautiful untrue things," is the privilege and proper aim of
art.[12] The whole essay on "The Decay of Lying" enlarges on
this equation of "lying" with art. Wilde performs here a
transvaluation of values. Given a new context, "lying" denotes "an accurate description of what has never occurred."
Like "lying," the word "insincerity" assumes a new reference:
it becomes "a method by which we can multiply our
personalities." If the artist appears insincere, that is because
he refuses to conform to the stock responses of the crowd.
Uninhibited by any rigid code of morals, the artist can carry
out his acts of transcendence when he projects his individu-

11 *Victorian England: Portrait of an Age* (Oxford Paperback edn.,
London, 1960), p. 186.
12 Frank Kermode traces the background of this idea of the artist
as "liar" in *Romantic Image* (Vintage edn., New York, 1964), pp.
44-48.

ality in the shape of new sensations, original forms and points of view. Wilde sees in the "lie" of art his ideals of novelty and fidelity to inward revelations.

The personality, Wilde submits, transcends mere intellect; for "it is a dynamic force of its own, and is often as superbly unintelligent as the great forces of nature."[13] Liberation and expansion of consciousness attends every movement of the personality; personality sustains dandiacal wit, in which the mind is brought into full play, happily embellishing façades, and then stripping them of ornamentation with ceremonial aplomb. In the paradoxical epigrams of the dandy prevails "the rhythm of reassuring platitudes, of proverbial certainties, and cutting across them the intransigencies of individual thought," giving the pleasure of "affirming the *ancien régime* and rebelling against it at the same time."[14] While Yeats regarded the mask as a figure of the mind's metamorphosis and its possibilities for cyclic renewal, Wilde regarded the mask of antithetical personalities—the dandies versus the sentimentalists—as an instrument for freeing the mind from fixed attachments, from the constricting hold of obsolete norms. Both for Yeats and Wilde, the mask allowed the mind to exercise its energy on "the whole range of human life and circumstance."

Throughout his career Wilde never ceased discoursing on the supremacy of art over life. What he wrote and what he lived through both testify in the fullest degree to his involvement, even if at times by negative skepticism, in the human predicament. In *Salome*, for instance, Wilde captures the moods of a sensibility—by turns pessimistic, subjective, relativist, and detached—in terms of dramatic relationships mastered by a single obsession. Whatever mood or situation Wilde explores, there emerges a world out-

[13] Quoted by H. Montgomery Hyde, *Oscar Wilde: The Aftermath* (London, 1963), p. 493.
[14] Richard Ellmann, "Romantic Pantomime in Oscar Wilde," *Partisan Review*, XXX (Fall 1963), 349.

look circumscribed by the cultural ambience of nineteenth-century England.[15]

At first glance it would seem difficult to admit that Wilde, whose fame as an aesthete took on the proportions of a *Punch* hero, or Bunthorne in *Patience*, could be so concerned with a terrifying "romantic agony," or with what J. Hillis Miller calls "the disappearance of God" from the horizon of that turbulent century. Unlikely as it might seem, Wilde was in fact also disturbed by issues that transcend mere private dilemmas. Two of the thematic motifs that suggest his preoccupation with the human condition are: sin in "The Sphinx," in *Dorian Gray*, in *Salome*, in the comic villains, in *Reading Gaol*; and, in almost all his writings, the experience of doubt and dread arising from the clash between pagan appetite and Christian morality. Wilde's sudden leaps from proud self-indulgence to humility and contrite self-abnegation (as in the letters, or in *De Profundis*) fall into what has been called the secular pattern of conversion, which is incipient or overtly fulfilled in the lives of the artists and intellectuals of the age. This pattern is dominated by a pervasive feeling of guilt, damnation, and a foreboding of tragic failure. Initiated first by an apprehension that the truths of the self no longer coincide with the facts of the ordinary world, the experience culminates in the tension of the "two voices" that drive the individual to ultimate withdrawal, indifference, or surrender to some absolute creed, religious or secular.

Readers have noted how Wilde's fictional characters often move toward an exposure of their own true selves, toward a clearing up of mystery. One observes this tendency in the recurrent theme of the protagonist's search for identity; the personages in the plays have either a secret past or an unknown deed around which the action pivots. Dorian

[15] See William A. Madden, "The Victorian Sensibility," *Victorian Studies*, VII (September 1963), 67-97.

Gray's picture, for example, propels the whole train of events leading to the disclosure of his true self. In the social comedies, dandiacal wit undeceives and, in the process, evokes sudden realizations and discoveries. Sensibility and intelligence fuse in Wilde's farcical wit, producing "a most instructive commentary not only on the manners of his time, but also on its possibilities for good as well as evil."[16]

It is certainly misleading to focus attention only on the "decadent" affectations of Wilde's style, on the idiosyncratic use of "perfection," "exquisite," "mystical," "charming," "delicate," without heeding the conventions which govern the language, thought, and uniformity of tone of his works. Amid the paraphernalia of the age—antimacassars, Biedermeier furniture, the Albert Memorial—Wilde emerges with a self-imposed, stylized costume. The borrowed clothes he has retailored for himself to suit his own personal needs become in due time worthy of parody by *Patience* and by *Punch*. Beyond the flamboyant knee-breeches, velvet doublet, pale lavender gloves, thick flowing hair, is the framework of mind which multiplied posings and converted them into modes of giving value to reality. The pose then transformed the artist into the dandy who became the hero of the age, whether in Baudelaire's artificial paradise or in Yeats' later Byzantium. In Wilde's case, the dandy lived on a precarious ledge between the ivory tower (the self) near the seashore and the glamor of the city (the world). Existence seems to have congealed in the pose; and the emblematic gesture, the symbolic stance, has become Wilde's unique *Lebensform*. Form and feeling crystallized in the mask by means of which Wilde confronted the discords between man and the forces of civilization and fate.

It is therefore difficult to perceive Wilde's value today if we simply dismiss the oddity of a freakish, cynical jester

[16] H. V. Routh, *Money, Morals and Manners as Revealed in Modern Literature* (London, 1935), p. 187.

acting as social prophet and arbiter of taste in a situation where his audience has either retreated into the "buried self" or surrendered to the lure of material comfort and smug respectability. We need, in short, a preliminary understanding of Wilde's ironical method. A. E. Dyson provides a clue to the sharp relevance of his social satire: "The unusualness of Wilde's irony is that the norms are to be found neither in what he says nor in the reversal of what he says, but in the confrontation of moral humbug parading as righteousness with moral goodheartedness parading as flippancy."[17] Wilde is, after all, in the tradition of "metaphysical" wit. His social comedies have of late profited from formalistic analysis; one critic, for instance, delineates the pattern of the archetypal "courtship dance" in *The Importance of Being Earnest*.[18]

The ironical pose, the shifting of perspectives, and the playing up of multiple senses of words can all be viewed as functions of the dramatic sense. They result from the attitude that masks or personae are necessary to the task of embodying a person's philosophy of life in a time when commonly agreed standards of valuation are lacking. Like the leaders and statesmen of the age, writers as a rule enact their chosen roles. They amplify their public voice, sounding like expert ventriloquists, striving to mediate between their anguished yearning for a harmonious order in culture and society, and their immediate knowledge that everywhere "mere anarchy is loosed upon the world." Wilde shares a predicament similar to those of Tennyson, Arnold, Browning, and many others who experienced the difficulties of establishing the self's identity in their individual careers.

Wilde's mind, on the evidence of his poems and plays, did not on its own initiative always move in the realm of ab-

17 "The Socialist Aesthete," *The Listener*, LXVI (August 24, 1961), 273.
18 Otto Reinert, "The Courtship Dance in *The Importance of Being Earnest*," *Modern Drama*, I (February 1959), 256-57.

stractions. His true vocation as a verbal performer clearly demanded an audience. But the meaning and tone of his attitudes inhere in their literary forms, in the distinctive wit that profoundly animates them. Wit refers to the perception of unity in dissimilar facts, or to the violent yoking of contraries, which produce a sudden release of repressed instincts leading to an epiphany. Wit employs ironic juxtapositions for the exposure of deceit, distortions, and fraud, which in turn brings about a clarification of the strange element in the commonplace. Wit also satirizes, turns half-truths topsy-turvy, wrecks comfortable platitudes.

The atmosphere of religious instability fostered the kind of spontaneous, critical play of the mind that is in essence Wilde's wit. Wit furnished the introspective self with an efficient vehicle for sublimating obsessions and externalizing disproportions. Wit, with its purgative effect, was able to control the "multitudinous stream" of phenomena and render it intelligible to men. Wit thus exorcised the irrational demons of the self. To Wilde, "Morality is simply the attitude we adopt towards people whom we personally dislike." One of his spokesmen remarks: "If one tells the truth, one is sure, sooner or later, to be found out"—that is, depending on whose truth is involved and in what context the utterance is made. Imitating the rhythm of popular proverbs, Wilde's wit assures but subtly undermines; he wants to belong, yet rebels.

It has been the fashion to explain away Wilde's contradictions by reference to his homosexuality, his pampered youth, and other eccentricities which have found their most exciting exponent in Frank Harris. Who is the authentic Wilde—the devil's advocate, Bunthorne, or any of Wilde's fictive protagonists?[19] In his novel, we watch Dorian Gray

[19] See Arthur H. Nethercot, "Oscar Wilde and the Devil's Advocate," *PMLA*, LIX (September 1944), 833-50; and also Edmund Wilson, "Oscar Wilde: One Must Always Seek What Is Tragic," *The New Yorker* (June 29, 1946), 70.

"wonder at the shallow psychology of those who conceive the ego in man as a thing, simple, permanent, reliable and of one essence. To him man was a being with myriad lives and myriad sensations, a complex multiform creature that bore within itself strange legacies of thought and passion, and whose very flesh was tainted with the monstrous maladies of the dead."[20] We read in *De Profundis* Wilde's claim to immortality: "to truth itself I gave what is false no less than what is true as its rightful province, and showed that the false and the true are merely forms of intellectual existence."[21] Here we touch directly the insights, the ideas of perspective and of a relativistic point of view toward reality, that impart philosophical weight and relevance to Wilde's creative work.

From Pater to Yeats and Henry James, the fundamental problem of the artist expressed itself in the quest of the permanent structure of truth. At the outset of the seventies and eighties, the Victorian moral premise of ethical sympathy through feeling considerably weakened; skepticism flourished and doubts intensified under the impact of radical thought and worsening social disunity precipitated by local and international crises. A case in point is the aging Ruskin who, when he attacked Whistler's paintings and by implication the principles of new artistic trends, exemplified thereby the split between moral determination and aesthetic detachment. Pater, the contemplative artist, sought not to judge or act but to comprehend with the aid of classical "fixities." He sought for the best that has been thought and said, for a culture that would refine and realize the essence of a soul. Marius, Sebastian van Storck, and Florian Deleal in "The Child in the House," among others—these heroes dedicated themselves to absolute self-expression. Self-

<hr>

[20] *The Portable Oscar Wilde*, ed., Richard Aldington (New York, 1964), p. 300.
[21] *Letters*, p. 466.

expression as an art, the exaltation of temperament as the motive for spontaneity and style, art's supremacy over nature and convention in its harmonious fusion of form and content —these strands combined in Pater's integral experience of the flux of time.[22] Wilde, likewise, embodied this same vision in nostalgia for a lost purity and innocence in *De Profundis*; in most of the tales in *A House of Pomegranates* and *The Happy Prince*; in the breathless complication and resolution of *Dorian Gray*; in the pivotal disclosures of the poetic drama and society comedies.

One can argue that the problem of time, whether in the form of unravelling of plot or the motifs of the quest and the journey, pervades Wilde's works no less than those of other Victorian artists. Jerome Buckley suggests the persistent engagement of the Victorian artist with the fourth dimension of reality, time:

> The Victorians were clearly moving into the world of modern physics where all things would exist in a time-continuum and the fixed object would become but a range of charged energies and continuous events. But they strove more strenuously than we have striven to find meanings in the present process. In his never quite successful paintings, Rossetti—to cite an interesting example—paid far more attention to color than to draftsmanship with the result that the edges of the object wavered and the image of solidity yielded to the impression of change and a changeful life beyond the canvas.[23]

Change of orientation toward time, subsuming the idea of process and permanence, is a fairly common thematic concern in the literature of the period. When we reach the closing years of the century, the human mind seems to ex-

[22] John Pick, "Divergent Disciples of Walter Pater," *Thought*, XXIII (March 1948), 114-28.
[23] "The Fourth Dimension of Victorianism," *The Victorian Newsletter*, No. 21 (Spring 1962), 3.

perience an anxiety as it expects a fulfillment of some kind, the nature of which becomes the central subject of dream and speculation. The temper of decadence heavily accentuates the "neurosis"; the syndrome assumes bewildering shapes which somehow elude Arthur Symons' clinical inferences: "an intense self-consciousness, a restless curiosity in research, an over-subtilizing refinement upon refinement, a spiritual and moral perversity."[24] Together with such characteristics, we perceive the presence of antithetical features existing side by side: a cult of action and of inaction, diabolism and evangelism, artificiality and naturalism, and so forth. There is, in short, a massive and complex structure of dispositions, attitudes, and values which defy any simple categorical accounting in the ordinary literary histories.[25]

Underlying all these crisscrossing currents of thought and belief is the preoccupation with experience as a mode of orientation for the self-seeking identity. Romanticism of course emphasized this focus on individual consciousness as a creative power, an inventor of values, an artificer of reality. Romanticism aspired to establish unity between man and nature amid the seeming discords of fact and feeling in actual life. By the middle of the century, however, art and literature began to stress with threatening implications the chaotic flux of history in terms of geological as well as biological time. Ambiguity, indecision, "prismatic" truths, historicism in Biblical scholarship, "the alien vision," ultra-self-consciousness, divided wills—all these features of spiritual history may be endlessly illustrated with quotations from

[24] "The Decadent Movement in Literature," *London Quarterly Review*, 129 (January 1918), 89-103. See also Clyde de L. Ryals, "The 19th Century Cult of Inaction," *Tennessee Studies in Literature*, IV (1959), 51-60.

[25] See Paul West, "A Note on the 1890's," *English*, XII (Summer 1958), 54-57; Russell M. Goldfarb, "Late Victorian Decadence," *Journal of Aesthetics and Art Criticism*, XX (Summer 1962), 369-73; Clyde de L. Ryals, "Toward a Definition of *Decadent* as Applied to British Literature of the Nineteenth Century," *JAAC*, XVII (September 1958), 89-92.

poems, notebooks, autobiographies. To Yeats, sensibility, the "structure of feeling" which appears coherent in balanced and stable civilizations, had lost its "artificially created illusions."[26]

In *De Profundis*, Wilde defined his symbolic relation to the age in his acceptance of life as "complex and relative." The complex web of "multitudinous facts," wrote Arnold in "On the Modern Element in Literature," has called forth the distinguishing effect and quality of contemporary imaginative literature. In the conclusion to the *Renaissance*, in his essays on style and on the romantic poets, Pater considered the relativity of values as a justification for the aesthetic susceptibility of the artist to the process of experience. Wilde gathered together these two strands in Victorian thinking and unified them through comic ambiguity and paradox and through the concept of masks and of dramatic illusion. In practice he imparted to his works the organic force of a temperament at once unique and representative; unique in the matter of style and the manner of composition, but also representative in the matter of historical and intellectual awareness of the problems of his time. As Symons testifies in this regard: "Wilde is a typical figure, alike in 'the art of life' and the art of literature, and, if he might be supposed for a moment to represent anything but himself, he would be the perfect representative of all that is meant by the word 'Decadence' as used in the 'nineties' of last century and the 'noughts' of this."[27]

Despite the numerous studies on the influence of Pater and Arnold on Wilde, the singular importance of the "Wildean" quality in his criticism of art and literature has hardly received any comment with an attempt at synthesis. Few have considered the pertinacity of his random speculations, for example:

[26] *Autobiography* (New York, 1938), p. 326.
[27] *A Study of Oscar Wilde* (London, 1930), p. 24.

Modern life is complex and relative. Those are its two distinguishing notes. To render the first we require atmosphere with its subtlety of *nuances*, of suggestion, of strange perspectives: as for the second we require background. That is why Sculpture has ceased to be a representative art; and why Music *is* a representative art; and why Literature is, and has been, and always will remain the supreme representative art.[28]

In *Axel's Castle*, Edmund Wilson mentions Wilde sporadically in his treatment of Yeats' work. In *The Last Romantics* Graham Hough scarcely deals with Wilde as a thinker in his own right, though he pays some attention to *Dorian Gray*. The accounts of Winwar, Pearson, and their numerous predecessors are interesting and illuminating for their biographical facts, though frequently gossip and fable intermingle with documentary reports. Most critical-biographical essays are vitiated by their eccentricity, partisanship, or wayward diagnosis. There are some recent inquiries concerning "the truth of masks," which Yeats adopted as an axiom and made the premise of his system, *A Vision*; and the nature of the paradox and other devices that shape "virtual illusions," as illustrated by dialogue, confession, fantasy, comedy, and allegorical narrative.[29] But so far there exists no thorough account of the varied motivations and topics which recur in *Dorian Gray*, in the poetic drama and the comedies, in the essays and poems. What is needed above all is a critical scrutiny of the individual works and an appreciation of the vision of truth embodied in forms which are significant and enduring. This study is written with that aim in mind.

[28] *Letters*, p. 460.
[29] See George Steiner, "Life of Letters," *Kenyon Review*, xxv (1963), 176-77; N. J. Endicott, "The Letters of Oscar Wilde," *University of Toronto Quarterly*, xxxii (April 1963), 297-300; Roy Harrod "Oscar Wilde," *Times Literary Supplement* (July 27, 1962), 541; also "Imitating Art," *TLS* (June 29, 1962), 469-71.

Wilde's "stock"—to place him in the critical market—may be in for a long-anticipated boom, especially now that the taste of the audience favors irony, paradox, and ambiguity of meaning. For one thing, recent reviews of the collected letters cry out for an intensive discussion and evaluation of his writings. It is actually because of "the amount of felt life" the works give that we are compelled to see in Wilde a contemporary of our times. Just as Henry James and the metaphysical poets are intimately with us in their modernity, so Wilde proves a sensitive and instructive companion in our present predicament. His personality fascinates our minds; we are curious about the literary expressions of such a personality. Though he confused the spheres of art and morality, Wilde nonetheless wrestled with realities as painful and inescapable as those we confront daily. His passionate engagement with the human condition also embraced the function of literature in society and the value of art to life.

Like James, Wilde tried to fashion a method whereby the critical intelligence of the artist, in projecting a world of its own, transforms psychic experience into an art-work whose form and content are indivisibly bound, reflecting the texture, the fabric of life itself. He believed that fiction "can make things probable; can call for imaginative and realistic credence; can, by force of mere style, compel us to believe."[30] Such a statement implied a humanistic interpretation of literature as both *dulce et utile*. Interest in Wilde's critical and aesthetic principles will naturally lead us to consider further what profit can be gained from a study of his works. Even his early poems, one will find, yield a pleasure commensurate with the generosity and intelligence one brings to them.

[30] Cf. Edouard Roditi, "Oscar Wilde and Henry James," *University of Kansas City Review*, xv (Autumn 1948), 52-56.

I · Image and Rhetoric in
the Early Poems

At the height of Wilde's notoriety, *Poems* appeared in July 1881.[1] Although five editions sold quickly, the indifferent and sometimes hostile reception of the book by the public was enough to hint that most of the poems were, if not imitative, of a mildly shocking sort. Opinion may be sampled in the judgment of an arbiter no less than Oliver Elton who, it seems, had set the tone for future appraisals when he said:

> It is not that these poems are thin—and they *are* thin, it is not that they are this or that—and they *are* all this and all that; it is that they are for the most part not by their putative father at all, but by a number of better-known and more deservedly reputed authors. They are in fact by William Shakespeare, by Philip Sidney, by John Donne, by Lord Byron, by William Morris, by Algernon Swinburne, and by sixty more, whose works have furnished the list of passages which I hold in my hand at this moment. The Union Library already contains better and fuller editions of all these poets: the volume which we are offered is theirs, not Mr. Wilde's. . . .[2]

Dr. Bernhard Fehr has devoted a whole book, *Studien zu Oscar Wilde's Gedichten* (Berlin, 1918), to Wilde's assiduous and amazingly successful imitations of Milton, Keats, Rossetti, Swinburne, Tennyson, Thomas Hood, and countless authors; he has also investigated the influence of Dante, Flaubert, Pater, Whistler—one can, indeed, cite the whole corpus of original sources. Researches

---

[1] For the circumstances of publication see *Letters*, pp. 76-77.
[2] Hesketh Pearson, *Oscar Wilde* (New York, 1946), p. 46.

of this kind abound; what we lack is a study of the poems as formal aesthetic objects.[3] Wilde's poetry has usually been regarded as the genuine testimony of an intuitive mind; the poet, it may be, tried to falsify his original impulses by wholesale copying; or by appropriating the vocabulary, manners, and styles that were classic models, or were then in fashion. Unfortunately, few have examined the poet's dominant themes and imagery in order to define the resources and motives of his imagination. This chapter hopes to prelude further discussion of the aesthetic qualities of Wilde's poetry.[4]

A good example of Wilde's early manner is "Panthea."[5] It consists of thirty stanzas with six iambic pentameter lines to each stanza, rhyming ababcc, the last line being a hexameter. Its grammatical mood, exclamatory and assertive, sustains the pitch of a choral hymn. From the beginning, the speaker's straightforward affirmations thwart any possible qualification of the truisms:

For, sweet, to feel is better than to know,
    And wisdom is a childless heritage,
One pulse of passion—youth's first fiery glow,—
    Are worth the hoarded proverbs of the sage:
Vex not thy soul with dead philosophy,
Have we not lips to kiss with, hearts to love and eyes to see!

[3] The following works may be cited: E. J. Bock, "Walter Pater's Einfluss auf Oscar Wilde," *Bonner Studien zur englischen Philologie*, VII (1913); Ernst Bendz, *The Influence of Matthew Arnold in the Prose Writings of Oscar Wilde* (Gothenburg, 1914); and especially Albert J. Farmer, *Le Mouvement Esthétique et Décadent en Angleterre: 1873-1900* (Paris, 1931), pp. 132-46.

[4] I take account of previous studies: Anonymous, "The Poetry of an Aesthete," *Dial*, II (August 1881), 82-85; H. E. Woodbridge, "Oscar Wilde as a Poet," *Poet Lore*, XIX (Winter, 1908), 439-57; J. D. Thomas, "Oscar Wilde's Pose and Poetry," *The Rice Institute Pamphlet*, XLII (October 1955), 32-52.

[5] See the text in *Works*, pp. 768-72. The poems not included in this edition may be found in *Poems* by Oscar Wilde, Volume I of the *Complete Works*, ed., R. Ross (New York, 1921).

The situation appears simplified, given these confident resolutions. The address to another person, "sweet," pales off into the rapid accumulation of certainties and assurances. Since the questions are rhetorical, no room for dialogue is entertained. Thoughts proceed symmetrically, in a series of contrasts and equations: "to feel is better than to know"; "youth's first fiery glow" / "hoarded proverbs of the sage," and so forth. The long sixth line, usually an emphatic conclusion, closes many of the stanzas; except for some running-over of the last lines, the stanzas stand as independent wholes.

The argument of the poem is simple: let us live pleasurably (1-4) since the gods are indifferent (5-12). The sequence of stoic despair and resigned acceptance (13-15), which recalls FitzGerald's *Rubaiyat*, is climaxed with the intrusion of a wholly unprepared conviction (stanza 16): "We are resolved into the supreme air, / We are made one with what we touch and see...." This hymn of harmony goes on to the end (16-30) in a crescendo of unrestrained rejoicing. Wordsworth's pantheism, the principle of evolution, microcosm and macrocosm, organic development, reciprocal dependence in nature, "Oenone" and "The Lotos-Eaters"—all these strands unite in a lofty oratorical descant. Notice how the string of monosyllables suggests the steady passage of time. With the magnitude of the physical and temporal panorama, the poet's vision encompasses all creation:

> With beat of systole and diastole
> One grand life throbs through earth's giant heart,
> And mighty waves of single Being roll
> From nerveless germ to man, for we are part
> Of every rock and bird and beast and hill,
> One with the things that prey on us,
> and one with what we kill.

Lacking any objective situation of doubt or conflict, except perhaps for the notions of pain in disease, of disappointments and remorse, "Panthea" derives its strength from its sweeping, eloquent rhythm. Wilde's epithets seem to be survivals of Theocritean pastorals: "diapered fritillaries," "silver-fretted night," "merry bright-eyed Elves," and other worn-out phrases. Indeed, the common idiom of the poems is consciously decorative and artificial. "Apologia" has "gorgéd asp of passion," and "dull failure be my vesture"; "The Grave of Keats" uses romantic phraseology throughout, e.g.: "gentle violets weeping with the dew / Weave on his bones an ever-blossoming chain." In "Requiescat," however, the language becomes spare, direct, and concrete, as the nature of the subject requires.

Other poems, like "Humanitad," "The Garden of Eros," "The Burden of Itys," "Charmides," are largely built in a slow, elevated and ceremonious manner. Wilde exploits the resources of strong fantastic impressions which are conveyed by an intimate correspondence between sound and sense, the richness of texture superimposing itself over the logic of argument. Sensuous, palpable qualities predominate; argument and action are subordinated to the associations evoked by the full, smooth orchestration of words. In "The Garden of Eros," we meet "gorgeous-coloured vesture," the soul twisted in all its "mighty questionings," and the awkward line: "Its new-found creeds so sceptical and so dogmatical." Wilde's florid diction and the tedious catalogue of classical allusions do not at all make the pursuit of beauty a rejuvenating task. "The Burden of Itys," with its rustic paraphernalia, displays archaic fossils, fanciful but petrified, just as "Humanitad," a discursive medley of philosophic themes obviously inspired by Swinburne, manipulates familiar exotic property. With "Charmides," we cannot help being reminded of Keats' *Endymion*, Arnold's pastoral elegies, the cadence and alliterations of Swinburne (e.g., "he paddled with her polished throat"). "Ravenna," with its 332 lines, moves like a mechanized travelogue. Its gaudily decked couplets are sometimes melodiously elegiac; but most often, they are burdened with too much adjectival embroidery so that, despite the narrative momentum, the blank verse continually halts at long stretches of static description.

Wilde's five long poems cited above all use the stanza of "Venus and Adonis" except for a lengthened concluding line. The lines are decasyllabic, with alternate rhymes in the first four lines, concluding with a rhymed couplet, the last line being of seven feet or fourteen syllables. Wilde does not really *feel* this stanzaic and metrical form; he adopts it mainly for the congenial space it affords for lavish decorative musings on an actual or imagined setting. While the pattern fits the meditative pace, the meter drags, counteracting any variation in movement or setting. In "From Spring Days to Winter," "Chanson," "Serenade," and "Endymion" Wilde attempts an analogy to musical forms— a corollary to his pictorial techniques; but despite his virtuosity, his early poems—like "The New Helen," "Ballade de Marguerite," "Magdalen Walks," and most of the sonnets— are drab "literary constructions."[6] They possess no distinctive quality apart from their illustrating Pre-Raphaelite stylistic features. While his poetic devices are conventional and at best "pure," Wilde's themes and topics are remarkably broad in scope and betray a seriously inquiring mind: liberty and politics are treated in "Ave Imperatrix," "Sonnet on the Massacre of the Christians in Bulgaria," "Libertatis Sacra Fames"; religious sentiments form the material for the poems in the section "Rosa Mystica"; philosophical issues give weight and substance to "Humanitad," and "Atha-

[6] H. J. C. Grierson, *The Background of English Literature* (Barnes and Noble edn., New York, 1963), p. 71. Grierson, in his chapter on "Arnold and Swinburne," estimates the value of Pre-Raphaelite poetry.

nasia"; literary values enliven "To Milton," "Vita Nuova," "The Grave of Shelley," and others.

Wilde admittedly does not possess the capacity for "analytic despair" in the pure exercise of which the French decadents showed classic sophistication.[7] The example of *Les Fleurs du Mal* (1857), with its transposition of sensual experience onto a moral plane of existence, asserts itself but intermittently in Wilde's poems. Tension in the encounter of ambiguous or paradoxical forces is often diffused, if not factitiously resolved in lyric instants where the spirit easily attains a dubious supremacy. Insight gives way to ego-centered exultation.[8] Even the elaborate fiction of "Charmides," its basic story loaded with mythical and symbolic nuances, blurs under the dense layers of superfluous ornamentation. Thus, despite the unaffected simplicity of "Requiescat," or the synthetic brilliance of "Her Voice," the "impressions" and the exercises in French forms, one can validly say that to read through Wilde's poems seems, as B. Ifor Evans testifies, like passing through "a 'beautified' room in some over-expensive boarding-house with rococo decorations, classical statuary, and objets d'art, mingled in elaborate profusion but with little taste."[9]

"Celtic" magic, picturesque scenes, and the harmonious interweaving of syllables may help preserve some poems as specimens of the imagistic and melopoeic style. Wilde undoubtedly lacks an abiding dramatic faculty; except perhaps *The Ballad of Reading Gaol*, his monologues (for example, "The Sphinx") serve the purposes of the poet more than the needs of the projected persona. That is to say, Wilde, unlike the gallery of live masks that constituted his

[7] I differ from the strictures of Hoxie Neale Fairchild, *Religious Trends in English Poetry* (New York, 1962), v, pp. 152-53.

[8] Wendell Harris, "Innocent Decadence: The Poetry of the Savoy," *PMLA*, LXXVII (December 1962), 629-36.

[9] *English Poetry in the Later Nineteenth Century* (London, 1933), p. 309.

personality, could not divorce himself from the speaking voice of his poems; the person speaking in the poem is often indivisible from the poet. He forcefully represents himself in the situations of his poems so much so that many regard them as intentionally autobiographical. What assumptions can be said to lead to this orientation of Wilde's creative instincts?

Rossetti, one of Wilde's masters, proclaimed apropos of the artist's duty that "the hand should paint the soul." His emphasis on pictorial elements and on accurate descriptive details demands sincere candor and a naïve naturalness which are required to render the beatific simplicity of nature. Grave, formal, and elevated subjects, rendered with visual fidelity, are made to incarnate symbolic messages, as in Holman Hunt's "The Light of the World," or in Rossetti's "The Blessed Damozel."[10] Now what is important is the total impression and the emotional response the poem or picture arouses. To arrive at this end, the artist intends meticulous depiction of a scene to present the surface not for its own sake but for its value as a realistic emblem of the spiritual life, as an allegory of subtle states of individuality. Details may also be organized so as to suggest a view of life or a flitting mood, the effect being strictly detached from ethical or utilitarian concerns: the projection of inward experience is the poet's chief concern. "Look in thy heart and write" was the implicit ruling principle. Every element— mystical overtones, earthbound naturalism, archaic language—is to be compressed within the frame of the poet's sensitivity. Wilde tacitly subscribed to such values as Rossetti and the Pre-Raphaelites exemplified in their work. Color, mass, and rhythm adjusted themselves to the "I" con-

[10] For treatments of the poetic persona in the nineteenth century and in general, see Robert Langbaum, *The Poetry of Experience* (New York, 1957) and George T. Wright, *The Poet in the Poem* (Berkeley and Los Angeles, 1962). Consult in particular Anna Jarney De Armond, "What Is Pre-Raphaelitism in Poetry?" *Delaware Notes* (19th series; Newark, Delaware, 1946), 67-88.

sciousness given full rein in utterance, using the processes of dream, vision, quest or hallucination to focus the conflicting impulses of the sensibility.[11]

One of Wilde's means of achieving unity is synesthesia, the condensation of various sensory impressions in a single tissue or network: "green thirst," "music of daybreak," "to build a rose out of music by moonlight."[12] Apart from this means, one thinks of Whistler, the French impressionists, and the vogue for Japanese block-printing as factors that contributed toward the tightening of construction and the clarity of delineation in Wilde's later poems.[13] By vivid color combinations and exact imagery, Wilde effectively sought to particularize, harden, and outline in opaque silhouettes and subtle chiaroscuro, as witnessed in "Impression du Matin," "Fantaisies Decoratives," "Impression: Le Réveillon," the last title being the painter's term for a strong employment of light against a somber background. His lumpy declamations yield now to the precise molding of plastic contours, to swift energetic lines like: "And in the throbbing engine room / Leap the long rods of polished steel." In "The Harlot's House," Wilde's craftmanship manifests a finer skill of execution and a firmer grasp of his material.[14] Although again the derivations obtrude—Poe's

[11] Cf. Kristian Smidt, "Point of View in Victorian Poetry," *English Studies*, XXXVIII (February 1957), 1-12; also E. D. H. Johnson, *The Alien Vision of Victorian Poetry* (Princeton, 1952).

[12] Stephen von Ullmann, "Synästhesien in den dichterischen Werken von Oscar Wilde," *Englische Studien*, LXXII (Leipzig, 1938), 245-56.

[13] See Earl R. Miner, *The Japanese Tradition in British and American Literature* (Princeton, 1958), pp. 79-85, 100-103, 236; Kelver Hartley, *Oscar Wilde: l'influence française dans son oeuvre* (Paris, 1935).

[14] "The Harlot's House" was printed in the *Dramatic Review*, April 15, 1885; "The Sphinx' was begun when Wilde was still at Oxford, finished in Paris about April 1883, and published in 1894. These dates are established in *Letters*, pp. 144, 174. The texts of the poems are in *Works*, pp. 778-79; 812-21. The chronology of Wilde's poems may be found in the reliable Stuart Mason, *A Bibliography of the Poems of Oscar Wilde* (London, 1907).

"The Haunted Palace," Baudelaire's *danse macabre*, grotesque motifs from Egyptian and medieval lore—the lines have an edge absent in the early poems. Cast in thirty-six lines arranged in tercets with linked rhymes, the poem deals mainly with the desertion of the poet by his loved one. Its dreamlike and dusky setting provides a fitting décor for the weird mechanical movements. Its haunting cadence heightens the queerly evocative images that pass in montage before the eyes:

> We watched the ghostly dancers spin
> To sound of horn and violin,
> Like black leaves wheeling in the wind.

> Like wire-pulled Automatons,
> Slim silhouetted skeletons
> Went sidling through the slow quadrille.

Wilde's revisions indicate a newly acquired maturity in the handling of organic metrical effects. Originally the bare registration of activity in the lines, "But she—she heard the violin,/ And left my side, and entered in:" ran limply and vaguely: "But she—she heard the violin / Upon the steps like a live thing," the latter phrase altered again to "like live things." Similarly, the subtraction of an adjective strengthened the mimetic effect of the last line which, in an early draft, went: "Crept like a little frightened girl." Wilde ignored metrical uniformity to heighten the dramatic projection of scene. He suppressed one beat and thus effectively signaled a change of viewpoint contrasting with the regular rhythm and order of the first two lines:[15]

[15] J. D. Thomas, "The Composition of Wilde's 'The Harlot's House'," *Modern Language Notes*, LXV (November 1950), 485-88; Bernhard Fehr, "Oscar Wilde's 'The Harlot's House'," *Archiv fur das Studium der Neueren Sprachen und Literatur*, CXXXIV (1916), 59-75.

> And down the long and silent street,
>> The dawn, with silver-sandaled feet,
> Crept like a frightened girl.

In his early poems, like "Ave Imperatrix," with its sequence of geographical facts ("The almond-groves of Samarcand," "The wind-swept heights of Trafalgar"), Wilde tried to achieve graphic vividness by particularization:

> In vain the laughing girl will lean
>> To greet her love with love-lit eyes:
> Down in some treacherous ravine,
>> Clutching his flag, the dead boy lies.

"Requiescat" has a subdued manner, alternating objective description and human response:

> Coffin-board, heavy stone,
>> Lie on her breast,
> I vex my heart alone
>> She is at rest.

With the poems labeled "Impressions," Wilde attains sharpness and tonal complexity in the depiction of scenes. Colors, tactile sensations, and a weird "animistic" vibration characterize physical movements, as in "Impression du Matin":

> A barge with ochre-coloured hay
> Dropt from the wharf: and chill and cold
>
> The yellow fog came creeping down

Sounds are registered too: the "clang of waking life" made by passing country-wagons, the birds' chirping, and so forth. "Impression: Le Réveillon," with the illumination splashed against a somber background, displays the poet's playful arrangement of hues; "Les Silhouettes" exhibits the melancholy mood borne out by the correspondences: "And like a withered leaf the moon / Is blown across the stormy bay."

Like the dainty simile of "The dawn is rising from the sea, /
Like a white lady from her bed," the comparisons in "Symphony in Yellow" underscore their pictorial value in their isolated positions:

> An omnibus across the bridge
> Crawls like a yellow butterfly . . .
>
> And, like a yellow silken scarf,
> The thick fog hangs along the quay.

Amid the surface polish and elegant decoration, we catch intermittently an inner tremor, an undercurrent of anxious privation which informs the process of articulation. This disturbing chord echoes from lines like "The dull dead wind is out of tune," from the emptiness that haunts "The Harlot's House," from the bleak solitary figure in "Impression du Matin":

> But one pale woman all alone,
> The daylight kissing her wan hair,
> Loitered beneath the gas lamps' flare,
> With lips of flame and heart of stone.

The juxtapositions of the last line convey a psychological effect similar to the gradual dissociation, in "La Fuite de la Lune," between inner psychic poise and the distortions from outside; the external world distracts with "a cry that echoes shrill / From some lone bird disconsolate," until nature becomes horribly animate and looms as an ominous mirror of the spiritual condition of the observer:

> And suddenly the moon withdraws
> Her sickle from the lightening skies,
> And to her sombre cavern flies,
> Wrapped in a veil of yellow gauze.

Withdrawal, abandonment, isolation—these situations are virtually prefigured in Wilde's "Helas!" as the loss of the soul's inheritance, and continued in the inferno of *The Ballad of Reading Gaol*. Of the dualisms embodied in the poetry, the antithesis between an instinctively driven body and a conscience-filled awareness acquires dramatic immediacy in "The Sphinx," the culmination of Wilde's verbal "posing."

"The Sphinx," ironically, takes over the rhyme-scheme of *In Memoriam*, converting the quatrain into long solid couplets. There are sixteen syllables, basically iambic, to each line. Its internal rhymes, flimsily veiled, afford a pretext for opulent imagery enhanced by the preponderance of adjectives. Clearly Wilde indulges here in word-play, mixing motifs, images, and vocabulary from Gautier, Baudelaire's "Les Chats," Poe's "The Raven," and the sybaritic luxuries of the "fleshly school." Contrasted with Poe's poem with its trochaic lines, the swift rhythm of its repetitions, and the continuity of the feminine rhymes, Wilde's poem proceeds in an undulating slowness. The caesuras of the lines produce a mesmeric beat of obsessive continuity. The "baroque" rhymes—"grotesque," "arabesques," "automatons," "skeletons," "hand," "saraband"—are in consonance with the nature of the subject.[16]

The bulk of the poem consists of the speaker's recollection of all the scenes in which the Sphinx figures. The Sphinx's history has been condensed in one vision of transcendence. The mosaic and the pageantry equal the fabulous identity of this enigmatic creature. In conceptual terms the poem expresses the polarities of the eternal because cyclic permanence of the Sphinx and the time-bound "I" afflicted with its sense of finitude: "A thousand weary centuries are thine while I have hardly seen / Some twenty summers cast their green for Autumn's gaudy liveries." Growing from this op-

---

[16] A reasoned appreciation of Wilde's verbal eccentricities is that of Kingsley Amis, Introduction to *Poems and Essays* by Oscar Wilde (New York, 1956), pp. 17-19.

position, the tension will later increase in the confrontation of pagan and Christian values. Right at the start, fancy fails to comprehend the passage of time, for time appears to the speaker like a "shifting gloom," a spiritual duration. This is concretely staged in the locale established in the opening lines: "In a dim corner of my room for longer than my fancy thinks / A beautiful and silent Sphinx has watched me through the shifting gloom." Strange that the Sphinx, "an exquisite grotesque," who is also "inviolate and immobile," incarnates in herself the turbulent flux of history. The speaker cannot resist her; in fact he is driven by a compulsive force emanating from within. Somehow the Sphinx seems to be an illusion precipitated from an anguished consciousness. The poet labors under a spell; suspended in this state, he witnesses all the focal moments in the Sphinx's existence. One perceives how the Sphinx simultaneously performs the roles of prophet, poet, and priest, as evidenced in the sense of the iterated apostrophe "Sing to me—" beginning on line 31. She then becomes the fertile matrix of revelations and of fascinating forms: ". . . what horrible Chimera came / With fearful heads and fearful flame to breed new wonders from your womb?" and from lines 120 on, the Sphinx is urged to resurrect her dead lovers. A hint of conflict occurs in lines 131-132: the poet counterpoints Christ with pagan materialism and voluptuousness. The seraphic raptures, intensifying in the thunderous evolution of episodes and the piling-up of details, evolve to a point where action alone could release its painful potency from within the self. The sadistic invocations near the end denote an abrupt shift of attitude: from the speaker's close identification with the Sphinx to complete rupture, abhorrence, and repulsion:

> O smite him with your jasper claws! and bruise
> him with your agate breasts!

> Why are you tarrying? Get hence! I weary of
> your sullen ways,
> I weary of your steadfast gaze, your somnolent
> magnificence.

The succeeding lines comprise a litany of repudiation and hateful derision hurled on the Sphinx. This negative recoil springs from the fateful dialectic of the poet's indecision. Indulgence, of course, brings eventual satiety and disgust. Since the Sphinx, in her monumental fixity, arouses passions but does not fully satisfy them, the worshipper suffers the pangs of inevitable chagrin. Bitterly disillusioned, he then seeks refuge in the symbol of the crucifix. And the crucifix, like the Sphinx before the reversal, offers a perfect equivalent to, and a concrete objectification of, the poet's dilemma:

> Go thou before, and leave me
> with my crucifix,
>
> Whose pallid burden, sick with pain, watches
> the world with wearied eyes,
> And weeps for every soul that dies, and weeps
> for every soul in vain.

While, in "Ave Imperatrix," his objective glance encompasses the Ganges, "portals to the East," and other tourist spots, in "The Sphinx," Wilde delves into the center of subjective processes where time becomes a "shifting gloom." The Sphinx symbolizes a godlike spirit of history: she dies and is reborn many times, her omniscient gaze focused on exquisite but grotesque scenes. Here the technical beauty of aesthetic surface controls the violent impulses latent in the subject. The strict metrical pattern, the ritulistic cadence, and the fine orchestration of sounds hold in poise the brutal sadistic possibilities in: "And let me touch those curving claws of yellow ivory"; "O smite him with

your jasper claws! and bruise him with your agate breasts!"
and so forth.

Among all Wilde's poems, "The Sphinx" alone betrays a
masculine energy that enlivens gorgeous landscape, fusing
religion, iconology, and historical facts within the current of
meditation and monologue. Its emphatic details are designed
to appeal to the visual, tactile, and olfactory senses, while
the Biblical reminiscences and the polysyllabic diction gener-
ate a pitch of excitement which sustains the tempo of the
spiritual drama. Wilde's adjectives are efficiently placed; the
pedantic resonant nouns—"lúpanar," "Oreichalch," "nenu-
phar," "Mandragores," "Hippogriffs"—enrich, with their
oriental mystery, the commonplace "horrible," "monstrous,"
"furious," "fantastic," and so forth. Wilde has been able thus
far to endow a private theme with a body of public references. The "impressionist" poems, apart from "The Sphinx"
and the later ballad, form a noteworthy if meager body in
Wilde's writings which consistently exploits a definite mode
of composition. They belong to the finest "literary poetry,"
stimulating a pleasure proper to their kind.

Viewed from the context of the outlook that motivates his
actions and words—the aesthetic "Byzantinism," the flair
for elegant and refined surface, the predilection to set up
ritualized encounters between pagan and Christian forces—
Wilde's poetic achievement may be considered as one
reading of truth and reality.[17] It gives a perception of reality
through a personal experience interpreted and objectified
by the resources of language. Wilde proposes that poetry
should be like "a strange crystal that mirrors all the
world."[18] The function of mirroring reality serves less an
imitative than an idealizing purpose; the dimensions of reality

[17] For a discussion of the poet's personality as revealed in the
poems, see Helene Richter, "Oscar Wilde's Persönlichkeit in seinen
Gedichten," *Englische Studien*, LIV (October 1920), 201-76.
[18] *Letters*, p. 217.

reach us only after their passage, in sensory experience, through the peculiarly tuned sensibility of an individual. Poetic language, as it joins universals and particulars, becomes an autonomous force. It tends to engender its own realm of being, creating values, struggling to triumph over necessity and contingency. In effect, the groundwork of poetic meaning is seen to rest ultimately on the poet as creative agent.

In trying to determine the essence of imaginative creation, the romantic poets perpetually wrestled with the problem of ideality and the flux of the everyday world. While romanticism generally regards self-expression, rather than public communication, as the criterion of artistic integrity, the problem of subjectivity, and the diffuseness of meaning which is bound to arise from the pressure of insights into transcendence, remains the perennial center of theoretical speculation. Form and substance, welded together inseparably in the poem, must be realized in language and not alone in the mind. On this assumption Wilde's poems suffer from flabby exaggeration, sentimental nostalgia, tired and antiquated phrasings; in short, Wilde has in many cases ignored the need to objectify his striving for balance, remaining content with the celebration of whatever certainty he has for the moment gotten hold of, whether it be hedonism or medievalism. Wilde's verse shows, according to Douglas Bush, "all the traditional elements of romantic Hellenism in all the refinement and purity of decadence," quite removed from the quotidian affairs of men.[19] Indeed, from the artificial bucolic stage of "The Garden of Eros"—

> The early primrose with shy footsteps run
> From the gnarled oak-tree roots till all the wold,
> Spite of its brown and trampled leaves, grew
> bright with shimmering gold.

[19] *Mythology and the Romantic Tradition in English Poetry* (Norton edn., New York, 1963), p. 418.

to the tense, bare contrasts of statement in *The Ballad of Reading Gaol*—

> For oak and elm have pleasant leaves
> That in the springtime shoot:
> But grim to see is the gallows-tree,
> With its adder-bitten root,

the radical transition implies a discontinuity, a shift in outlook: rhythm, diction, syntax, and imagery are transformed in the direction of greater intelligibility, amplified by more positively verifiable references to ordinary experience. The change signifies a greater respect for actuality and the impact of personal experience which eludes clichés and statistics.

Analysis of the motifs that run through Wilde's early poems will show that the distinctive quality which defines his work inheres in a fundamental commitment: the choice of decorative field or pattern, of "artifice liberated as pure design." In "Les Silhouettes," for instance, the impressions, treated as motifs, metamorphose into recurrent images and clusters of sensuous impressions, performing their role within a setting prescribed by the nature of the motifs. One can say that the stanzaic outline serves as a limiting framework analogous to the rigid vertical and horizontal lines that Aubrey Beardsley traces first to chart his sinuous calligraphy. Likewise, in plastic design, it is a linear stylization that governs the ornamental impulse. As Wylie Sypher points out, theoretical justification of the *Art Nouveau* movement of the time may be found in Wilde's critical principles, in statements like "All art is at once surface and symbol."[20]

Although such pieces as "La Fuite de la Lune" or "Symphony in Yellow" may be explained by alluding to the trends

[20] *Rococo to Cubism in Art and Literature* (Vintage edn., New York, 1963), pp. 223, 242.

of contemporary decorative art, or to the axioms of symbolism persuasively argued in Wilde's *Intentions*, an examination of the poems would reveal a complexity of issues in terms of feelings and ideas that continually recur as motives for whole poems, or as elements of tension within the parts. We have seen how Wilde gradually laid stress on the colorful impressions of the natural world, though the adjectives he employed may be weak and trite: "The sky is laced with fitful red," or "the pale green Thames / Lies like a rod of rippled jade." But, as he contends, the properties of the visible surface no longer suffice to represent interior processes: "Plastic simplicity of outline may render for us the visible aspect of life" but "those secrets which self-consciousness alone contains" escape categorical understanding.[21] The images that we perceive in Wilde's poems, whose power of qualification inheres in their quaintly disposed color-tonalities, appear then as a technique of visionary exploration. In other words, the impressions principally serve the requirements of symbolic representation.

By "visionary exploration" I mean the use of sensible or perceptible qualities which the poet embodies in language to shape a meaningful, harmonious universe. Wilde always strove, as the poem "Apologia" for instance indicates, to "burst the bars" of mortal finitude and know "the Love which moves the sun and all the stars!" Sustained partly by a belief in the power of ideal Forms, this aspiration manifests itself in a belief "in some divine eternity" ("The True Knowledge" in an idyllic, mystical "enchanted land / Whose slumbering vales forlorn Calypso knew" ("The New Helen"); or in an apocalyptic prospect of "some flame-girt Raphael" descending to free enslaved Italy. Underneath this impulse to discern a realm beyond worldly limitations lies the awareness of an antagonism between spirit and flesh, passion and

[21] *A Critic in Pall Mall*, collected by E. V. Lucas (New York, n.d.), p. 216.

belief, in short, the traditional dualities that inform the human predicament in major romantic poetry. This awareness infuses into Wilde's poems the urgency of a personal commitment in his subjects.

The dramatic oppositions offered in the poems unfold spontaneously from a knowledge of the human condition, its shortcomings and possibilities: "had I not been made of common clay / I had climbed the higher heights unclimbed yet, seen the fuller air, the larger day" ("Flower of Love"). The illustrious example of Wilde's hero, Dante, guides his pilgrimage to witness "the suns of seven circles shine." The exalted tone with which "the new Helen" is lifted to "thy re-arisen shrine," the merging of Greek beauty and Christian sanctity that recurs in the poems dealing with his Italian sojourn, accompanies the confrontation between the afflicted soul and the Redeemer in "E Tenebris":

> I shall behold, before the night,
> The feet of brass, the robe more white than flame,
> The wounded hands, the weary human face.

Ritual and iconology function as the correlatives for the resolution of diverging sentiments.

Eventually this consort between pagan feeling and Christian otherworldliness leads to an equivalence, by virtue of which the poetic apprehension of carnal beauty approximates the crowning vision of the *Divine Comedy*. In "Madonna Mia," the meticulous concern with a woman's "brown, soft hair close braided by her ears," with her "white throat, whiter than the silvered dove, / Through whose wan marble creeps one purple vein"—this scrutiny, this warm sketching of features, as though laboring to disclose the *quidditas* of each particular object, virtually becomes a ceremonial act: it initiates the tribute of praise accomplished in the utterance itself. His consciousness expands until the impact of the experience assumes a religious import; he vicariously feels

> Like Dante, when he stood with Beatrice
> Beneath the flaming Lion's breast, and saw
> The seventh Crystal, and the Stair of Gold.

Asserting that Wilde held the activity of expression as a means of capturing the dynamic essence of spirit through the passions and the dissolution of consciousness, Leone Vivante submits that Wilde's "conception of an active principle is that of absolute immanentism,"[22] as in "One fiery-coloured moment: one great love; and lo! we die" ("Panthea"). But "immanentism" should be appraised properly as one facet of Wilde's fundamental concern: to see through the refractions of phenomena the luminous sphere of Platonic Forms.

The aesthetic mode of concentration on evanescent moods and transient sensations, which forms the keynote of the poems in *The Yellow Book* and *The Savoy*, entails the deliberate massing of manifold details in each line. At the outset, however, Wilde loved to manipulate stereotypes and hackneyed locutions without a thought for dramatic complication, as in "Ravenna," "Ave Imperatrix," and the political poems. Later, such allegorical figures as "Treason and the dagger of her trade," or "Murder with his silent bloody feet" disappear. Typical illustrations are substituted: the "travail of the hungry years" involves "A father grey with grief and tears / A mother weeping all alone." Since an imaginative work, however, is at once "surface and symbol," denotation and connotation, the poet contrives an interanimation between feeling and form. In harnessing the power of epithets to create impressionistic wholes, Wilde seeks to reveal the inner structure of the apprehending mind.

In the later poems, Wilde spins a texture at once musical and richly suggestive, with the emotional coloring of his diction permeating objects, human physiognomy, and fancied

[22] *English Poetry* (Carbondale, Illinois, 1963), p. 307.

sights. On the ornamental surface, the mobile and the inert combine: "A wild moon in this wintry sky / Gleams like an angry lion's eye" ("La Mer"); the pale dove "with silvered wing and amethystine throat" ("Athanasia"); "her sweet red lips / Burned like a ruby fine" ("In the Gold Room"). The metallic properties of minerals and jewelry give nature the permanence of artifice. Vitality seems arrested owing to an excess of verbal arabesques; statuesque figures or immobile landscapes—always the products of meticulous inventiveness —often result. Wilde's joining of human and nonhuman elements seems to shadow forth an active power, daemonic and irrational, lurking behind appearances: "The oranges on each o'erhanging spray / Burned as bright lamps of gold to shame the day," or "the slight lizard shows his jewelled head" ("The Grave of Shelley"). This tendency operates toward the immediacy of a carefully wrought artifact. In "Impression de Voyage," for instance, the landscape of the sea acts as a staged background: "The sea was sapphire-coloured, and the sky / Burned like a heated opal through the air." It establishes temporal and spatial distance between the enthusiastic visitor and the "fabled" Greece of myth and romance. It serves to intimate the speaker's receptiveness. Obliquely indicating movement toward the living actuality of Greece, the aural impressions—

> The flapping of the sail against the mast,
> The ripple of the water on the side,
> The ripple of girls' laughter at the stern

follow the movement of the poet's consciousness from the active involvement with the external world to a sensitive, passive acceptance of any stimulus from outside. Such is a specific case where the conjunction of animate and inanimate factors reflects the subjectivity of the poetic process. Frequently, nature as the source of decorative motifs—"the turquoise sky to burnished gold wss turned" ("Sonnet on

Approaching Italy")—reinforces the fated gravitation of the poet to the ideal realm of spiritual freedom. G. Wilson Knight, interpreting Wilde's fairy tales, ascribes to him the gift of a "seraphic intuition," in that Wilde, using jewel-symbolism as a transparent vehicle for transcendence, satisfactorily answers the question: "How, then, may the 'soul' and its jewelled and seemingly infertile Eros be related to love and the Christian values?"[23]

The quest for unity of being, which is a central motivation in Wilde's works, pursues its course beyond the fusion of qualities in synesthesia. The poise of heart and mind ceases to be elusive as soon as Wilde can embody it in figurative shapes: for example, in the mysterious faun of "In the Forest":

> He skips through the copses singing,
>   And his shadow dances along,
> And I know not which I should follow,
>   Shadow or song!

Or in these clearly drawn images: "The thin foam that frets upon the sea" ("Tedium Vitae"); "Huge Triton writhes in greenish bronze" (Le Jardin des Tuileries"). We remark too, on a larger scale, the atmosphere of "La Fuite de la Lune" suffused with a mute anguish as though it assumed the form of a spiritual landscape. Varied situations are used to condense discordant associations so that the poet can transcend the arbitrary realm of experience; for example, glimpses of eternity are embodied in a multiplicity of incarnations in "The New Helen"; in acts of resurrection signified by the growth and exfoliation of the "little seed" in the Egyptian girl's hand ("Athanasia"); in the reemergence of "Phèdre" into "this common world so dull and vain." The idea of permanence also inheres in Elysian retreats: "To the

[23] *The Christian Renaissance* (Norton edn., New York, 1962), p. 291.

land where the daffodils blow / In the heart of a violet dale!"
("Under the Balcony"); in mystical illuminations: "Her soul
aflame with passionate ecstasy" ("Queen Henrietta Maria";
see also "La Bella Donna della Mia Mente"); in the playful
mood of innocence ("Le Jardin des Tuileries"); in the absolute equilibrium of Greek art ("Theocritus," "Theoretikos");
or in violent amalgamations of death and life in "But gentle
violets weeping with the dew / Weave on his bones an ever-
blossoming chain" ("The Grave of Keats"; see also "Requiescat"). Culminating in the vision of a soul "half-divine"
("Lotus Leaves"), this aspiration toward transcendence
affirms its roots in personal certitude ("At Verona"):

> behind my prison's blinded bars
> I do possess what none can take away,
> My love, and all the glory of the stars.

This imaginative order does not, of course, dissolve the
agonizing distortions in life. Wilde employed other techniques and devices to organize phenomena in time and space,
making much of the sheer inconsequentiality of content. In
"Les Ballons," for example, the conceits have at best a
carnival gusto:

> Against these turbid turquoise skies
> The light and luminous balloons
> Dip and drift like satin moons,
> Drift like silken butterflies;
>
> Reel with every windy gust,
> Rise and reel like dancing girls,
> Float like strange transparent pearls,
> Fall and float like silver dust.

The rhythm of the lines, buoyant and rollicking, is
mainly due to the assonances of short *i*'s and long *i*'s, e.g.:
"Dip and drift like satin moons, / Drift like silken butter-

flies." The insistent repetition of consonantal clusters dictates the speed of the lines: "Dip and drift . . ."; "Rise and reel . . ."; "Fall and float. . . ." What distracts us are the sounds more than the sights. The sudden fade-in and fade-out of appearances possess no logic other than that of an exuberant fancy. When Wilde seeks to paint the "coy fantastic pose" of these balloons, he fashions surrealistic conceits: "Each a petal of a rose / Straining at a gossamer string," and so forth. But again the lavish decor serves to frame everything in fixed portraiture. The fantasy of frozen images that we perceive in retrospect acquires a thickness in the seduction-drama intimated in "Le Panneau." Whatever feeling of festive zest may be expressed here, the presentation of action and relationship through adjectives and descriptive qualifiers tends to bring about a stasis. The continuity of rhythm, the uniform syntax, the regular beat, conceal the human implications in the whimsical behavior depicted here:

> She takes a lute of amber bright,
>> And from the thicket where he lies
>> Her lover, with his almond eyes,
> Watches her movements in delight.

> And now she gives a cry of fear,
>> And tiny tears begin to start:
>> A thorn has wounded with its dart
> The pink-veined sea-shell of her ear.

Combining play, rococo furnishings, and passion, the drama points to the creative process as a form of idealization.

Fancy or invention, the faculty whose function Coleridge ranked below the secondary imagination, is for Wilde supreme. His method is one of deliberate contrivance and delicate artifice. External facts or objects are modified by association with human life, as in "The Grave of Shelley":

"Like burnt-out torches by a sick-man's bed / Gaunt cypress-trees stand round the sun-bleached stone." This scene in a common graveyard, where repose in death seems assured, is set in opposition to the noble restlessness of Shelley's grave:

> In the blue cavern of an echoing deep,
>   Or where the tall ships founder in the gloom
>   Against the rocks of some wave-shattered steep.

Wilde's exclamatory, sonorous style gains added vigor with the reconciliation of height and depth imaged in the poem.

Nature in general furnishes the poet with objective attachments to his feelings, nature provides physical settings to the decor of *Art Nouveau*. In fact, the style and practice of artists like Beardsley and Gustave Moreau depend on the abstraction of patterns from naturalistic settings, and the repetition of such patterns within a confined space. Wilde, however, tends to spiritualize his material. The psychological charge of a line like "The dull dead wind is out of tune" in "Les Silhouettes," seen in context, illustrates the poet's constant effort to make the objects and occurrences in nature part of the workings of the human spirit. In "Le Jardin des Tuileries," the speaker expresses his sympathy with the agile games of children by desiring to assume the form of a tree so that he might, despite winter, "break / Into spring blossoms white and blue!" for the children's delight. Allegorical personifications of summer and winter figure in "The New Remorse." Flowers signify modulations of response in "Chanson," while the sea, in "Sonnet to Liberty," mirrors "my wildest passions." Milton's spirit resides in "white cliffs and high embattled towers" ("To Milton"); eternity is imaged in the sea-gulls' love for the sea, the sunflower's love for the sun ("Her Voice"); affections vary according to the cycle of the seasons ("From Spring Days to Winter"); and in metaphoric crisis, "the long white fingers of the dawn" will "grasp and slay the shuddering night" ("By the Arno").

To illustrate the transposition of natural scenes to symbolic status, one may gloss "Wasted Days." The theme concerns the futile nature of beauty in a world where such beauty, being mortal, is condemned beforehand to extinction. The poet exemplifies this idea by ironic juxtaposition of a beautiful face portrayed in detail with a generalized setting. While the glory of youthful innocence arouses rapture—

> A fair slim boy not made for this world's pain,
> With hair of gold thick clustering round his ears,
> And longing eyes half-veiled by foolish tears
> Like bluest water seen through mists of rain—

the background scene connotes transience amid ripeness:

> Corn-fields behind, and reapers all around
> In weariest labour toiling wearily,
> To no sweet sound of laughter or of lute.

With his "white throat whiter than the breast of dove," and seemingly immortal, the boy dreams in a place blessed by a golden harvest—this abundance and the crimson sunset-glow converging in the topic of life's autumnal decline. The poet's mind has been touched by "the tears of things." In the encroaching darkness, the white throat of the boy and the bright corn-field will not only be obscured but totally obliterated: "In the night-time no man gathers fruit." Wilde has here successfully imposed on his material a coherence and a unity of progression. The mystical "Madonna Mia," possibly an early draft, lacks the intensity of pathos found in the octave of "Wasted Days." Compactness and ease were gained when Wilde revised the original sestet (c. 1877):[24]

[24] Mason, p. 54. Some other instructive revisions show Wilde's craftsmanship. Take the original first six lines of "Impression: Le Réveillon" (Mason, p. 48):

The sun is shooting wide its crimson rays
Behind, wide fields, and reapers all a-row
In heat and labour toiling wearily,
To no sweet sound of laughter or of lute.

The sun is shooting wide its crimson glow,
Still the boy dreams: nor knows that night is nigh,
And in the night-time no man gathers fruit.

The final version in the 1881 volume reads:

Corn-fields behind, and reapers all a-row
In weariest labour toiling wearily,
To no sweet sound of laughter or of lute.

Eastward the dawn has broken red,
The circling mists and shadows flee;
Aurora rises from the sea,
And leaves the crocus-flowered bed.

Eastward the silver arrows fall,
Splintering the veil of holy night. . . .

And compare it with the final version:

The sky is laced with fitful red,
The circling mists and shadows flee,
The dawn is rising from the sea,
Like a white lady from her bed.

And jagged brazen arrows fall
Athwart the feathers of the night. . . .

Note the human undertone in words like "fitful," "jagged," etc.

Compare the original third stanza of "La Fuite de la Lune" (Mason, p. 38):

And, herald of my love to Him
Who waiting for the dawn, doth lie,
The orbéd maiden leaves the sky,
And the white fires grow more dim,

with the final version:

And suddenly the moon withdraws
Her sickle from the lightening skies,
And to her sombre cavern flies,
Wrapped in a veil of yellow gauze.

Surely the final version, with its personification, harmonizes with the preceding lines.

For another example: precision is gained when the original line in stanza 13 of "Ave Imperatrix," "Set where the plain and mountain meet," is changed to the final line "Set at the mountain's scarpèd feet." See Mason, p. 17.

And careless of the crimson sunset glow,
The boy still dreams; nor knows that night is nigh,
And in the night-time no man gathers fruit.

Given the dualisms that make up Wilde's thematic pre-
occupations, the undeviating pursuit of the sublime comes
out as a salient feature of his uneven but daringly ambitious
poetry. Wilde, as symbolist, allowed his subjectivity to direct
the formal execution of a work to the extent that often the
required detachment gave way to passionate involvement.
The poet then found himself in a position where he must
urgently justify himself as speaker or protagonist of his
poems. Self-expression led to mannerism and stylization of
whatever material, vocabulary, and devices the poet found
congenial.

In Wilde's case one can trace a general tendency of
growth: from the mannerisms of the derivative sonnets, the
painterly "Charmides," the pastiche of "Ravenna," to the
linear grace of "Le Panneau," the sensuous contours of "The
Sphinx," and finally to the plain economy of *The Ballad of
Reading Gaol* (which I discuss in Chapter Six). Enumerat-
ing the artistic vogues that fluctuated within the last quarter
of the century, Edouard Roditi gauges their impact on
Wilde's poetry and arrives at this summary of his poetic
career: "The evolution of Wilde's descriptive style in his
poetry, from the museum-piece ornateness of his earlier
works to the simpler and more delicate art of his more
mature poems, was accompanied, moreover, by an analogous evolution of his poetry's intellectual content, from the
discussion of general problems of politics, ethics, or aesthetics
to a greater attention to personal impressions or to the elucidation of particular problems of the poet's life, such as his
temptations and moral conflicts."[25] This interpretation,
though largely valid, needs qualification since, as we have

[25] "Wilde's Poetry as Art-History," *Poetry*, LXVII (March 1946),
325.

seen, Wilde in his poems exhibited a precious, even learned, integrity of style and theme. One can observe in the *The Ballad of Reading Gaol* the engagement with sin, suffering, and purgation that motivated "Panthea," "The Sphinx," almost three-fourths of the whole poetry. And one can detect the mannerisms of "Ravenna" in "The Sphinx" and the later poems.[26]

One trait seems unquestionable: Wilde habitually chose statement and exclamation as the chief modes of poetic utterance. Although he experimented in ideas, he did not seek new forms or techniques to mirror the novelty of nuance or the intricacy and depth of his awareness—except, perhaps, in the minor "impressionistic" pieces. For his generation, the late romantic idiom of Tennyson and Swinburne and the Pre-Raphaelites sufficed; Yeats, in his "Celtic twilight" period, and some Georgian poets used this idiom. On the other hand, we have to reckon with the methods of the French symbolists like Rimbaud, Baudelaire, Huysmans, blending with English tastes as reflected in genre painting; the willow-pattern plates; *Biedermeierstil* furnishings; the fastidious sartorial dandyism of Brummell, Disraeli, Barbey d'Aurevilly, Bulwer-Lytton, not to mention the hovering presence of Byron. Wilde made much of these forces by forging an idiom of his own that would fulfill the deepest needs of his personality. This idiom drew ornate still-lifes, staged tableaux, rhapsodized on the wicked charms of the Sphinx, ornamented or idealized the façade of nature with its

[26] Wilde's "The Sphinx" borrows numerous lines from poems published earlier. Compare, for instance, the lines from "Ravenna" at the end of part four:

> One who scarce has seen
> Some twenty summers cast their doublets green,
> For Autumn's livery. . . .

with the lines from "The Sphinx":

> A thousand weary centuries are thine while
> I have hardly seen
> Some twenty summers cast their green for
> Autumn's gaudy liveries.

own stylized ingenuity. Wilde's style, with its formal and easy elegance, answered well the need for distancing his material and providing it with an elaborate perspective of hints and allusions. Within the convention of pure decorative poetry, his rhetoric proved efficient and authentic for his individual purposes.

Throughout his career Wilde persistently sought to compose a verbal artifice that would be absolute in itself. Envisaging a poem as a self-sufficient entity, he isolated certain experiences that would embody the intricate workings of a fully developed consciousness. He strove to present a complex experience in a mode of lyrical intensity that would successfully unify multiple ways of feeling and thinking in a meaningful totality. In sum, Wilde's poetics, empirical in method but idealistic in orientation, conceives of matter as a manifold of impressions. These impressions form the raw material of art which the artist struggles to organize and control in a fitting rhythmical pattern. The poetic process involves several stages of transformation: it proceeds from a revealing insight to a distancing of the situation, then to a crystallization of feelings in imagery, and ends in a synthesis of all elements in the linguistic form.

Communication of a vision of reality is, for Wilde, the aim of literary creation. Accordingly he tried to set up a theory of the imagination which would be the basis for the formulation of universal aesthetic standards. From Wilde's reasoned intuitions, the principle of "art for art's sake," viewed as an effort to check man's increasing alienation from nature and society, implies the fulfillment of the need for communication. Aestheticism, which presupposes a conception of art as the ordering of experience and with it the perception of value in both process and result, thus acquires its practical justification. And this is essentially what Wilde attempted to demonstrate in his novel, *The Picture of Dorian Gray*.

II · *The Picture of Dorian Gray* and the Form of Fiction

When *The Picture of Dorian Gray* appeared in 1891, the general reaction showed the widening split between the "nonconforming" artist and the reader. While Pater singled out the "really alive quality" of the dialogue, and Yeats praised it as "a wonderful book,"[1] the outraged comments in the newspapers vehemently decried the work's "immoral" message. The common reader was still addicted to the search for inspiring messages. And when he got something quite alien to his conventional expectations, his response naturally took a uniform crudeness: "dullness and dirt . . . unclean. . . . It is a tale spawned from the leprous literature of the French Decadents—a poisonous book, the atmosphere of which is heavy with the mephitic odours of moral and spiritual putrefaction."[2]

Who were the French Decadents alluded to? Certainly not the chaste Mallarmé, who exulted in Wilde's novel: "une rêverie essentielle et des parfums d'âme les plus étranges s'est fait son orage. Redevenir poignant à travers l'inouï raffinement d'intellect, et humain, et unie pareille perverse atmos-

---

[1] *Art and Morality*, ed., Stuart Mason (London, 1908), p. 119. This reprints all the known reviews of Wilde's novel, including his replies. See the review of W. E. Henley in *The Scots Observer* (July 5, 1890) in Mason, p. 63; *The Athenaeum* (July 27, 1891) calls the book "unmanly, sickening, vicious." For Yeats' comment, see *Letters*, p. 270n.

For speculations on the influential book on *Dorian Gray*, see Bernhard Fehr, "Das gelbe Buch in Oscar Wildes *Dorian Gray*," *Englische Studien*, LV (1921), 68-75; Walther Fischer, " 'The Poisonous Book' in Oscar Wilde's *Dorian Gray*," *Englische Studien*, LI (1917-18), 37-47; see also H. Lucius Cook, "French Sources of Wilde's *Picture of Dorian Gray*," *Romantic Review*, XIX (March 1928), 15-34.

[2] From the review in the *Daily Chronicle*, June 30, 1890; *Letters*, p. 263n.

phère de beauté, est un miracle que vous accomplissez et selon quel emploi de tous les arts de l'écrivain! . . . Ce portrait en pied, inquiétant, d'un Dorian Gray, hantera, mais écrit, étant devenu livre lui-même."[3] Mallarmé gives us a clue toward a larger comprehension of the novel than has hitherto been accorded to it. This pertains to his conception of the central image of the story, Dorian's immutable portrait, as having become ultimately the whole book itself.

It is precisely through this picture of a permanent youth, an image objectifying the inner motivation of the major characters, that Wilde successfully integrates the formal elements of his narrative. His narrative acquires focus by a style which the picture itself announces. For at the end, the picture "the monstrous soul life," suffers a change only when Dorian himself, by an act of slaying what it embodies in idea, also renounces his fidelity to what it has always stood for.

The portrait, not Dorian Gray, emerges finally as the authentic hero. After all it is not life but art that inspires Dorian as well as Basil Hallward and, indirectly, Lord Henry. Just as Basil directs his passion from the flesh and blood youth to his painting, from person to artifice, so Dorian responds only to the actress in Sibyl rather than to her daylight personality. Dorian is enraptured by personae, by masks, and not by persons. Thus, when Sibyl forsakes acting and surrenders herself to emotional possession, she loses Dorian's love: his hate virtually kills her. (Similarly, Wilde in real life adored the "eternal feminine" as incarnated by actresses and acquaintances like Ellen Terry, Lily Langtry, Sarah Bernhardt, or by his fictitious women.) Dorian's decision to marry Sibyl is therefore a betrayal of his true nature; in the cult of immoralism, the good may be found by acting in harmony with one's innermost self.

When Dorian first beholds his portrait, "the sense of his

[3] *Ibid.*, p. 298n.

own beauty came on him like a revelation." In Dorian's wish, a narcissistic motif appears for the first time: "If it were I who was to be always young, and the picture that was to grow old. For that—for that—I would give everything! . . . I would give my soul for that!"[4] By grace of the omniscient point of view, Dorian's wish spins out its own realization. The novel is a fulfillment of this wish; it is the bridge that joins the conditional mood and the declarative mood. Dorian's wish functions as the germ of the plot; it impels episodes and invents details of scene, description, and summary. It lays out the background of the Dorian-Lord Henry-Basil Hallward complex. It indirectly causes Dorian's disillusionment with Sibyl. When Basil comes to see and borrow the picture, Dorian is tempted by some perverse imp of the unconscious to kill the painter. This murder leads to dissipation, opium dens, and the infernal labyrinth of the concluding chapters, until finally we attend Dorian's ascent to the chamber where the deeds of the past, memory, and the remorse of the present converge, pushing Dorian to affirm his will to reconciliation through death.

Such is the skeleton outline of the narrative. There are actually two parts to the basic action concerning the nature and destiny of Dorian's character: the first part before Chapter XI, which consists of the exposition (I-III) and the Sibyl-Dorian relation (IV-X); the second part after Chapter XI, which includes the climactic murder of Basil, Jim Vane's death, and the resolution (XII-XX). Despite the heavy rhetoric, the "purple" saturation, and the verbal embroidery in the manner of Huysmans' *A Rebours* in Chapter XI, the plot as a sequence of beginning, middle, and end is clearly discernible.

Wilde himself calls this novel an "essay on decorative art," "all conversation and no action." He confesses: "I can't describe action. My people sit in chairs and chatter."[5] These

[4] *Works*, p. 34.   [5] *Letters*, p. 255.

assertions render suspect the notion of *Dorian Gray* as a novel in the usual sense of a series of incidents arranged so as to produce a single concentrated effect. Chapter XI disrupts the sequence of the action since—notwithstanding the return of Jim Vane—it snaps the thread of Dorian's involvement with youthful love. It aborts the romance only to lead Dorian to incidents that play on "the note of Doom" which Wilde considers the cohesive ingredient in his work.

Taken literally as a melodrama of vengeance, *Dorian Gray* deals with Jim Vane's sentimental vow to avenge his sister's death in circumstances that are linked with the counterfeit atmosphere of his mother's sordid life. Indeed, the mother's "make-up" is revealing. Wilde portrays Jim with the gross, stilted diction reminiscent of his early plays, *The Duchess of Padua* and *Vera*. But Jim is, to an extent, functional: with his mannequin features, he enacts the role of the detective in pursuit of the guilty man. In contrast, Wilde's depiction of Sibyl's pathetic figure betrays his instinctive sympathy for his characters. Despite her immersion in theatrical life, Sibyl's nature displays a clean simplicity: she can only accept or deny love.

In this detective-novel stage, Dorian's role of "Prince Charming" provides the element of fantasy; the story as a romance figuratively presents the wager of good *versus* evil. What informs the theme of pride and downfall is the literal drama of return and pursuit, the rise and decline of Dorian. Dorian's existence preserves, and is itself preserved by, the picture. When he kills Hallward, he denies the creator of his beauty; for the painter is solely responsible for his preternatural beauty and his vanity. Just as Adam denies his Creator, so Dorian commits the "sin" of pride. The denial of authority foreshadows, and underlies, the murders of Basil, Campbell, and the death of Jim Vane. Dorian falls from an exquisite innocence into a haunted state of awareness. In exploiting Campbell's secret enormities,

Dorian perverts science in order to get rid of his artistic creator.

Concern over genre, or the purely specific differentiae of *Dorian Gray*, is not an end in itself but a means toward defining its structure of values. One is reminded of Wilde's argument in emphasizing the primacy of the novel's existence as an imaginative work. He hopes here to demonstrate the value of renunciation as the moral poise gained from an intelligent discrimination of the issues involved in the hero's plight. Of course Wilde's pleading for his novel's positive qualities before a hostile audience must not be confused with the organic wholeness of the novel which is our primary interest.

Classified as "decadent," Wilde's novel pursues the attitude and style established by its main inspiration, Huysmans' *A Rebours*, which Lord Henry's gift to Dorian vaguely resembles. On the surface, it illustrates the temper of the milieu that we meet later in Whistler, Beardsley, *The Yellow Book*, and *The Savoy*. It lays considerable stress on decoration, psychological experimentation, fantasy, abnormalities, the correspondence between odors and states of guilt and innocence; the purging of illusions by crude materialism; the contrast between consciously planned actions and instinctive drives—a variety of topics deriving from *Faust*, the Gothic novels, Pater's studies on the Renaissance, Gautier and the French Symbolists; and many other sources. Generalizations have indeed been made about the decadent novel and its subjects: the attenuation of emotion, the detailed analysis of ennui, moral disintegration, psychic alienation.[6] In dealing with a rarefied atmosphere and the fetish of form and language, the decadent novel supposedly conveys a static condition in which time and space are fused in elaborate patterns. These patterns represent Axel's or Des

[6] Richard A. Long and Iva G. Jones, "Towards a Definition of the 'Decadent Novel,'" *College English*, XXII (January 1961), 245-49.

Esseintes' mad pursuit of worldly pleasures and sensory hallucinations, their flair for the *outré* and the bizarre. How valid are these generalizations?

Called an escapist testament, a breviary of neo-hellenism, *Dorian Gray* bears indisputable affinities with aestheticism. But in truth the novel presents a spirit active and vivifying in its intellectual restlessness, with its adventurous energy seeking release in some fitting, viable form. One can interpret the scenes of dawn in the novel, when Dorian emerges from his nocturnal haunts, as prefiguring the consciousness rising from its dream to cast a defining light on the surrounding world. At this point, Wilde's handling of time and space, which has been so far overlooked, demands scrutiny. Edwin Muir considers a novel dramatic when the progression and resolution of action figure in time.[7] A character novel, on the other hand, has an action with a static nature; action is continuously reshuffled in space while the fixity and the circumference of the characters endow the parts with their proportion and meaning. Whereas the dramatic novel engages itself chiefly with time, the character novel is preoccupied with space as its field of action.

Now Wilde's novel, as the title suggests, revolves within a space definitely circumscribed, urban in locale, and urbane in taste. Within this field and at the center of it is the enigmatic canvas. Dorian's room, the idyllic garden, Lord Fermor's house in "a labyrinth of grinning streets and black, grassless squares," Piccadilly crowds and theaters, Sibyl's dressing room, a storeroom in the attic, innumerable dining-rooms, a secluded conservatory—all these comprise the physical setting in which eloquent gestures, decisive and expressive, bespeak more of spiritual crises than outright adventures. Even the hunt, a concrete analogue of Dorian's fugitive role, signifies a short interval which connects limited, enclosed spaces. This shrunken world, relatively

[7] *The Structure of the Novel* (London, 1954), pp. 63ff.

speaking, is required by the aim of intensity. Since novelty and multiplicity of sensation, both of which Dorian elects as his dominating passions, abound more in the city than anywhere else, the city with its gorgeous courts and loathsome gutters assumes the function of a vast stage where life solidifies in the rigid shapes of an art-work. This is exactly the effect produced by the massive catalogue of jewels, treasures, bric-a-brac, in Chapter XI. Absolute stasis, caused by the enchantment over exotic wealth, tends to hold up the development of either physical or psychological action; that is, the novel tends toward lyrical condensation, not an epic sweep or dramatic mobility. Even the syntax of sentences sags with its excessive load of decorative epithets, substantives, phrasal units arranged in an endless procession.

It would be instructive to compare the dense texture of Chapter XI and the depiction of Dorian Gray's room or of Basil's studio with the shabby home of the Vane family, and the squalid slums of the London underworld. In all these descriptions, the same degree of skill and effort seems to have been expended. Consequently, whatever distortion may prevail in the extravagance of Dorian's life and the misery around him is restored to balance by the justice of narrative proportion. Each part receives the same painstaking treatment. To joyful outbursts on the glories of fashionable dandyism, Wilde counterpoints starkly realistic details which are either subtly insinuated or rendered in the process of accumulation. For example, juxtaposed with Dorian's raptures over Sibyl's voice with its "wild passion of violins" is the vulgarity of the "hideous Jew . . . smoking a vile cigar," who has "greasy ringlets, an enormous diamond blazed in the centre of a soiled sheet."[8] Opposed to the slick glamor of Lord Henry and the blaxing luxury of drawing rooms are the impressions of grotesque scenes, such as the dancing saloon with "its tattered green curtain.

8 *Works*, p. 49.

. . . The floor was covered with ochre-coloured sawdust, trampled here and there into mud, and stained with rings of spilt liquor. . . [Dorian] looked round at the grotesque things that lay in such fantastic postures on the ragged mattresses. The twisted limbs, the gaping mouths, the staring lustre-less eyes, fascinated him."[9]

Restriction of space in the novel entails a corresponding withdrawal of characters into intense self-awareness which initially affects plot, diction, spectacle, and thought. This psychological trait prompts the unremitting attention paid to surfaces of objects, contours, masses, outlines of appearance that evoke the greatest density of sensations. This mode of treatment logically follows from such typical impulses as Dorian reveals ("I love beautiful things that one can touch and handle. . . .") or from Lord Henry's preaching ("all experience is of value"). Organized around the vital process of Dorian's sensibility, the texture makes no pretense to detached objectivity. Wilde takes advantage of what E. M. Forster considers the novelist's privilege of an un-hampered point of view.[10] Wilde uses a primitive version of stream-of-consciousness technique in some sections, nota-bly in Dorian's ponderings and reveries, to capture the character's unique apprehension of his inwardness and the "tone of things."

Wilde exploits visual and aural sensations to establish the moral correlatives of the psyche. A case in point is Jim Vane's despondency on the eve of his departure. The narrator projects his fate through the image of the flies buzzing around his "meagre meal," with the "loud rumble of omni-buses" and cacophony of the city as signs of the hostile pres-sure of an alien world. (Jim, symbol of the vengeful con-science, is slain by leisurely society: he is accidentally shot by hunters in a country retreat.) Sound and sight conspire in this situation:

[9] *Ibid.*, p. 142.   [10] *Aspects of the Novel* (London, 1927).

His mother was waiting for him below. She grumbled at his unpunctuality, as he entered. He made no answer, but sat down to his meagre meal. The flies buzzed round the table, and crawled over the stained cloth. Through the rumble of omnibuses, and the clatter of street-cabs, he could hear the droning voice devouring each minute that was left to him.[11]

Wilde's analysis of subjective experience and the flux of feelings dictates a stylistic *ordonnance* of this kind. His style corresponds not only to the requirements of the individual natures he explores, but also to the ambience of cosmopolitan refinement, with its "thickness" of manners, intimations, rituals. Applied to other personages, like Campbell, Hallward, and Sibyl, this mode of presentation operates with efficient and telling economy.

Another example of concrete description serving a thematic purpose is the first two paragraphs of the novel, in which Wilde sketches deftly the landscape of Basil's studio:

The studio was filled with the rich odour of roses, and when the light summer wind stirred amidst the trees of the garden there came through the open door the heavy scent of the lilac, or the more delicate perfume of the pink-flowering thorn.

From the corner of the divan of Persian saddlebags on which he was lying, smoking, as was his custom, innumerable cigarettes, Lord Henry Wotton could just catch the gleam of the honey-sweet and honey-coloured blossoms of a laburnum, whose tremulous branches seemed hardly able to bear the burden of a beauty so flame-like as theirs; and now and then the fantastic shadows of birds in flight flitted across the long tussore-silk curtains that were stretched in front of the huge window, producing a kind of momentary Japanese effect, and making him think of

[11] *Works*, p. 64.

those pallid jade-faced painters of Tokyo who, through the medium of an art that is necessarily immobile, seek to convey the sense of swiftness and motion. The sullen murmur of the bees shouldering their way through the long unmown grass, or circling with monotonous insistence round the dusty gilt horns of the straggling woodbine, seemed to make the stillness more oppressive. The dim roar of London was like the bourdon note of a distant organ.[12]

Here the tonalities of surface and color in furniture, clothing, insects all appeal to an irrational stratum of awareness. Synesthesia furnishes one means of ordering things: the movement of scent and perfume coordinates distance and space, while visual, gustatory, and olfactory impressions coalesce in "the gleam of the honey-sweet and honey-coloured blossoms of a laburnum." One notes also the striking device whereby Wilde attributes life to inert artifacts. Opposites give rise to each other and are seen to be ultimately identical: "now and then the fantastic shadows of birds in flight flitted across the long tussore-silk curtains. . . ." Art souvenirs of antique civilizations combine with vivid tokens of spring and natural beauty to establish a world of half-fancy and half-reality. Under Wilde's touch, inanimate objects wake to life. Everything then breathes with organic energy and innocent charm.

Our knowledge of character in the world of this novel chiefly derives from the exposure in methodical sequence of typifying gestures or acts. They are disposed on strategic occasions: for example, when Jim Vane impulsively swears vengeance; or in the studied languor of Lord Henry's phrases and postures. Given the poses of the characters, we conceive of space here principally as the stage of behavior, with appropriate foreground, background, props, etc. Such actions

[12] *Ibid.*, p. 18.

as we see are executed for the sake of substantiating an idea which a character embodies. To this extent, Wilde's characters seem flat: we can always predict Lord Henry's opinions, Dorian's reactions, Basil's scruples. Granted Lord Henry's pervasive influence, which fills the book like a contagion, fixing the smell and shade and the whole panorama of every dramatic encounter in social exchange or in monologue, we can foretell probable consequences. From the moment the portrait registers a curve on its lips, we can intuitively forecast the limit to this magic, and the recognition and catastrophe that will soon follow.

One can easily demonstrate the affinities of the novel to a "well-made" play in its adroit management of the curve of incidents. But while Dorian may be a type in this play, he is still fluid in substance, as we see from his responsive liveliness, his energy of commitment, his impressionability. Up to the end, any move he determines to make seems urged on by shifting moods and spontaneous feelings. Take his deliberations to destroy the picture: the short sentences, with their staccato beat and jerky rhythm, suggest an actively scrupulous mind. Unlike Lord Henry's monolithic firmness of conviction, Dorian's susceptibility acquires depth in the choices and discriminations he makes. These discriminations embrace complex issues, antinomies in truth, perplexed by a profound sense of hovering retribution.

Since Dorian's awareness evolves in time, it is incorrect to classify *Dorian Gray* as a novel in which the element of space predominates. In the first place, the novel portrays the attempt of a young man to transcend the flux of temporal experience. This subject is handled by manipulating the concept of time which underlies the evolution of plot. Consequently we find that the factor of time governs the psychological experiences of the protagonist, and determines the states of his consciousness. Dorian's naive simplicity passes through stages of love, bitter disappointment, pride, ecstasy, solitary introspection, horror, humiliation, anguish, ennui, despair—the entire gamut, to be sure. These are manifold "events" within his consciousness. Each stage offers a problem that requires eventual resolution; each thesis generates an antithesis until, out of their conflict, a new synthesis is born. Such a dialectic seems to control the attraction and repulsion of characters among themselves, epitomized in Dorian's fluctuating love and hatred of his portrait.

In the anguished state of Dorian's life, the simple incidents that gradually entangle him come about with inexorable continuity. Realism becomes tempered by the remoteness of the supernatural picture from quotidian life. Unexposed, the portrait remains a mere artifact shrouded in mystery; exposed, it reflects the actuality that visible appearance and facts conceal. Could it be that Dorian, if he desires to know his true self, must ruin the good and beautiful? Wilde's narrative authority works through the changes of the portrait; thus, art becomes a vehicle of truth. The picture registers Dorian's acts in facial alterations, rendering the spiritual in concrete terms. This ironically fulfills Dorian's aim to unite the body and the spirit. Yet even his identity blurs in the end: Dorian's corpse, loathsome in decrepitude, can be identified only by means of his loathsome jewelry.

In the beginning Dorian accepts from Lord Henry a "poisonous" book which tells of men who tried to realize in their brief lifetimes all the passions found in the history of human experience. This fantastic record soon becomes a reality as Dorian imitates what it describes. Note that Dorian's lineage, his birth, childhood, and adolescence, all remain obscure, just as his name remains a secret to Sibyl and James Vane. His identity is never fully redeemed from its shadowy origin. London gossips about his debauchery, his association with drunken sailors and thieves, in a frantic quest for sensations; it is up for the reader to spell out the nature of his immoralism.

Although Dorian's immoralism, obscure throughout and obliquely referred to now and then, is never definitely compromised, still some primal urge drives him to hide and at the same time confess the secret of his total self. In a sense his fetish is not beauty but the need to know his integral self. And the talisman for this project is the portrait. Unlike other literary versions of the "double," e.g., Dr. Jekyll, William Wilson, the portrait functions less as a conscience than an emblem.[13] It furnishes us the criterion of Dorian's growing lucidity as he follows the progress of his degeneration. It lays open the portentous disequilibrium that disturbs the spirit. Dorian's need to know indicates the absence of unity of being and sensibility. When he tries to break the cycle of corruption, the moral conflict ends; the novel ends, too. Somehow, for the fate-stricken Dorian, ideas and feelings lose their power. The ambiguity of Dorian's crimes affords an expansive field for the exercise of the reader's susceptibility, just as a kindred ambiguity of the specters in *The Turn of the Screw* provokes our curiosity. Wilde once defended himself by saying: "Each man sees his own sin in Dorian Gray. What Dorian Gray's sins are no one knows. He who finds them has brought them"[14]—although we know that he is guilty of murder.

What then are the specific attributes that distinguish Wilde's work as a unique contribution to the genre of the novel?

In 1884 Henry James initiated a new period in aesthetic inquiry when he questioned the current orthodox practice of insisting on a moral message that can be directly drawn from the novel at a glance. He held the principle, later fully developed in "The Art of Fiction," that the task of the

[13] Cf. Leon Lemmonier, *Oscar Wilde* (Paris, 1939), pp. 158-59.
[14] *Letters*, p. 266.

novelist is to grasp experience "which is an immense sensibility," "the very atmosphere of the mind." For James the novelist possesses "the power to guess the unseen from the seen, to trace the implications of things, to judge the whole piece by the pattern."[15] Wilde assumed this vision of the artist when he affixed his witty preface to *Dorian Gray*. The preface no doubt is a synthesis of the ruling ideas that vitalized the creative instincts of a whole generation—Pater, Whistler, James, Yeats—and the tradition they gave rise to.

Despite Wilde's flippant ridicule of James' "elaborate subtlety" and "refined realism," his practice affirms James' dictum that the moral "sense of a work" immediately depends on the "amount of felt life concerned in producing it." Wilde likewise professed that "the moral life of man forms part of the subject matter of the artist, but the morality of art consists in the perfect use of an imperfect medium." Wilde disapproves of James' manner because it involves "analysis, not action" as its aim; it has more "psychology than passion." Unwittingly Wilde is characterizing the manner of *Dorian Gray*. We can justifiably say that because the narrative focus often isolates the spiritual struggle in Dorian's self, with the spotlight steadfastly thrown on the objective awareness that he exercises in moments of crisis, the primary issue in the novel is lucidity of discrimination; the secondary issue concerns itself with the antinomies of sense and soul, the clash of good and evil, and other opposites.[16]

[15] "The Art of Fiction," *Myth and Method*, ed., James E. Miller, Jr. (Nebraska, 1960), p. 13. See Oscar Cargill, "Mr. James' Aesthetic Mr. Nash," *Nineteenth Century Fiction*, XII (December 1957), 177-87.

[16] Of relevance are the following discussions, most of them repetitive and some vitiated by lack of proportion: Ted R. Spivey, "Damnation and Salvation in *The Picture* of Dorian Gray," *Boston University Studies in English*, IV (Autumn 1960), 162-70; Ernest A. Baker, *The History of the English Novel* (New York, 1938), IX, pp. 216-23. On certain motifs in Wilde's novel, the following are

Analysis of psychological states figures in Wilde's fantasy to a considerable degree, chiefly as a response to the necessity of plot. Antagonisms among varying temperaments that surround Dorian do not happen in terms of overt hand-to-hand combat; rather, they occur as collision of wills, aims, likings, and the infinite ramifications of impulse and conscious intent. To Lord Henry's proposal of buying the picture, Basil says "no." To Dorian's passion over Sibyl, Lord Henry reacts with mocking shrewdness. Dorian's evasions, outright refusals, negative subterfuges, and shiftings of attitude all stem from his anxiety to keep faith to the vow he swore before his portrait. His gestures culminate in the supreme nihilism of murder, anticipated by Sibyl's suicide and followed by Jim Vane's accident, Campbell's slow wasting, and his death. Dorian's stab on the picture, a final assent to self-contradiction, comes with graceful inevitability.

Lord Henry, the presumed Mephistopheles of this Faustian drama, seems to have maneuvered everything from beginning to end. His cynical logic and the unflagging bravura of his sophistry are modulated by a tact that his entrances and exits indicate. Like the epigrammatic villains in the comedies, Lord Henry converts the traditional *raisonneur* into an incisive critic of manners. He caricatures people's faces and gestures in his private game of parody. He has Wilde's sharp, cruel eye for the hypocrisies of aristocratic society and the comic absurdities of life. Despite the fact that he does not act—he never practices what he preaches— Lord Henry gives us the strongest proof that Wilde, instead of being a dreamer, actually performs best as a satirist of mores and social behavior.[17]

---

interesting: Victor A. Oswald Jr., "Oscar Wilde, Stefan George, Heliogabalus," *Modern Language Quarterly*, x (December 1949), 517-25; Oscar Maurer, Jr., "A Philistine Source for Dorian Gray?" *Philological Quarterly*, xxvi (January 1947), 84-86.

[17] Correlate Dorian's attitudes with the "healthy" optimism of the contributors to *Fifty Years*. Sir Ian Malcolm, for example,

Although Lord Henry never does what he says, yet without him the novel could not exist. For he promotes the action at crucial points: (1) he reveals to Dorian the horror of growing old, thus inducing the youth to utter his fatal wish; (2) he buttresses Dorian's egoism when Dorian hears of Sibyl's death; (3) he convinces Dorian that all repentance is vain. Notwithstanding his influence, Lord Henry provides us not with merely a "satiric sketch," as Pater suggests, but a split personality. Professing subversive opinion, he does not however commit any malfeasance or give the slightest hint of scandal. Scorning action and cultivating exotic tastes, he nevertheless drives Dorian to a frenzied pursuit of active pleasure.

From a wider perspective, Lord Henry belongs in the deepest sense to a symbolic reality. His idiosyncrasies, his methodical incursions, awaken the real Dorian Gray embedded in the tissue of mundane superficialities. He is father to the Narcissus in Dorian that is caught within multiple contradictions; he affects radically the destiny of the novel's protagonist. But while he is the evangelist of sensuous perfectionism, his intelligence leaps forth with vigor, complementing Dorian's sensitivity. Dorian and Lord Henry together form an indivisible unity. From an allegorical standpoint, Dorian represents the experiencing self while Lord Henry represents the rationalizing self. Dorian acts, Lord Henry abstracts. It is possible also to discern in Lord Henry the intelligence of Wilde, in Dorian, his sensibility. At any rate, the dichotomy persists and pervades the whole work.

---

pp. 38-45, celebrates "*Jeunesse dorée*," gilded youth; Sir Arthur Quiller-Couch writes nostalgically of Dorian's milieu, pp. 52ff.

The historical and temporal depth of the novel derives from covert allusions and scattered references to the Roman emperors in Rome's declining years, to corrupt Italian princes, and to mythical personages, as referred to in R. D. Brown, "Suetonius, Symonds, and Gibbon in *The Picture* of Dorian Gray," *Modern Language Notes*, LXXI (April 1956), 264.

Compared with Lord Henry and Dorian, Basil Hallward, the other major figure, crystallizes the condition of a precarious self-sufficiency. Opposed to his secret passion for another man, the society of his time and its strict ethical code force Basil to conform to certain patterns of conduct. Consequently he acquires the status of spokesman of standard morality. He thus escapes his calling as an androgynous dandy by adopting the mask of collective conscience. At times he assumes the role of chorus to the tragic complications of Dorian's life. He sublimates his feelings in art, thus separating morality from nature. He insures himself from being a victim of perversion by always yielding to Dorian and Lord Henry. He middle class attitude, as shown in his compassion for Sibyl's mother, proves the counterpart to Lord Henry's distinction of birth and mind, to Dorian's fortuitous beauty. His death implies the defeat of sentiment when faced by an absolute faith in art. If Basil practically introduces the novel to us in his capacity as the maker of the miraculous portrait, he also concludes the novel as a victim of his own creation. His existence images the complete circuit of Dorian's action.

Using these typical traits and general outlines of the important characters, we can easily chart and diagram the conflicts and tensions that retard or accelerate the action of plot. However, their meaning within the thematic pattern—insofar as conflict is a function of character as given fact—must needs be defined. We must know the tenor of which the characters and their behavior are metaphoric vehicles. A handful of antitheses will subsume the topics of description and dialogue in the book, such as youth's magnificence, life's brevity, life as art, social corruption, and so forth.

At the heart of the narrative action, governing its pace and direction, is the irrational phenomenon of the portrait. This mystery is in turn contained within a form ordinarily given to a transcription of average, normal processes of thought and behavior. The reader shares Dorian's surprise at this inexplicable fact. The unexpected suddenly happens, upsetting all predictions of common sense: "Surely his wish had not been fulfilled? Such things were impossible. . . . And, yet, there was the picture before him, with the touch of cruelty in the mouth."[18] Mirrorlike in effect, Dorian's picture participates in the life and fortunes of its original. Lord Henry's axiom that life has its elaborate masterpieces, that sometimes a "personality" assumes "the office of art," has been realized here without much ado. Wilde therefore begs at the outset the reader's willing suspension of disbelief. Grant the work its mystery and everything follows patly like clockwork. Given the dualism in Dorian of narcissistic pride and instinctive restraint that tends to discipline the libido, the novel's denouement follows with spontaneous naturalness.

Quite peculiar to the narrative substance is its position within a frame built from a miraculous phenomenon as *donnée*. The story proper hinges on the fulfillment of a wish that Dorian's youth be eternal; only when he violates the terms of the "contract" do the normal laws of life reassert themselves. From the suspension of normal law, the mood of uncanny artificiality emerges. Through the ingenuity of Campbell, guilty of sins we do not know, Basil's body disappears in a way we shall never know. We hear often the confused gossip of the London multitude. Dorian's sins are reported indirectly, and this poses a problem: if the novel "imitates" action, Wilde has to create some kind of conflict.

Conflict develops accordingly from the confrontation of characters. Dorian's character proves intriguing, when this *fin-de-siècle* Faust turns out to be an instrument of a didactic tale. Is he just a physiognomy designed for an illustration of a type? Or is he a created character with a palpable

[18] *Works*, p. 78.

roundness of his own? By means of sustained interior dialogue, Wilde renders Dorian's most intimate confidences in set situations and tableaux. Dorian agonizes over Sibyl's suicide, he repents—but only for a while. He discovers himself invulnerable to pity; his cruelty soon mars the portrait. But he does not aspire to the status of a reality. He acts an ideal role in exemplifying a synthesis of sensibility and perversion, a rare yet plausible type. In other words, Dorian's character is a condition in which extremes meet; his acts signify the temporary triumph of one extreme over the other.

Lured by the siren of beauty in art, Dorian, however, succumbs to sensual dissipation. Rejecting good and bad, he yields nonetheless to an inner fatality, a passionate indifference which makes him incapable of feeling compassion for others. Becoming less perfect and even less human, he is also spiritually debased. Since pity and suffering ruin the sensitive enjoyment of voluptuous refinements, Wilde in actual life hated pain and suffering; only in *Reading Gaol* does he attempt to gain a sense of balance. Similarly, Dorian yields to the ravages of sensory delights. His case therefore bears a marked internal inconsistency. Opposing universality of taste to the relativity of awareness, he tries to unify soul and sense, passion and thought, by concentrating on limited aspects of experience. But such intensity suffers from narrowness of sympathy; and melancholy, ennui, desperation, and remorse are the result.

If we examine the logic behind Dorian's hopeless violence in demolishing the image of his conscience, an act itself prompted by the conscience within, the necessity of the act discloses itself. Dorian wanted to get rid of the guilt attached to his past so that he could relinquish all duties and obligations, and pursue freely his affections for Hetty Merton (Sibyl's ghost?). Could it be that he has forgotten his wish? Now he has become the portrait in his ageless glamor while the portrait has assumed the lineaments of his human self,

human in the sense that its face grows more distorted whenever Dorian commits a vicious deed. How can one exist without the other? At the start, we have accepted the premise of
imitation by the picture of the moral value of Dorian's conduct in terms of pictorial commentary. So far there has been
no positive change. What this signifies is the failure of
Dorian's nerve in endeavoring to arrive at an all-embracing
reconciliation, a marriage of self and its appearances. Finally
death lends the ultimate oneness.

Dorian's predicament exemplifies only one form, yet the
most general, of the ordeal to attain unity of self. This theme,
elaborately meditated upon in *De Profundis*, distinguishes
one dominant strand in Wilde's literary compositions.
Throughout the novel, opposing forces move within the
stream of the plot. Antitheses between passion and spirit,
consciousness and unconsciousness, feeling and artifice drive
the characters to take up differing positions, differing
judgments. Wilde gains a perspective on these conflicts by
partly confining them within the range of Lord Henry's
sophisticated survey; the latter's intellect delineates issues
from a well-defined viewpoint. In Chapter IV, for example,
Lord Henry constantly poses the disparity between soul
and body. Yet he does not ignore the possibility of harmony
between them: "There was animalism in the soul, and the
body had its moments of spirituality. . . . Who could say
where the fleshly impulse ceased, or the psychical impulse
began?"[19] Both logic and sentiment, pain and pleasure, have
resemblances and differences. Lord Henry himself defines his
mission: "To note the curious hard logic of passion, and the
emotional coloured life of the intellect—to observe where
they met, and where they separated, at what point they
were in unison, and at what point they were at discord—."[20]

We see now that Dorian's love for Sibyl is an attempt to

[19] *Ibid.*, p. 56. [20] *Ibid.*, p. 55.

abolish egoism and merge the self in empathic projection with the person of the beloved. But this love, being exclusive, fails. Love succumbs to the sin of self-consciousness, to its self-defeating fidelity to an art of transcendence. The obvious reason of course is the fact that Sibyl, no longer immersed in her act, becomes aware of her spectators: she loses unity of self as person and actress. She denies the imaginative, poetic detachment which, for Dorian, gave an ideal aura to her life. No doubt Dorian has mistaken dramatic illusion for the reality. Consequently, love fails to unify art and life—the art solidified in theaters, paintings, books; the life manifest in the hideous grin of Dorian's portrait, the dismal gutters, the filthy houses of lust.

Just as love, in Dorian's case, proves futile to unify warring forces, so does the willed dream of Huysmans' Des Esseintes fail to absorb all the possible experiences of mankind in a single moment. Dorian had hoped to partake of "that vivid life that lurks in all grotesques." He strove to spiritualize the senses. Likewise, Des Esseintes tried to "multiply personalities," being for Dorian that "wonderful young Parisian in whom the romantic and scientific temperaments were so strangely blended," who "became to him a prefiguring type of himself."[21] Both these protagonists simply revolve within a circle of contradictions: desiring to transcend the flux of historical experience, they exploit experience itself to the extent that a mystical asceticism may grow out of self-titillation—strange dialectic, indeed! Dorian simply echoes Pater in theorizing that he should never "accept any theory or system that would involve the sacrifice of any mode of passionate experience," experience being the obsessive goal. When Wilde, however, intrudes the information that Dorian "never fell into the error of arresting his intellectual development by a formal acceptance of creed or system,"[22] he is talking outside of the novel's context.

[21] *Ibid.*, p. 102. [22] *Ibid.*, p. 106.

Dorian's intellectual development remains circular in its fanatic adherence to epicureanism. Dorian descends to a lower type when he loses the sense of good and evil. He commits the cardinal error in practicing Lord Henry's hedonism, leading to the distortion of the beautiful portrait and his hopeless floundering. Instead of annihilating time, Dorian's unchanging youth shortens it; when his thirty-eighth year arrives, he finds himself still dissatisfied, restless, afflicted.

Paradoxically, Dorian's struggle to escape the laws of time and contingency restricts both his spatial and temporal reach. Spatial range, as we have seen, is limited. Duration in time means only a progression within a closed circuit; its terminal is the *cul de sac* of satiety and revulsion. Like Des Esseintes, who tormented himself between the extremes of sensuality and purity, Dorian staggers between ennui and flight from his nobler self. What is Jim Vane's vengeance but a form of nemesis? Character, then, is fate.

In his early fiction, Wilde examined the impulse of "duty" in "Lord Arthur Savile's Crime," and showed his talent for producing clever, gratuitous mystifications; witness "The Sphinx without a Secret," "The Model Millionaire," and "The Canterville Ghost." In "Pen, Pencil and Poison," the artist's diabolic inspiration and morbid fatality convert sin into a sacramental act. In "The Portrait of Mr. W. H.," the power of the "lie" quickens truth and self-knowledge. In *Dorian Gray*, Dorian's relation with his picture exemplifies duty counteracting self-indulgence: when he stabs the picture, Dorian commits a contradiction—he defies the power of time which ruins the portrait, but from which he himself is liberated. His remorse exists, curiously enough, in time. When he ceases to be a spectator of life and acts violently, he puts an end to the suspension of time; he destroys his beauty and the reason for his existence. The end products of Dorian's life are "a ruined body which is continuous with his personality and his society, and a work of art which will symbolize forever his power to explore the hell of reality."[23]

It would be superfluous to make more explicit the battle between good and evil forces in Dorian's mind. Despite his resolve to shape his life into art, he still flinches and wavers under the piercing impact of life itself, life uncontrollably fertile and spontaneous. The organic vitality of life set over against the artifices of culture and fixed rituals; the vigor of desire and repugnance, of imagination against mechanical knowledge; of natural feeling and intuition against the reflexes of habitual and routine existence—these values, deducible from the interaction of characters and circumstances, helped to organize the luxuriance of rhetoric and imagery within a meaningful frame. They also endow the conventional cast of the plot with symbolic implications.

Wilde's triumph in the novel form consists in the careful management of an interesting story as such, without sacrificing the virtue of style and the order of dramatic complications which express the judgment of the author. By manipulating situation, as when Dorian, the priest of beauty, is juxtaposed with ugly surroundings, Wilde achieves the end in which the judgment of experience upon character is objectively expressed. Choice of viewpoint exposes social foibles and individual absurdities. From this angle, *Dorian Gray* answers the requirements of a novel of social criticism. If fiction is sustained by entertainment value and justified by moral purpose, then Wilde's novel supplies both.

Assessed on the basis of literary and cultural history, *Dorian Gray* exemplifies the pervasive trend in the latter half of the Victorian period toward intense analysis of mental states.[24] In the past the novel generally conceived of meaning

[23] Morse Peckham, *Beyond the Tragic Vision* (New York, 1962), pp. 318-19.
[24] This has been frequently discussed, e.g., Leon Edel, *The Modern Psychological Novel* (New York, 1955). Cf. Oscar Wilde, *Reviews* (London, 1908), pp. 482-83: "Action takes place in the sun-

and value as something imposed by an external authority, such as church, state, family. Gradually, however, the novel tended to view man as the sole creator of his own existence, thus relegating the myths of religion to a remote past. Symbolism gave rise to the technique of making the external world an outward analogue or extension of the psyche. Plunging into the mind and subconscious realm, Dickens, George Eliot, and others sought to transcribe the vicissitudes of the inner self as demanded by an outlook which decreed that what is significant is not truth in fact but truth in relationships; that is, not the statistics of Moll Flanders' world but the relationships of Middlemarch. This practice suggests the collapse of traditional norms of conduct, which is now almost a sociological platitude. The evolution of "terror" fiction, its changes of scope and emphasis, indicates the mutations of the novel form in the latter part of the century. Whereas Gothic romances showed us the success of naturalistic devices, occult lore, and ingenious contraptions, the ghost and mystery stories of Collins, Stevenson, Henry James, and others reveal the increasing ascendancy of a totally subjective viewpoint. Eventually the mind became the principal setting, while dreams and delusions became pivotal elements of narrative.

Parallel to this change is the heightened concern with the artist's predicament in an industrial, bourgeois civilization.[25] Attention centered itself on biographical facts, on the ambiguities of art's connection with reality. The confession appeared as a favorite mode of self-expression. When the artist withdraws from social encounters to passive intro-

---

light, but the soul works in the dark . . . thought seems to proceed not on logical lines, but on lines of passion. The unity of the individual is being expressed through its inconsistencies and its contradictions. In a strange twilight man is seeking for himself. . . ."

[25] See Raymond Williams, *Culture and Society 1780-1950* (Anchor edn., New York, 1960), pp. 178-79, 183-85; Walter E. Houghton, *The Victorian Frame of Mind* (New Haven and London, 1957), pp. 115, 126-27.

spection, we find Beardsley and his "elegant" caricatures; we behold the estranged lives of poets, their exile or suicide. We discover Wilde in Reading Gaol; after his release, we see him descend into the squalid "pits" of Paris. Whatever commitment the artist had the courage to carry out into action was narrowed down to a dedication to his craft and the exaltation of the creative process to the realm of an absolute. Aesthetic experience fed on itself by being the paramount subject matter of fiction.

In the light of the development of the novel after Henry James, *The Picture of Dorian Gray* earns for itself a significant place in the tradition. In setting a portrait, a work of art, at the center of the action, Wilde effects the interplay of natural perception and moral judgment in the novel. From the reader's viewpoint, the picture suggests the treatment of angle and distance—the ways of telling and of showing—which make up the perennial issues of the aesthetics and criticism of fiction.[26]

[26] For a recent discussion of technical problems, see Wayne Booth, *Rhetoric of Fiction* (Chicago, 1961).

III · Aesthetics and Literary Criticism

CONTEXTS

Scholars and informed readers are generally agreed that Wilde's criticism merits study only as a patchwork affair or as a polished form of public entertainment.[1] And yet his criticism preserves its quality of being earnestly suggestive in posing just the right questions. Although one cannot doubt a certain adventurousness, an *ad hoc* quality, in Wilde's penetrating insights, yet the doubt remains as to whether, apart from the liveliness of the prose, there is any intrinsic originality in his theories. But of course originality, in a broad sense, concerns focal adjustments and a strategy of emphasis.

Wilde as a critic, except perhaps for his flippantly satiric tone, is not wholly a consistent and systematic thinker.[2] What

---

[1] The publication dates of the essays in *Intentions* (1891) are as follows: "The Decay of Lying," *Nineteenth Century*, January 1889; "Pen, Pencil and Poison," *The Fortnightly Review*, January 1889; "The Truth of Masks," first appeared as "The True Function and Value of Criticism," in *Nineteenth Century*, part I on July 1890, with the subtitle "With Some Remarks on the Importance of Doing Nothing"; Part II on September 1890. "The Portrait of Mr. W. H." appeared first in *Blackwood's Magazine*, July 1889. Further particulars regarding the publication of these pieces can be found in the *Letters*.

Wilde began writing articles for *Pall Mall Gazette* on October 14, 1884; *Dramatic Review* on March 14, 1885; *Nineteenth Century* on May 1885; *Society* on July 4, 1885; *Saturday Review* on May 7, 1887; *Woman's World* (as editor) on June 1887; *The Lady's Pictorial* on December 1887; *The Speaker* on February 1890.

[2] See Alice I. Perry Wood, "Oscar Wilde as a Critic," *North American Review*, CCII (July-December 1915), 899-909; Albert J. Farmer, *Le Mouvement esthétique et "décadent" en Angleterre* (Paris, 1931), pp. 154-69. Wilde's aesthetics is seriously discussed and fruitfully compared with the expressionist movement in modern Germany by Guido Glur, "Kunstlehre und Kunstanschauung des Georgekreises und die Aesthetik Oscar Wildes," *Sprache und Dicht-*

unity and logic his essays show depend chiefly on the recurrence of a dominant point of view—either of aesthetic
purity or of radical individualism; and the repeated discussion of topics like decorative art, the value of the Pre-
Raphaelite movement, romanticism and classicism, and so
forth. Wilde's critical writings as a whole revolve largely
around his inquiry into a fundamental problem, namely, the
relations of life to art. Transcending the simple equivalence
of image and idea, fact and cognition, the problem concerns
the question of human identity. The self demands a new
mode of understanding, a deeper probing into its substance:

> Plastic simplicity of outline may render for us the visible
> aspects of life; it is different when we come to deal with
> those secrets which self-consciousness alone contains,
> which self-consciousness itself can but half reveal. Action
> takes place in the sunlight, but the soul works in the dark.
> There is something curiously interesting in the marked
> tendency of modern poetry to become obscure. Many
> critics, writing with their eyes fixed on the masterpieces
> of past literature, have ascribed this tendency to wilful-
> ness and to affectation. Its origin is rather to be found in the
> complexity of the new problem, and in the fact that self-
> consciousness is not yet adequate to explain the contents of
> the Ego.[3]

Wilde observes further that modern thought now proceeds
"not on logical lines but on lines of passion"; man constantly seeks himself amid inconsistencies and contradictions. Objective forms of art, like sculpture and drama,
no longer suffice to illuminate the contemporary crisis, this
"strange twilight," of post-Renaissance man. Can art shelter
man from despair, from "the division and terror of the

---

ung, Band 3 (Berne, 1957), Chapter II, 31-59. See also Aatos Ojala,
Aestheticism and Oscar Wilde (Helsinki, 1954-55).

[3] *Reviews*, p. 482.

world"? Wilde agrees with Hardy that "ideal physical beauty is incompatible with mental development, and a full recognition of the evil of things."[4]

Like Arnold, Mill, and other Victorian sages, Wilde complains of "that strained self-consciousness of our age" which impels man to doubt, question, and disbelieve. But this self-consciousness is the source not only of romantic art but of all Western culture. It manifests itself in eclectic tastes and in the accelerated pace of intellectual activity. The self-conscious artist begins to contemplate his own universality as he brings about the influx of Greek and Christian traditions, the intermingling of Eastern and Western cultures.

This awareness of universality pervades modern man's thinking to such a degree that he continually strives to acquire that "divine natural prescience of beauty" which is the ruling spirit of antiquity. Perhaps in this nostalgia lies the reason why the analytic mind fails to be sensitive enough to register the sensuous element of contemporary art. While the Greeks loved plastic clearness of outline, modern man tends to indulge in picturesque effects of light and shade. Modern poetry lacks clear outline and restrained form; it is plagued by "violence and vagueness."

Modernity, for Wilde, means a consciousness expanded in both dimensions of time and space. It means historical insight and an appreciation of other cultures, enlarging one's range of sympathies and enhancing one's susceptibilities. Exercising his curiosity and his subtle reasoning powers, modern man participates in the "collective life of the race." Wilde's interpretation of the modern temper arises from his acute sense of historical perspective. This is confirmed by his essay "The Rise of Historical Criticism," which anticipates modern archetypal criticism and the discipline of cultural anthropology.[5]

[4] *Ibid.*, p. 446.
[5] *Intentions and other Writings* (Dolphin edn., New York, 1960),

In his essay Wilde recounts how during the sixth century B.C. in Greece, a significant change in man's attitude came about when a heightened freedom of the intellect spurred men to revolt against authority and inspired them to foster the "speculative spirit of innovation." Man began to see that behind legend and miracle lies the rational order of nature. Soon historical criticism emerged as a mode of ascertaining the truth of events and their causes, analyzing "the general relations which phenomena of life hold to one another" and penetrating to the substratum of historical fact which underlies myth.

Historical criticism then refers to the awakened interest in the workings of the mythopoeic spirit in civilization. Wilde observes that elements of Greek mythology, "spiritualized by the purifying influence of Christianity," reappear as "plausible residuum" in European culture. Ancient historians were generally ignorant of the method by which the historical critic could detect the unconscious survival of archaic customs in the symbolism and formulas of present-day civilization. While the old chroniclers saw only the historical event in a marriage feast, the historical critic could perceive its ritualistic implications. Such an awareness of archetypal patterns in human behavior is already evident in *Prometheus Bound* or in *De Rerum Natura*. What the historical critic does is to formulate a law which will connect "the different manifestations of all organic bodies, *man included*, which is the germ of the philosophy of history."[6]

Wilde then introduces the issue between human freedom and divine providence in history: "While the conceptions of law and order have been universally received as the governing principles of the phenomena of nature in the sphere of

---

p. 106. See *Works*, pp. 223-66. Edward Tylor's *Primitive Culture* came out in 1871, Frazer's *The Golden Bough* in 1890 (and expanded in 1911-1915).

6 *Works*, p. 264.

physical science, yet their intrusion into the domain of history and the life of man has always been met with a strong opposition, on the ground of the incalculable nature of the two great forces acting on human action, a certain causeless spontaneity which men call free will, and the extra-natural interference which they attribute to God."[7] The canons of historical criticism, questioning the ideas behind Nemesis and Providence, arose from the historian's philosophical doubt and psychological relativism. In contrast with the "stationary" rules for the assessment of evidence in the courts, Wilde states that the "science of historical probability" pursues a progressive course and "changes with the advancing spirit of each age." The historian elucidates the characteristics of human nature as it develops under varying circumstances. Given the premise of general human nature, history moves in a cycle: "In Thucydides the philosophy of history rests on the probability, which the uniformity of human nature affords us, that the future will in the course of human things resemble the past, if not reproduce it. He appears to contemplate a recurrence of the phenomena of history as equally certain with a return of the epidemic of the Great Plague."[8]

In reading history from the standpoint of contemporaneity, Thucydides the rationalist becomes the first modern spirit. He exemplifies, Wilde writes, "that natural reaction against the intrusion of didactic and theological considerations into the sphere of the pure intellect, the spirit of which may be found in the Euripedean treatment of tragedy and the later schools of art, as well as in the Platonic conception."[9] Modernity then is equivalent to contemporaneity. To "realize" the nineteenth century one must grasp all those factors and tendencies which have contributed to its formation. The critic must exhibit urbanity and cosmopolitan preferences. If the critic's judgment is to be universally

[7] *Ibid.*, p. 263.   [8] *Ibid.*, p. 265.   [9] *Ibid.*, p. 246.

valid, he must "bear within himself the dreams and ideas and feelings of myriad generations," for to him "no form of thought is alien, no emotional impulse obscure."[10]

Since the value of tradition centers on this awareness of the best that has been thought and done in the past, Wilde, following Arnold, directs our attention to deliberate culture acquired through a study of the best models. Individuality presupposes culture; culture disciplines the natural temperament and predispositions. Like the Platonic visionary, the poet becomes the spectator of all existence.

At this point Wilde's historical relativism suffers a radical change in assuming an antihistorical or ahistorical orientation. His attitude that the poet can be omnipresent resolves the nostalgia for the "golden age," whether medieval or Hellenic, which characterizes a great part of the Victorian sensibility. In the favorite genre of Victorian poets, the romance of idyll or saga, facts blend with fancies, thus destroying time and mutability. Wilde holds that since the "external forms of modern life are hardly, as yet, expressive of the spirit of the age," the poet cannot surrender the "truths of the imagination" to the "truths of fact."[11] Although the scientific and industrial revolution enhanced "close observation and the sense of limitation" required by art, Wilde still thought of romance as a faithful picture of "humanity."

The universality of recurrent themes, of ideas and forms evolving in time, is therefore an unquestioned phenomena in art and literature. Art escapes history in expressing nothing but itself; "the only history that it preserves for us is the history of its own progress."[12] It never reproduces its own age because it conforms to its own laws and conventions. It operates beyond the exigencies of historical vicissitudes since it conforms strictly to the law of plastic form, of embodied

[10] *A Critic in Pall Mall*, p. 254; also pp. 269-70.
[11] *Miscellanies*, p. 135.   [12] *Ibid.*, p. 41.

repose, which absorbs all the accidents of reality. From the 1876 essay on historical criticism to "The Decay of Lying" (1889) and "The Critic as Artist" (1890), Wilde passes from historical relativism to pure aesthetic idealism qualified by traits of naïve realism and a contemplative form of common sense.

ATTITUDES AND IDEALS

The shift of attitudes, the passage from one school of thought to another, may be seen in Wilde's devotion both to pure aesthetic formalism and to a love of the sensible world. Although Wilde wavered between the espousal of romantic ideals and the imitation of classic objectivity, he tried to support a viable compromise—Byzantinism, a frame of reference deducible from this passage: "In Byzantium the two arts met—Greek art, with its intellectual sense of form, and its quick sympathy with humanity; Oriental art, with its gorgeous materialism, its frank rejection of imitation, its wonderful secrets of craft and color, its splendid textures, its rare metals and jewels, its marvellous and priceless traditions."[13] Byzantium witnessed the marriage of "the intellectual art of the West" and its concern for "imitative presentation" and "ideal motive," with oriental decorative art; this union is present in the "elaborate perspective and subtle aerial effects" of some European embroidery. While Western art is committed to thought and action, Islamic art, for instance, instead of seeking to mirror life, avoids it altogether and concentrates on geometrical virtuosity.

Wilde's allegiance to Pre-Raphaelitism originates from this liking for decoration. The early Italian masters whom the brotherhood took as their models set their intense realism of detail and religious vision against the conventions of academic art. What the Pre-Raphaelites accomplished is the infusion of "plastic feeling" into the "mere facile prettiness"

[13] *Pall Mall*, pp. 150-51.

of classical portraits, yielding a "rare combination of Greek form with Florentine mysticism." But Wilde later objects to this mystical strain, preferring the visualized synthesis of "pure Hellenic joy and serenity" that he surprisingly finds in Whistler.

Wilde isolates the oriental nature of Western decorative art in its quality of "frank rejection of imitation, its love of artistic convention," its aversion to the literal representation of nature. A work of art, though possessing a primitive surface, translates experience into conventions. In arguing that "simplicity and direct utterance are *not* the dominant characteristics" of folk literature, Wilde debunks the superstition that the early stages of folklore were naive. "Our historical sense is at fault. . . . Every century that produces poetry is, so far, an artificial century, and the work that seems to us the most natural and simple product of its time is probably the result of the most deliberate and self-conscious effort."[14]

By virtue of the artificial and thus sophisticated nature of his craft, the designer represents for Wilde the exemplary artist. The designer, who confines himself to the intensive exploitation of his medium, subordinates appearance to decorative intentions, to "geometric plan and abstract line and color," thus opposing naturalistic mimicry and reportorial catalogues. The human figure, as an "expressive unit of design," contains all the principles of decoration. Echoing Ruskin, Wilde calls the decorative artist a realist because he chooses the Greek ideal of clarity rather than transcendental mysticism as a guide: "The metaphysical mind of Asia will create for itself the monstrous, many-breasted idol of Ephesus, but to the Greek, pure artist, that work is most instinct with spiritual life which conforms most clearly to the perfect facts of physical life."[15]

[14] *Reviews*, pp. 356-57.   [15] *Pall Mall*, p. 248.

Wilde, trying to merge his inheritance from Ruskin and his borrowings from Whistler, makes a distinction between two types of art: impressive and expressive. While impressive art (Japanese art) glorifies its material, expressive art (Michelangelo's paintings) annihilates it. Impressive or Gothic art projects a purely pictorial subject, while expressive or Renaissance art employs subjects replete with historical associations and memories.

The principal difference then between impressive and expressive art is that the former emphasizes its material while the latter annihilates it. Owing to this difference we have "healthy" and "unhealthy" art:

> From the point of view of style, a healthy work of art is one whose style recognizes the beauty of the material it employs, be that material one of words or of bronze, of colour or of ivory, and uses that beauty as a factor in producing the aesthetic effect. From the point of view of subject, a healthy work of art is one of the choice of whose subject is conditioned by the temperament of the artist and comes directly out of it. In fine, a healthy work of art is one that has both perfection and personality. . . . An unhealthy work of art, on the other hand, is a work whose style is obvious, old-fashioned and common, and whose subject is deliberately chosen, not because the artist has any pleasure in it, but because he thinks that the public will pay him for it.[16]

Wilde admires in tapestry the "superb Gothic design and the bright colors," with the brilliant tones so cunningly placed. Compared with the masterpieces of Italian Renaissance art, with its "wide expanse of waste sky, elaborate perspective, posing nymphs and shallow artificial treatment," Gothic art displays that robust energy and exuberance consisting of "the complete filling up of every corner and square and inch

[16] *Intentions*, pp. 212-13.

of surface with lovely and fanciful and suggestive design."[17] Wilde points out that the very limitation of his material forces the decorative artist to abandon chiaroscuro and other tricks, obeying the dictates of space limitations. Pictorial design relies on surface and chromatic texture, just as the sensuous life of verse relies on the "inventive handling of rhythmical language."

In the paintings of Burne-Jones and the handicrafts of Morris, Wilde sees intellectual sympathy, mood, and cultivation which rest not on idle fancy but on the "studied result of accumulative observation and delightful habit." Analogously the poet should treat language as a "fine material." He should have that spirit in which the maker of lace embroidery explores "the fancy and grace" of intricate geometry. Wilde does not mind "raising" literature to the level of upholstery—Michelangelo was just a "furnishing upholsterer"—and brought to the level of the antimacassar![18]

Wilde's elevation of decorative art to the supreme rank springs from his romantic attachment to concrete detail. He censured the generality, the "colorless and empty abstractions" of eighteenth-century poetry and the vague sentimentalism of the German transcendentalists. He preferred Blake's will to particularity. It was his axiom that to all "noble, realistic and romantic work" belongs the "love of definite conception," clarity, and the sense of limit, because "the more distinct, sharp and defined the boundary line, the more perfect is the work of art; and the less keen and sharp the greater is the evidence of weak imitation, plagiarism and bungling."[19]

PRINCIPLES

In "The Decay of Lying," Wilde's partiality for expressive, "Byzantine" art receives theoretical formulation:

[17] *Miscellanies*, p. 321.   [18] *Ibid.*, p. 301.
[19] *Pall Mall*, p. 247.

1. Art never expresses anything but itself. It has an independent life, just as thought has, and develops purely on its own lines.

2. All bad art comes from returning to Life and Nature, and elevating them into ideals. Life and Nature may sometimes be used as part of Art's rough material, but before they are of any real service to Art they must be translated into artistic conventions.

3. Life imitates Art far more than Art imitates life.

4. Lying (the telling of beautiful untrue things) is the proper aim of Art.[20]

The primary tenet that art is self-sufficient informs the organic unity of form and content that Wilde discerns in a perfect work of art. Contrary to the popular belief that art conveys feelings through its subject, art actually "rejects the burden of the human spirit and gains more from a new medium or a fresh material than she does from any enthusiasm for art, or from any lofty passion, or from any great awakening of the human consciousness."[21]

The artist achieves universality when he, desiring to comprehend his age, abstracts himself from it. Wilde even objects to a novel told from a single point of view, since "life to be intelligible should be approached from many sides, and valuable though the permanent ego may be in philosophy, the permanent ego in fiction soon becomes a bore."[22] All good work, therefore, is modern and universal. Now since art finds its own perfection within itself, it should not be judged by an "external standard of resemblance" or criterion of being true to life. Verisimilitude is not its goal. Art invents forms and ideal archetypes more real than living

---

[20] *Intentions*, pp. 41-42. Compare the aesthetic principles in the following: Clive Bell, *Art* (London, 1914); Roger Fry, *Vision and Design* (London, 1920); and Herbert Read, *The Meaning of Art* (Penguin, 1931).

[21] *Intentions*, p. 36.   [22] *Miscellanies*, p. 83.

man. "Life holds the mirror up to Art, and either reproduces some strange type imagined by painter or sculptor,
or realizes in fact what has been dreamed in fiction."[23] Life
being simply "the desire for expression," art presents
"various forms through which the expression can be
attained."[24]

Art, Wilde argues, transcends human finitude because it
mirrors man in all his infinite variety, concentrating on "one
moment of perfection, beyond any possibility of growth or
change."[25] In the figures around the urn in Keats' ode, we
perceive the single exquisite instant transfixed in the poise of
living energy. Compared with art, life shows itself deficient
in form; its tragedies seem farcical, its comedies a grotesque
horror. As life grows more complicated and diffuse, men will
turn more and more to art not only for pleasurable sensations but also for that spiritual repose it provides. Whereas life is narrowed by circumstances and its "sordid security,"
art gives us the freedom to choose our time of "initiation" and
"ecstasy."[26] If life must first be transmuted before it can
reflect the spirit, so nature must first be reworked before it
can acquire human import.

Nature, in Wilde's thinking, is matter struggling into
mind. Nature, which quickens into life in human brains, is
created by man: "Things are because we see them, and what
we see, and how we see it, depends on the arts that have
influenced us. To look at a thing is very different from
seeing a thing. One does not see anything until one sees its
beauty."[27] Wilde's theory of knowledge includes two postu-

[23] *Intentions*, pp. 33-34.   [24] *Ibid.*
[25] *Miscellanies*, p. 87.
[26] *Intentions*, p. 67. For Wilde's affinities with the symbolists, see
Louise Rosenblatt, *L'idée de l'art pour l'art dans la littérature an-
glaise pendant la période victorienne* (Paris, 1931), pp. 243-94. See
also William York Tindall, *Forces in Modern British Literature* (New
York, 1956), pp. 258-61.
[27] Quoted by Laurence Housman, *Écho de Paris* (London, 1923),
p. 22.

lates: (1) what exists is mainly appearance, (2) the appearances we see depend on our subjective apparatus of seeing and interpreting. Wilde seriously entertained the notion of reality as mere appearance, the result of perception: "Try as we may, we cannot get behind the appearance of things to the reality. And the terrible reason may be that there is no reality in things apart from their appearances."[28] Wilde's hypothesis leads to the conception of nature as an artistic creation. Nature suggests "dramatic moods" to which the artist's temperament gives bodily shape. Art, Wilde keeps repeating, is only mind expressing itself under the conditions of matter; landscape is simply the mood of a man's mind.

What is meant then by the "imitation of reality" is not the imitation of truth but the faithful expression of the inner experiences and psychic states of the individual. Since the artist sees things not as they really are but as they appear to him under pictorial conditions, he translates the rough material of life into the specific conventions of his art. Seeking to mediate "formal grace" and "absolute reality," the artist abides by the precept that "to paint what you see is a good rule in art, but to see what is worth painting is better."[29] Art reveals nature's lack of design, her "absolutely unfinished condition." Nature being but a collection of phenomena external to man, "people only discover in her what they bring to her."[30] The artist draws his rough material, even hints of his method, from life, but "to use life as an artistic method" engenders nothing but chaos. Wilde elaborates further:

> Art deals with appearances, and the eye of man who looks at Nature, the vision in fact of the artist, is far more important to us than what he looks at. . . . Art begins with abstract decoration. Art takes life as part of her rough material, recreates it, and refashions it in fresh forms,

[28] *Ibid.*   [29] *Miscellanies*, p. 318.   [30] *Ibid.*, p. 435.

is absolutely indifferent to fact, invents, imagines, dreams, and keeps between herself and reality the impenetrable barrier of beautiful style, of decorative or ideal treatment.[31]

The principle that art enables man to transcend his limited condition should not lead us to forget the fact that before the artist can transmute his images and symbols into form he must confront and grasp the crude distortions and painful actualities of life. Wilde believes that there are two forces that comprise "our conscious intellectual tradition": the Hellenic spirit and the spirit of romance. The classic spirit deals with the type, with the permanent and essential truths of life; thus in sculpture "the subject predominates over the situation." In contrast the modern romantic spirit treats of the exception, the momentary event, beauty in its concrete radiance; thus in painting "the situation predominates over the subject."[32] The romantic spirit guides the Pre-Raphaelite movement, which Wilde conceives as a renaissance because it is "a new birth of the spirit of man, like the great Italian Renaissance of the fifteenth century, in its desire for a more gracious and comely way of life, its passion for physical beauty, its exclusive attention to form, its seeking for new subjects for poetry, new forms of art, new intellectual and imaginative enjoyments."[33]

Believing that creativity depends on individual freedom and initiative, Wilde stresses the value of the artist's personality. The artist is even free to explore the aesthetic possibilities of remorse and sin, since his chief interest is his own spiritual progress. Romantic art, as a revolt against empty reductive formalism, justifies itself by its verbal precision, varied melody, and "a sustaining consciousness of

[31] *Intentions*, p. 24.
[32] *Miscellanies*, pp. 244-45.
[33] *Ibid.*, p. 243. Cf. M. H. Abrams, *The Mirror and the Lamp* (New York, 1953), pp. 328ff.

the musical value of each word as opposed to that value which is merely intellectual."[34]

Although Wilde asserts the supremacy of form, he never completely ignores subject matter. Because each material has a value that suggests varied qualities, technique alone will not suffice; the artist must render "the correspondence of form and matter, the delicate equilibrium of spirit and sense,"[35] then could not the artist combine "romantic feeling with realistic form?"[36]

Wilde, in some of his critical pronouncements, considers fallacious the antithesis of idealism and realism. In spite of inconsistencies, his effort to reconcile subjective and objective viewpoints appears as a persistent endeavor. Thus he regards the true artist as a realist, for "he recognizes an external world of truth; an idealist, for he has selection, abstraction, and the power of individualization."[37] But facts must be subordinated to form: "to stand apart from the world of nature is fatal, but it is no less fatal merely to reproduce facts."[38] Art not merely holds the mirror up to nature, it recreates nature. In Greek mythology, Wilde discerns the success with which abstract ideals and feelings become personified, as in the representation of the shape and essence of floral beauty in the fair bodies of nymphs and deities. The artist must recognize actuality if he desires "flawless marble" to incarnate "the burden of the modern intellectual spirit" or "become instinct with the fire of romantic passion."[39] Wilde contrasts the metaphysical temper of romanticism with the Greek artist's conviction that a work is "most instinct with spiritual life which conforms most clearly to the perfect facts of physical life also."[40]

Another example of Wilde's attempts to resolve the difference between "Greek modes of thought" and "medieval feel-

[34] *Miscellanies*, pp. 253-54.   [35] *Ibid.*, p. 97.
[36] *Ibid.*, p. 73.   [37] *Ibid.*, p. 91.   [38] *Ibid.*
[39] *Ibid.*, p. 264.   [40] *Ibid.*, pp. 32-33.

ing" is his idea that the Pre-Raphaelites fused spiritual motive and technical execution, "the intricacy and complexity" of modern experience, the classic "clearness of vision and its sustained calm," and the romantic "variety of expression and the mystery of its vision."[41] Wilde defines the inspiration of Pre-Raphaelitism: "It is really from the union of Hellenism, in its breadth, its sanity of purpose, its calm possession of beauty, with the adventure, the intensified individualism, the passionate colour of the romantic spirit, that springs the art of the 19th century in England, as from the marriage of Faust and Helen of Troy springs the beautiful boy Euphorion."[42]

The Pre-Raphaelites, in short, had style. Style refers to "that masterful but restrained individuality of manner by which one artist is differentiated from another."[43] Style, the "union of personality with perfection," is distinguished by severe simplicity, awareness of possibilities and limitations, and restraint of manner gained by submission to law—qualities acquired only when taste has become critical and self-conscious. Wilde regards subject as nothing but "thought, emotion or impression which a man desires to embody in form and color."[44] He explains that the artistic urge draws strength from the "pattern-producing faculty" by which the artist can project the objective correlative of his intuitions. The virtue of style lies in the command of the maximum expressive powers of one's medium.

Wilde asks, "Why do Holbein's portraits impress us with a sense of their absolute reality?" Because he "compelled life to accept his conditions, to restrain itself within his limitations, to reproduce his type and to appear as he wished it to appear."[45] Unless objectified and organized in a unified form, a cry of pain or of joy does not have any aesthetic significance: "The real experiences of the artist are always those

[41] *Ibid.*, p. 247.   [42] *Ibid.*, p. 245.   [43] *Ibid.*, p. 91.
[44] *Ibid.*, p. 255.   [45] *Ibid.*, p. 19.

which do not find their direct expression but are gathered up and absorbed into some artistic form which seems, from such real experiences, to be the farthest removed and the most alien."[46]

The mature artist, abhorring didacticism and the "weak prettiness of lifeless abstraction," keeps in mind the desideratum of form, which involves "cadenced meter," not direct utterance or "pathos of feeling." For beauty is nothing but "materialized" form. Accuracy produces that intensity of vision, the most vivid realism, as in Whistler's "pure melody of color"; the painter has arranged his pigments like chords in a musical composition so that "the harmony that resides in the delicate proportions of lines and masses becomes mirrored in the mind. The repetitions of pattern give us rest."[47]

One literary mode of rendering experience into form is the adoption by the poet of a persona. Since the persona fulfills only what the situation of the poem demands, it guarantees sincerity of tone and purges morbidity: "What is morbidity but a mood of emotion or a mode of thought that one cannot express? The public are all morbid, because the public can never find expression for anything. *The artist is never morbid. He expresses everything.* He stands outside his subject, and through its medium produces incomparable and artistic effects."[48] Wilde exhorts the artist to deny "the claims of the emotional faculties, the claims of mere sentiment and feeling, for personal experience of joy or sorrow is not poetry, though it may afford excellent material for a sentimental diary."[49] Wilde, however, sometimes temporarily severs subject from treatment: "The idea of the book is not bad, but the treatment is very unsatisfactory, and combines the triviality

[46] *Ibid.*, p. 255.
[47] *Intentions*, p. 121. See Edmund Wilson, *Axel's Castle* (New York, 1931), pp. 1-25; A. G. Lehmann, *The Symbolist Aesthetic in France 1885-1895* (Oxford, 1950).
[48] *Intentions*, p. 212.   [49] *Miscellanies*, pp. 170, 255.

of the tourist with the dullness of good intention"; the novel is "sometimes complex and intricate in expression, but then the subject itself is intricate and complex."[50]

Emulating Plato, Aristotle, the English Romantics, and Schiller "who tried to adjust the balance between form and feeling," Wilde tried to clarify the dialectic between spontaneity and self-consciousness, between instinctive expression and rational craft. The artistic spirit, bridging conscious and subconscious realms, becomes a force which energizes technique and transforms the resources of the medium into vital patterns. "Workmanship" concerns "the entire subordination of all intellectual and emotional faculties to the vital and informing poetic principle."[51]

Wilde says that the "self-conscious aim of life" is to find a "mode of expression." Art offers life "certain beautiful forms through which it may realize its energy to express itself."[52] He urges the passion for creation to be sharpened by a critical awareness which culture gives; "the various spiritual forms of the imagination have a natural affinity with certain sensuous forms of art," and culture helps us "to discern the qualities of each art, to intensify as well its limitations as its powers of expression."[53]

Although Wilde emphasizes technique, he does not completely ignore spiritual motivations, as attested by his analysis of the basic drive behind Whitman's innovations: the poet of objects and organic process wanted to articulate "the lofty spirit of a grand and free acceptance of all things that are worthy of existence."[54] Wilde also praises "the lofty spiritual visions" of Blake and Rossetti. His preoccupation with style, overshadowing the focus on subject, leads him to favor an art of suggestion in which "every mood has its color, every dream its form." He commends individuality, not extravagance or eccentricity, of manner. Disdaining rule and

[50] *Reviews*, p. 482. [51] *Pall Mall*, p. 4. [52] *Miscellanies*, p. 42.
[53] *Ibid.*, p. 247. [54] *Reviews*, p. 201.

rational stratagems, besieged by "discordant despair of doubt or the sadness of a sterile scepticism," the poet will be "always curiously testing new forms of belief, tingeing his nature with the sentiment that still lingers about some beautiful creeds, and searching for experience itself, and not for the fruits of experience."[55] The artist's detachment presupposes "negative capability," enhancing the beauty of formal treatment, which is "always a source of joy; the mere *technique* of verse has an imaginative spiritual element; and life must, to a certain degree, be transfigured before it can find its expression in music."[56]

CRITICAL THEORY AND PRACTICE

Like the artist, the critic exercises the imaginative faculty to transfigure his impressions into some durable form. Wilde takes criticism as a species of independent artistic creation. The critic as artist, relying on private intuitions, reproduces the work that he criticizes in a mode that is never imitative, and part of whose charm consists in the rejection of any resemblance between the criticism and the work criticized. In this way criticism assumes exactly the same relation to creative work that creative work does to the world of perception or of thought.

Although the Greeks had no art critics, they possessed the critical spirit which demands that "subtle tact of omission," and that "fine spirit of choice and delicate instinct of selection" which invents new forms. Repudiating dogmatic monism, Wilde chooses flexibility, liberal interpretation, and fidelity to one's impressions. He leaves the critic to decide for himself whether to compose a "synthetic impression of the work of art as a whole, or perform an analysis or exposition of the work itself."[57] Whether in rigorous textual exegesis or

[55] *Miscellanies*, p. 39. Obviously Wilde is paraphrasing Pater.
[56] *Reviews*, p. 283.
[57] *Miscellanies*, p. 95.

historical narration, the critic's job is "to deepen the mystery of art, . . . to raise round it, and round its maker, a mist of wonder."[58] To intensify art's mystery, the critic must intensify his own personality; the more strongly this personality enters into the interpretation, "the more real the interpretation becomes." His temperament, absorbed in the work, vitalizes his judgment.

The critic then must preserve the dynamic nature of the intellect, developing a capacity for disinterested, sensitive apprehension of values. Susceptible to the flux of impressions, the critic will grasp the unity of his impressions "through constant change," for art is concerned with "things beautiful and immortal and ever-changing."[59] Instead of dominating the work, he should let the work dominate him so as to purge his egotism, the "egotism of ignorance" and of "information."

Objecting to the pragmatic and utilitarian estimate of art, Wilde asserts that art has nothing to do with the "sane criticism of life." He dismisses the doctrine that art must have a mission, or must adjust itself to humanitarian causes or orthodox creeds. Art has no rationale except its own being; "the art which has fulfilled the conditions of beauty has fulfilled all conditions."[60] Assailing the dictum that art must be judged by the moral and ethical ideas it embodies, Wilde holds that we do not look in a painting "for any sentiment but beauty, or technique." (The slogan "art-for-art's sake" refers not to the final cause of art but to a "formula of creation.") He believes that "the intellect can be engaged without direct didactic object on an artistic and historical problem," since the intellect desires "merely to feel itself alive."[61] Wilde shares Browning's fascination: "It was not thought that fascinated him, but rather the processes by which thought moves."[62]

[58] *Ibid.*, p. 67. [59] *Intentions*, p. 116.
[60] *Miscellanies*, p. 263. [61] *Ibid.*, p. 266. [62] *Ibid.*, p. 216.

To discover the objective formula of a particular work, Wilde employed both formal analysis and intuitive empathy. He refrained from futile incursions into the biographical circumstances of a work except when the work is so uniquely obscure that "for a full appreciation of their style and manner some knowledge of the artist's life is necessary."[63] On the other hand, an account of Rossetti's life would be distractive and superfluous, since the poet "reveals himself so perfectly in his work."[64] Of Coleridge, Wilde writes:

> The real events of Coleridge's life are not his gig excursions and his walking tours; they are his thoughts, dreams, and passions, his moments of creative impulse, their source and secret, his moods of imaginative joy, . . . and not his words merely but the music and the melancholy that they brought him; the lyric loveliness of his voice when he sang, the sterile sorrow of the years when he was silent.[65]

Strongly interested in the mechanics of the creative process, Wilde hopes to investigate "the conditions that preceded the perfected forms, the gradual growth not of the conception but the expression."[66] His critical approach, tentative and pluralistic, often takes the form of appreciations which employ imagery to elucidate the intellectual appeal and evocative power of a particular work. His approach is similar to Pater's, whose *Imaginary Portraits* (1887) succeeded in giving "a sensuous environment to intellectual concepts." Pater's criticism traces the progress of a dialectic in which one factor is seen in context being reconciled with its opposite, thus forming a larger whole: "The philosophy is tempered by personality and the thought shown under varying conditions of mood and manner, the very permanence of each principle gaining something through the change and

63 *Pall Mall*, p. 123.   64 *Reviews*, p. 149.
65 *Ibid.*, p. 140.   66 *Miscellanies*, p. 276.

color of the life through which it finds expression."[67] Wilde also tried to project himself into past epochs: into early nineteenth-century English society in "Pen, Pencil and Poison," into the Elizabethan milieu in "The Truth of Masks" and "The Portrait of Mr. W. H."

"Unwieldy in handling abstract ideas," Pater's prose style, Wilde says, is "most felicitous when [it] deals with the concrete, whose very limitations give him finer freedom, while they necessitate more intense vision."[68] His prose, a mirror of the personality, has developed from the early exquisite diction and studied rhythm to the rich, precise, and tactful economy of the philosophical works, which are all free from surplus verbiage. Wilde attributes to such a style the Greek "purity of outline and perfection of form," coupled with a medieval "strangeness of color and passionate suggestion": "a strange blending of philosophy and sensuousness, of simple parable or fable and obscure mystic utterance."[69] He discerns in the involved syntax and rhetoric the mechanism of Pater's imagination, its power emanating from

those side-issues suddenly suggested by the idea in its progress, and really revealing the idea more perfectly; or from those felicitous afterthoughts that give a fuller completeness to the central scheme, and yet convey something of the charm of change; or from a desire to suggest the secondary shades of meaning with all their accumulating effect, and to avoid, it may be, the violence and harshness of too definite and exclusive an opinion. For in matters of art, at any rate, thought is inevitably coloured by emotion, and so is fluid rather than fixed, and, recognizing its dependence upon the moods and upon the

[67] *Pall Mall*, p. 71. Wilde approves of the critical method of Symonds' *The Renaissance in Italy* (1875-86).
[68] *Miscellanies*, p. 254.
[69] *Ibid.*, pp. 253-54.

passion of fine moments, will not accept the rigidity of a scientific formula or a theological dogma.[70]

When one has grasped the design of thought, then the clarity, simplicity, the "unity and elaborate charm" of Pater's musical style reveals itself.

Although technique signifies only an extension of temperament, Wilde believes that "the proper school to learn art in is not Life but Art." He points out that rhyme is "not merely a material element of metrical beauty, but a spiritual element of thought and passion also."[71] The poet "does not first conceive an idea, and then say to himself, 'I will put my idea into a complex meter of fourteen lines,' but realizing the beauty of the sonnet-scheme, he conceives certain modes of music and methods of rhyme, and the mere form suggests what is to fill and make it intellectually and emotionally complete."[72] All bad poetry "springs from genuine feeling" that lacks a controlling structure.

At times Wilde can be as detailed as today's New Critics: he counsels poets to avoid "Asiatic" effects of over-decoration and diffuseness.[73] He advises them not to rhyme "forefathers" with "rapiers," "chord" with "abroad"; and to eschew inversions, and such archaic clichés as "rude Boreas," "Aurora" for Dawn, or "Flora decks the enamelled meads," including cockneyisms and colloquialisms which comprise not the poetry of Parnassus but the "poetry of Piccadilly." Wilde believes that assonances in an unrhymed poem sound unpleasing; and unfinished short lines of five or six syllables ruin the music of blank verse. He is for "the brave Dorian mode of thoughtful and intellectual verse," the "light and graceful forms of old French song"; the "romantic manner

[70] *Pall Mall*, pp. 255-56. In *A History of Modern Criticism* (New Haven and London, 1965), IV, pp. 407-16, René Wellek describes Wilde's criticism as an unsteady shifting between panaestheticism, aesthetic idealism, and decorative formalism.

[71] *Intentions*, p. 30.

[72] *Ibid.*, p. 121.   [73] *Pall Mall*, pp. 5, 35, 91, 130, 365.

of antique ballads," and that "moment's monument," the sonnet. Alarmed that language is degenerating into "a system of almost algebraic symbols," Wilde emphasizes nuance, etymology, and density of association.

Despite his statements that objective clarity and directness are qualities the artist should strive for, Wilde's criticism often dispenses with analysis and definition and lapses into vague, polemic rhapsody. While censuring the "boisterous" spirit of Morris' *Odyssey* (1887), Wilde exults: "there is yet a vigour of life in every line, a splendid ardour through each canto, that stirs the blood while one reads like the sound of a trumpet."[74] He praises its "honest and direct diction," but owing to the impassioned presentation, the poem is unable to preserve the full flow and calm fervor of the Greek hexameter. Just as Wilde could qualify his judgment in detail, so he could bluntly indicate faults. Swinburne's "magnificent rhetoric," in *Poems and Ballads* (1878), is "always too loud for his subject"; alliteration has tyrannized over him to the extent that his eloquence "conceals rather than reveals." The poet's mannerisms, as in the wearying iteration of words like "fire" and "sea," and in the shrill monotony of rhymes, shows virtuosity; but, Wilde asks:

Does it really convey much? Does it charm? Could we return to it again and again with renewed pleasure? We think not. It seems to us empty. . . . Out of the thunder and splendour of words he himself says nothing. We have often had man's interpretation of Nature; now we have Nature's interpretation of man, and she has curiously little to say. Force and Freedom form her vague message.[75]

In distinguishing "unimaginative realism" from "imaginative reality," Wilde seems to engage in an amusing

[74] *Ibid.*, pp. 43-44.
[75] Wilde praises highly Yeats' *The Wanderings of Oisin and other Poems* (1889) in *Pall Mall*, pp. 212-15.

but pointless permutation. But he was definitely serious in his concern with the subtle presentation of truth in fiction's raw "slice of life." He thought that the novel, besides rendering manners and motives in plot, must also portray the immediacy of psychological conflict "by action not by analysis, by deeds not by description."[76] Style enforces the internal necessity of a work and compels belief. Wilde, however, finds some novels so "life-like that no one can possibly believe in their probability." Again he warns us not to confuse artistic with moral truth. When novelists reflect, they are inevitably dull; they fulfill their proper office when they try to "observe life with keen vision and quick intellect, to catch its many modes of expression, to seize upon the subtlety, or satire, or dramatic quality of its situations, and to render life for us with some spirit of distinction and selection."[77]

Wilde admired Balzac for converting "facts into truths," for imbuing his characters with the "contagious illusion of life." He did not merely depend on documentation, but rather toiled to effect a fusion of "the artistic temperament with the scientific spirit." Applying to his material the force of his personality, Balzac transcended the ephemeral quality of his subject, inventing a world distilled from intense moments in which characters "have a fierce vitality about them, their existence is fervent and fiery-colored; we do not merely feel for them but we see them—they dominate our fancy and eager scepticism."[78]

Three Russian novelists seem to have satisfied Wilde's demand for reliable narrative authority and convincing dramatization. He found in Tolstoy's novels "the grandeur and the simplicity of an epic."[79] He approved of Turgenev's practice of choosing "a few details to portray significant moments and moods of many lives."[80] Probing deeper into

[76] *Ibid.*, p. 179.   [77] *Reviews*, p. 418.
[78] *Pall Mall*, pp. 48-50.   [79] *Ibid.*, p. 67.   [80] *Ibid.*

the "hidden springs of life," Dostoevsky's realism seems "pitiless in its fidelity, and terrible because it is true"; but Wilde senses in his work "a note of personal feeling," not egotistic but compassionate. He explains the credibility of Dostoevsky's characters:

> We grow to know them very gradually, as we know people whom we meet in society, at first by little tricks of manner, personal appearance, fancies in dress, and the like; and afterwards by their deeds and words; and even then they constantly elude us, for though Dostoieffski may lay bare for us the secrets of their nature, yet he never explains his personages away; they are always surprising us by something that they say or do, and keep to the end the eternal mystery of life. . . . We see things from every point of view, and we feel, not that fiction has been trammelled by fact, but that fact itself has become ideal and imaginative.[81]

Ambivalence qualifies Wilde's response to English novelists. His comment on Kipling's *Plain Tales from the Hills* (1887) grows out of his antinaturalistic bias: "The mere lack of style in the story-teller gives an odd journalistic realism to what he tells us. . . . He is our first authority on the second-rate, and has seen marvellous things through keyholes, and his backgrounds are real works of art."[82] But writing of "low comedy in fiction," he muses on "the thrilling touch of actuality the simple mention of the 'gas bracket' give us." Meredith's personages "not merely live, but they live in thought. One can see them from myriad points of view. They are suggestive. There is soul in them. They are interpretative and symbolic."[83] On the other hand, Dickens, populating "with grotesque monsters a curious world of dreams," gives form to the most enigmatic fancy.[84]

---

81 *Ibid.*, p. 69. 82 *Intentions*, p. 125.
83 *Pall Mall*, p. 82. 84 *Reviews*, p. 143.

In his criticism of poetry and the novel, Wilde tried to strike a balance between realistic and nonrealistic approaches. Whether or not he successfully did so, it is clear that his attempted combination of historical knowledge and intuitive experience reflects the fundamental issue in literary and art criticism concerning ends and means: criticism as analytic evaluation, or criticism as scholarly research. Undecided about this issue, Wilde nonetheless kept the larger horizon of human purposes constantly in sight.

IMPLICATIONS

At no moment of his career was Wilde ever free from strong personal commitment to his aesthetic principles; and whenever his views on art were questioned or ridiculed by the philistine middle class, he always returned to the attack, patiently explaining his stand in straightforward discourse or attacking in oblique witticisms. He never shirked the challenges which the situation of a writer in late nineteenth-century England entailed. Even the decadent pose of withdrawal, if indirect and negative, was a gesture of commitment to the social conditions in which the artist found himself.

In his review of Whistler's *The Ten O'Clock* (1885) lectures, Wilde states his belief that the artist cannot be disengaged from his social and historical context: "An artist is not an isolated fact; he is the resultant of a certain *milieu* and a certain entourage, can no more be born of a nation that is devoid of any sense of beauty than a fig can grow from a thorn or a rose blossom from a thistle."[85] The statement implies a coalescence of Wilde's "Byzantine" inclinations and his social sympathies. Wilde denounces the corrupting vulgarity of the commercial class and the callow materialism of its mores. He believes in the unity of life and culture: "If

[85] *Miscellanies*, pp. 65-66.

you go into a house where everything is coarse, you find things chipped and broken and unsightly. . . . If everything is dainty and delicate, gentleness and refinement of manner are unconsciously acquired."[86] His conviction is that

> True art must have the vital energy of life itself, must take its colours from life's good or evil, must follow angels of light or angels of darkness. The art of the past is not to be copied in a servile spirit. For a new age we require a new form . . . . There can be no great sculpture without a beautiful national life, and the commercial spirit of England has killed that; no great drama without a noble national life, and the commercial spirit of England has killed that too. . . . In estimating the sensuous and intellectual spirit which presides over our English renaissance, any attempt to isolate it in any way from the progress and movement and social life of the age that has produced it would be to rob it of its true vitality, possibly to mistake its true meaning. And in disengaging from the pursuits and passions of this crowded modern world those passions and pursuits which have to do with art and the love of art, we must take into account many great events of history which seem to be most opposed to any such artistic feeling.[87]

Art then is a form of humanism in action, embodying "a desire on the part of man for a nobler form of life, for a freer method and opportunity of expression."[88] Wilde hopes that soon "beauty shall be confined no longer to the bric-a-brac of the collector and the dust of the museum, but shall be, as it should be, the natural and national inheritance of

[86] *Ibid.*, p. 289.
[87] *Ibid.*, pp. 245, 263. Compare Ruskin's ideas in "Traffic," *The Crown of Wild Olive*, 1866.
[88] *Ibid.*, p. 245.

all."[89] In announcing that the humanistic end of art motivates all radical changes in style and ideology, Wilde
subscribes to the ideals of the romantic revolt begun by
Blake and the English Romantics, culminating in the Pre-
Raphaelite and Aesthetic Movement. But his romanticism,
exposed to the preachings of the later Ruskin, Arnold,
and Morris, metamorphoses into a curious form of artistic
individualism which he calls "socialism." In "The Soul of
Man Under Socialism" (1891), Wilde contends that individualism will inevitably flourish in a socialist state where
the economic needs of men are taken care of.[90]

Defying all restrictions on the artist, Wilde in the same
spirit refuses to impose a single canon of taste on the masses.
His largeness of mind accords with the persuasion that art's
end is "to show the rich what beautiful things they might
enjoy and the poor what beautiful things they might
create."[91] Wilde's effort to overcome dualism again manifests
itself when he joins together the social relevance of art and
the purely formal or decorative criterion: ugliness implies
purposelessness, "want of fitness," "badly made," uselessness
(such as ornament in the wrong place), "extravagant,"
"spendthrift"; beauty signifies "purgation of all superflui-
ties," "divine economy." Where ugliness betrays impractical
execution, beauty shows "rightness of principles" working
toward freedom, comfort, and flexibility; beautiful decoration depends on "the use you put a thing to and the value
placed on it."[92] Thus beauty and function go together.

Beauty tied to function represents, on one level, Wilde's
understanding that a work of art exists at once in time and
in eternity. With the publication of Darwin's *On the
Origin of Species* (1859), the scientific revolution of the cen-

[89] *Ibid.*, p. 71.
[90] *Intentions*, p. 208. See George Woodcock, *The Paradox of Oscar
Wilde* (New York, 1950). Cf. *Pall Mall*, pp. 31, 425-28.
[91] *Miscellanies*, p. 71.
[92] *Ibid.*, pp. 293ff.

tury reached a climax. Man's conception of time changed: time assumed the form of a developmental process, a process of becoming. Wilde's view of history was not so much adapted from the Greek philosophers and historians as it was prompted by the intellectual currents of his age. (We now see "creative evolution" and the continuous emergence of novelty in Bergson, Pierre Teilhard de Chardin, and in the existentialist "care" for endless self-fulfillment.) To Pater the work of art embodies both the artist's personality, the product of a certain milieu, and the formal structure which transcends history in its appeal to a universal and innate sense of truth and beauty in man. Similarly Wilde perceived the universal patterns in myth, literature, and historical phenomena. And yet, though art is timeless, the criticism and appreciation of art are subject to the standards and conventions of a given period. Wilde not only saw the object lucidly and steadily but he also apperceived the contexts and angles from which the object can be viewed.

The idea of aesthetic contemporaneity results from the attempt to determine the significance of present experience in relation to the roots of that experience in the past. Wilde's historical sense drew him toward empiricism and individualism, both of which underlie laissez-faire economics and evangelicalism.[93] Facing the polarity of romantic and classic norms, Wilde evolved a theory of style which contains ambiguous implications in its effort to be inclusive. Style becomes not merely a transcript of concrete fact but a faithful record of the person's sense of interpretation of fact. This idea of style recalls Pater's in his essay on "Style" and in the conclusion to *Studies in the History of the Renaissance* (1873). But into this subjectivism Wilde introduced the temper of Gothic and decorative art. The fusion or com-

---

[93] See D. C. Somervell, *English Thought in the Nineteenth Century* (London, 1929), pp. 99-128; Graham Hough, *The Last Romantics* (London and New York, 1947), pp. 119ff; Walter E. Houghton, *The Victorian Frame of Mind*, pp. 313-15, 336-37.

promise took the shape of "Byzantinism," that is, a simultaneous liking for abstract design and sensuousness, for the formal properties of natural appearance. Wilde qualified his definitions in cases when social issues were involved and the position of the artist in society became a personal predicament; then he assumed his masks of the Christlike clown, the dandy, and the rebel. This urge to unify contradictory impulses present in Wilde's eclectic and immensely diversified range of critical interest culminates in *De Profundis* in which he tried to harmonize Christ and Apollo.

What the scope and depth of Wilde's thinking finally brings out is the crucial need for modern criticism to develop a balanced awareness of both the personal and the traditional elements, "the structure of the past and the texture of the present," in a particular work.[94] Employing both historical and impressionistic approaches, the "critic as artist" must try to integrate the knowledge of concrete data with the exercise of sensibility, enabling him to "appreciate a work of art from every point of view." This need for "roundness," for an intimate and absorbing contact with the multiphased process of experience, probably accounts for Wilde's implicit recognition that only in dramatic form can he bring to life his aesthetic attitudes, ideals, values, and principles.

[94] Philip Appleman, "Darwin, Pater, and a Crisis in Criticism," *1859: Entering An Age of Crisis*, eds., Philip Appleman, William A. Madden, and Michael Wolff (Bloomington, Indiana, 1959), pp. 81-95.

IV · Structure and Style in the Poetic Drama

Wilde wrote his first play, *The Duchess of Padua*, around September 1882, a year after the publication of his poems. While it was being staged in New York, he wrote the renowned Henry Irving, praising the actor's talent and at the same time noting what he considered the problem of the poetic theater in modern times. Irving's style, Wilde believed, linked the stage and literature in harmony:

> You are the one artist in England who can produce poetic blank-verse drama. . . . You have created in the theatre-going public both taste and temperament, so that there is an audience for a poet inside a theatre, though there is none or but a small audience for a poet outside the theatre. The public as a class don't read poetry, but you have made them listen to it.[1]

What Wilde valued above all is the actor's histrionic sensibility. He esteemed the skillful exercise of this sensibility in a craft directed toward reproducing the rhythm of emotion in speech. Using rhythmic speech to create a live illusion, drama ushers the audience into a condition of sensitive response.

Wilde's letter involves, in effect, the central issue of poetic drama, namely, the fusion of verse and dramatic situation. This fusion could be realized only in such ideal cases as T. S. Eliot had in mind in exploring this problem: "the audience, its attention held by the dramatic action, its emotions stirred by the situation between the characters,

[1] *Letters*, p. 286.

should be too intent upon the play to be wholly conscious of the medium."[2]

With *Vera* (1882) and *The Duchess of Padua*, Wilde launched his career as a playwright. He confessed that he aspired to "the fame of a Hugo." Despite his posings, his thoughts about the theater indicate a definite awareness of its peculiar challenges. His letters reveal his knowledge that drama is essentially a synthesis of varied elements; picture, movement, and feeling must be magically orchestrated in actual performance. He conceives of form as an imitation of action, as the idealizing principle of events in time:

> All good plays are a combination of the dream of a poet and that practical knowledge of the actor which gives concentration to action, which intensifies situation, and for *poetic effect, which is description, substitutes dramatic effect*, which is Life. . . . The dream of the sculptor is cold and silent in the marble, the painter's vision immobile on the canvas. (Italics mine)[3]

Theory is, of course, different from practice. *The Duchess of Padua*, like Wilde's early poems, suffers from a "surplusage" quite alien to the rapid pace of its intrigues. Unable to capture the hearty simplicity of Shakespeare's "low" personages, Wilde often lapses into bathos and fustian. What we have as a result is a historical melodrama soaked in romantic gush. Consider the florid oratory of the characters; for example, the pompous, pseudo-Elizabethan exclamations of

[2] *On Poetry and Poets* (New York, 1961), p. 76. Consult also Ronald Peacock, *The Poet in the Theater* (New York, 1946), and *The Art of Drama* (London, 1957), pp. 211ff. See Henrik Ibsen, "The Task of the Poet," pp. 3-4; W. B. Yeats, "Language, Character, and Construction," pp. 37-44; Christopher Fry, "Why Verse?" pp. 116-24, in *Playwrights on Playwriting*, ed., Toby Cole (New York, 1960).

[3] *Letters*, p. 125. For further thoughts on the theater, see Wilde's lectures in *Decorative Art in America*, ed., Richard Butler Glaenzer (New York, 1906), pp. 33-35.

the Duchess. Like the Duchess, Guido Ferranti is made to speak in falsetto as he invokes cosmic powers:

> O damnèd stars,
> Quench your vile cresset-lights in tears and bid
> The moon, your mistress, shine no more tonight.[4]

The play as a whole has no unity of action in the sense of inevitable transitions from scene to scene; love and duty, the combating forces, are obscured by exaggerated pathos and sentiment. After the Duchess' strident self-accusations in the closing scene, the tone of her last utterance strikes one as an abrupt intrusion:

> No, I have sinned, and yet
> Perchance my sin will be forgiven me.
> I have loved much.[5]

G. Wilson Knight, despite the play's glaring improbabilities, calls it "a neat enough projection of Renaissance villainy, controlling a subtle interplay of good and evil."[6] What actually gives the play a semblance of unity is the revenge motif established by two elements: the symbolic dagger, emblem of duty and family honor; and the specter-like Moranzone (inspired by the ghosts of the Jacobean tragedies) who, revealing Guido's past, assigns to him his fateful task. Evidently Wilde is trying to contrive a Hamlet persona; but Guido proves a bungling courtly lover. At first he seizes his duty as a moral obligation, vowing to fulfill it at the first opportunity. The complication and inner conflict are at once signalized by his dropping of the dagger on seeing the Duchess, before Act I closes. Anticipating Guido's fate, Moranzone sums up the whole plot:

> Nay, nay, I trust thee not: your hot young blood,
> Undisciplined nature, and too violent rage

[4] *Works*, p. 629.   [5] *Ibid.*, p. 360.
[6] *The Golden Labyrinth* (New York, 1962), p. 306.

Will never tarry for this great revenge,
But wreck itself on passion.[7]

As an apprentice's work, this play discloses characteristic qualities illustrating Wilde's mode of dramatic composition. One will observe the crucial ironies founded on mistakes of judgment: in Act III, the Duchess, misinterpreting Guido's hints, slays the Duke; rejected in turn by Guido, she condemns him as the murderer. At the end of Act IV, Guido, to protect the Duchess, claims the responsibility. Taking the poison reserved for Guido, the Duchess in Act V vainly tries to save her lover; but human nature, interpreted as simple natural instinct, triumphs. This sequence of timely recognitions, while building up suspense, operates toward the fullest exposure of character. For character consists mainly of certain dominant motivations displayed in speech and gesture. When the Duchess reflects, "I did not know him, / I thought he meant to sell me to the judge," and when she cries out to Guido in prison: "We are each our own devil, and we make / This world our hell,"[8] she expresses in the most succinct manner Wilde's all-embracing purpose: to sustain an action leading to the fullest revelation of character. Like Browning, therefore, Wilde intends to present "character in action," the anatomy of the soul. The action of this play spins from the passions of love and revenge. With the supremacy of love, duty becomes eclipsed; what is supposed to be a revenge tragedy becomes a Romeo-and-Juliet opera. We observe a movement toward greater subjectivity not only in the set speeches but also in the haunted harping on "Sin's teeming womb," which converts dramatic reality into lyrical meditation.

With the unfinished *A Florentine Tragedy* (circa 1895), Wilde efficiently applies the "know-how" learned from his acquaintance with the mechanics of social comedy. He tries

[7] *Works*, p. 565. [8] *Ibid.*, p. 626.

to avoid isolated lyricism in an effort to produce a unity of dialogue and scene. The play embodies a single unified action complete in itself, with its stages of complication, crisis, and comic twist as resolution.

When Simone the husband enters the scene where Guido and Bianca have been flirting and conspiring together, tension begins and mounts up to the duel scene. We have here the conventional "triangle" elaborated with subtle indirection. We know the illicit love between Guido and Bianca largely through the fluctuating tones of muted defiance and condescension the merchant betrays. Simone's address to Guido mimics Browning's Duke in "My Last Duchess," with a difference: behind his rustic mask is hidden the shrewd tactful trader and the skillful swordsman. As humorist he resembles the remorseless Duke of Padua, and anticipates the practical wit of Herodias. Cunningly aware of the situation, Simone seems to hear the lovers' asides with a sensitivity that somehow redeems his drab reticence. Wilde ties together with sure economy the details of event, emotional coloring, and attitudes in Simone's speech:

> Good night, my lord.
> Fetch a pine torch, Bianca. The old staircase
> Is full of pitfalls, and the churlish moon
> Grows, like a miser, niggard of her beams,
> And hides her face behind a muslin mask
> As harlots do when they go forth to snare
> Some wretched soul in sin.[9]

The mention of "pitfalls" and "harlots" signals Simone's awareness of his wife's betrayal and Guido's complicity. Wilde transposes thoughts and feelings into concrete physical details which at the same time serve to depict the setting and the physical behavior of the characters. Finally pragmatic reason wins over instinct. Like the preceding play,

[9] *Ibid.*, p. 683.

which ends in the superimposed description of the Duchess' face ("the marble image of peace, the sign of God's forgiveness"), *A Florentine Tragedy* concludes with a reversal:

BIANCA: Why
    Did you not tell me you were so strong?
SIMONE: Why
    Did you not tell me you were so beautiful?[10]

The questions point to the playwright's unrealized intent to lead the action to a final elucidation of personalities.

It seems that Wilde conceives of characters basically as lines of force that evolve and intersect one another, disposing themselves in schemes that would define exactly their individual natures. In *The Duchess of Padua*, the force of vindictive courage yields to passion when it meets the beauty and virtue of the Duchess. In *A Florentine Tragedy*, watchful cleverness defeats naive sentiment and social rank. Both plays, like the next two pieces *La Sainte Courtisane* (c. 1897) and *Salome* (1891), deal with the presentation of the self of the protagonists as they appear in temporal succession.

Hesketh Pearson, in his biography, suggests that *La Sainte Courtisane* is an expansion of Wilde's theory, first enunciated in "The Portrait of Mr. W. H.," that whoever converts others, loses his own faith.[11] But that is only the germ of the dramatic action. In a short space Wilde sketches a lively interaction of values through imagery, scene, thought, and behavior. In the fearful excitement of Myrrhina's interlocutors, Wilde projects images of fertility, lunar influence, and elemental animism that qualify our conception of the princess' role as a character whose intelligence stems from a fine voluptuous worldliness. But there

[10] *Ibid.*, p. 685.
[11] *Oscar Wilde*, p. 211. Leon Lemonnier, in *Oscar Wilde*, suggests Wilde's borrowing from *Thais* by Anatole France for the story of *La Sainte Courtisane*; and from Maeterlinck's plays for the prose style of *Salome*. *Salome* was originally written in French.

is one desire she has not yet satisfied: to become holy—that is, to be a saintly courtesan.

In the fervor of her wish to meet the fabled hermit, Myrrhina summons up in the mind fanciful images, a richness of context mirroring her innate exuberance: "Has he a house of reeds or a house of burnt clay or does he lie on the hillside?" and so forth.[12] Her monologue betrays a mind which abhors a vacuum of fact and mere data. Curiously enough she endeavors to picture the hermit's barren figure, his spiritual occupation, by lush, sensuous imagery: "What does he do, the beautiful young hermit?" and so forth.[13] Displaying no concern for the man's impoverished plight, Myrrhina, like her "sister" Salome, elevates the fulfillment of her desire to the realm of an ethical absolute. In the hermit's devotion to ritual and faith, we find a force of equal intensity. His luxuriant phrases contradict his abstinence. Hearing Myrrhina's words, his convictions strengthen, impelling him to convert the princess by urging on her the need to repent. But her temptations prove stronger. Like thesis and antithesis, the saint and the sinner comprise an indivisible partnership. Each one intensifies by contrast the qualities of the other.

The world of the play gradually reveals itself as one where arbitrary, impulsive motions prevail and where logic proves useless. Opposites attract and extremes are ultimately identical: Myrrhina incarnates the pleasure principle, Honorius the spiritual principle. Both are united in the absoluteness of their allegiances. Aside from this symmetrical pattern, what helps to maintain the intelligibility of discourse is the tone of confession: although subject to caprice, it is uniform throughout. Behind the mask of appearance resound the voices of actors suspended in a dream or trance. Vocabulary functions most effectively at the minimum level

12 *Works*, p. 687.   13 *Ibid.*, p. 688.

of sound and their associations. Wilde exploits here a type of address and rhetoric, refined in *Salome*, in which extravagance of imagery is highly stylized:

> The dust of the desert lies on your hair and your feet are scratched with thorns and your body is scorched by the sun. Come with me, Honorius, and I will clothe you in a tunic of silk. I will smear your body with myrrh and pour spikenard on your hair. I will clothe you in hyacinth and put honey in your mouth.[14]

In the end Honorius discovers the "good" in Myrrhina's life: "The scales have fallen from my eyes. . . . Let me taste of the seven sins." It seems that perfection requires an encompassing of extremes, or a transvaluation of values. Myrrhina, likewise, abandons pleasure as her sole "good" and chooses renunciation. Spirituality then unfolds itself as a complement to hedonism in the characters' decisions; their opposition actually makes up a unity which the whole play images in a paradoxical form. Myrrhina seems to be driven by a compulsion to exhaust all possibilities of whatever moral value. She embodies the cause of the turnabout in the play as she apprehends the symbolic role of her duty to Honorius: "That thou shouldst see Sin in its painted mask and look on Death in its robe of Shame."[15] Eventually, Honorius succumbs to Myrrhina's power. In transposing their roles, Wilde projects the idea of the interchangeability of roles in life which he has exemplified before in "Pen, Pencil and Poison," "The Truth of Masks," and "Lord Arthur Savile's Crime." Myrrhina, while exposing the false grandeur of her promiscuity, unveils the resolute concreteness of her desire to become what she is not. On the other hand, Honorius chooses that which is contrary to his standard of values. Climaxing a process of conversion, such choices reveal

14 *Ibid.*, p. 689.   15 *Ibid.*, p. 690.

aspects of the self which the characters seek to realize through engagements in the conflicting circumstances of life.

The theme and design of *Salome* is amply prefigured in the devices of presentation and portrayal used in *La Sainte Courtisane*. In both we have antithetical protagonists, an old saint and a young debauched woman (Salome is supposedly a virgin). We have also sustained repetitions, puzzling menaces, and the pervasive atmosphere of evil. Compare the beginning of *Salome*, specifically the words of the Page of Herodias, with the exposition of *La Sainte Courtisane*. Like the tentative probings of a detective's mind in search of the guilty man, the beginning of the latter play casts a provocative spell as the two men conjecture about Myrrhina's identity. Out of a few physical features, they weave a fabric of dazzling beauty. With a musically modulated language, they evoke wonder, mystery, and the thrill of unplumbed depths. To their gaze Myrrhina appears as an embodiment of sensual joy and spiritual devotion. Dressed in gorgeous finery she is an emperor's daughter; etherealized, she then becomes a Venus. The shuffling of a few decorative details observed in motion furnishes emotional continuity:

SECOND MAN: She has birds' wings upon her sandals, and her tunic is the colour of green corn. It is like corn in spring when she stands still. It is like young corn troubled by the shadows of hawks when she moves. The pearls on her tunic are like many moons.

FIRST MAN: They are like the moons one sees in the water when the wind blows from the hills.[16]

Salome amplifies and extends the manner of *La Sainte Courtisane*. It exploits the Biblical style that Wilde polished and thickened in his prose poems and fairy tales. Wilde also employs multiple parallelisms that dictate a slow, fluent

[16] *Ibid.*, p. 686.

evolution of image and idea in soliloquy or conversation. Physical atmosphere functions as a sensible manifestation of the clash of values. Ultimately the play's language and the ways it transforms the material of experience serve to distinguish the selves of the *dramatis personae* in their varied appearances on the stage.

Wilde handles the course of feelings of the characters in *Salome* by a principle of implied relations analogous to the technique of Hebrew poetry. The syntax of the Scriptures is essentially artificial and "constructive," as scholars have pointed out.[17] It consists of a mode of juxtaposing ideas whereby relations are expressed with hardly any of the connectives that usually bind thought-units in a normal sentence. Whereas, in English, prose employs subordination and poetry uses meter and rhyme, Biblical style proceeds toward "infinite predication." This effect is produced through accumulation by the parallel placement of syntactical members. They arise from patterns of sentences that are formed by the parallel disposition of clauses and phrases of approximate similarity or length. What is generally called "balladic" in this play, its "pastiche of erotic psalmody," its echo of the "Song of Songs," acquires henceforth a degree of propriety.

It would be enlightening to compare the rhythmic repetitions in the following passages. Here is Mark's account of the Salome story:

> And when a convenient day was come, that Herod on his birthday made a supper to his lords, high captains, and chief estates of Galilee;

[17] The findings are ably summarized by Annette M. MacCormick, "Hebrew Parallelism in Doughty's *Travels in Arabia Deserta*," *Studies in Comparative Literature*, ed., Waldo F. McNeir (Baton Rouge, 1962), pp. 29-46. See especially the detailed analysis of Wilde's Biblical style by Ojala, Part II, pp. 202-06. Cf. L. Finkelstein, "The Hebrew Text of the Bible: a Study of Its Cadence Symbols," *Symbols and Society*, eds. L. Bryson *et al.* (New York, 1955), pp. 409-26.

And when the daughter of the said Herodias came in, and danced, and pleased Herod and them that sat with him, the king said unto the damsel, Ask of me whatsoever thou wilt and I will give it thee, unto the half of my kingdom.

And she went forth, and said unto her mother, What shall I ask? And she said, The head of John the Baptist.

And she came in straightway with haste unto the King, and asked, saying, I will that thou give me by and by in a charger the head of John the Baptist.

And the King was exceeding sorry; yet for his oath's sake, and for their sakes which sat with him, he would not reject her.

And immediately the King sent an executioner, and commanded his head to be brought; and he went and be-headed him in the prison,

And brought his head in a charger, and gave it to the damsel: and the damsel gave it to her mother.

(VI, 21-28; King James Version)

And here is part of Wilde's play:

FIRST SOLDIER: The Tetrarch has a sombre look.
SECOND SOLDIER: Yes, he has a sombre look.
FIRST SOLDIER: He is looking at something.
SECOND SOLDIER: He is looking at someone.
FIRST SOLDIER: At whom is he looking?
SECOND SOLDIER: I cannot tell.

How similar this is to Maeterlinck's nervous accumulation of hints in his dialogues; for example:

STEPHANO: Again the comet of the other night!
VANOX: It is enormous.
STEPHANO: It seems to be pouring blood upon the castle.
    (Here a shower of stars seems to fall upon the castle.)

VANOX: The stars are falling on the castle! Look! Look! Look!

STEPHANO: I never saw such a shower of stars! You should say Heaven wept.

VANOX: The sky is turning black, and the moon is strangely red.

STEPHANO: It is raining torrents.

(La Princesse Maleine, Act I, Scene I)

Of the play's "childish prattle," which turns Flaubert's exotic Orient into a nursery tale, Mario Praz comments: "It is childish, but is also humoristic, with a humor which one can with difficulty believe to be intentional, so much does Wilde's play resemble a parody of the whole of the material used by the Decadents and of the stammering mannerism of Maeterlinck's dramas—and as parody, *Salome* comes very near to being a masterpiece."[18] To qualify Praz's sensible view, let me cite Wilde's own rationale for whatever value it has. In a letter to Lord Alfred Douglas, he says: "The Ballad is the true origin of the romantic Drama, and the true predecessors of Shakespeare are not the tragic writers of the Greek or Latin stage, from Aeschylus to Seneca, but the ballad writers of the Border. . . . The recurring phrases of *Salome*, that bind it together like a piece of music with recurring *motifs*, are, and were to me, the artistic equivalent of the refrains of old ballads."[19]

What gives unity to *Salome* inheres more in the even tone and texture of its language than in the bold outline of the characters. In exploiting the resources of language, Wilde captures the quality of the sublime, the sense of magnitude

---

[18] *The Romantic Agony* (New York, 1956), p. 298. For Maeterlinck's themes and techniques, consult the following: Henry Rose, *Maeterlinck's Symbolism* (New York, 1911), pp. 1-58; Granville Forbes Sturgis, *The Psychology of Maeterlinck* (Boston, 1914); W. D. Halls, *Maurice Maeterlinck* (Oxford, 1960); and Guy Doneux, *Maurice Maeterlinck* (Bruxelles, 1961).

[19] *Letters*, p. 590.

in the terrible, illustrated by Salome's hunger for carnal possession of Jokanaan. Wilde himself speaks of the thread of fatality, or the "note of Doom" that runs throughout the play. It is chiefly Salome who imposes the tight organization of the play and its singleness of impact. Her rhapsodic invocations to the saint are a virtual embodiment of the sublime, the hyperbolic effect justified by Longinus in *Peri Hypsos*: "Actions and passions which bring one close to distraction compensate for and justify every boldness of expression."[20] Salome's speech, languid and somnambulistic, seems to echo from a distance. Circular and densely metaphoric, dynamic yet restrained, her manner of address represents perfectly the oracular style which stimulates strong emotion: "I am amorous of thy body, Jokanaan! Thy body is white like the lilies of a field that the mower hath never mowed," and so on.[21] Brutality and delicate grace combine in the lofty, sensuous invocations. Longinus underscores the efficacy of this mode of expression: "Shall we then not believe that the arrangement of words—that music of rational speech which is in man inborn, which appeals not to the ear only but to the mind itself—as it evokes a variety of words, thoughts, events, and beautiful melodies, all of them born with us and bred into us, instills the speaker's feelings, by the blended variety of its sounds, into the hearts of those near him so that they share his passions? It charms us by the architecture of its phrases as it builds the music of great passages which casts a spell upon us. . . ."[22]

Wilde's device of witty pointlessness in dialogue functions toward the same end. As Kenneth Burke suggests, it intensifies a great variety of emotions by "climactic arrange-

[20] *On Great Writing*, tr., G. M. A. Grube (New York, 1957), p. 51. Wilde also uses synesthesia, e.g., "Thy voice was a censer that scattered strange perfumes, and when I looked on thee I heard a strange music."
[21] *Works*, pp. 543-44.
[22] *Ibid.*, pp. 51-52.

ment."[23] Such a formal design moves by psychological, not logical, progression. Its energy animates a pattern of utterances in which conscious and unconscious motivations heighten and clarify one another. A good example of this design would be the prolonged sequence in which Herod promises Salome a variety of things so that she may free him from his oath. Throughout the play, the characters tend to be isolated from one another, being superficially connected to the main episode: Herod's marriage feast. This sense of isolation infuses a strangeness into the individual voices we hear, reinforcing the fact that the context of their talk is but vaguely implied. Take the ritualized scene of which this is a condensation:

> SALOME: (to Jokanaan) . . . Suffer me to kiss thy mouth.
> JOKANAAN: Never! Daughter of Babylon! Daughter of Sodom! Never!
> SALOME: I will kiss thy mouth, Jokanaan. . . .
> THE YOUNG SYRIAN: . . . Look not at this man, look not at him. I cannot endure it. . . . Princess, do not speak these things.
> SALOME: I will kiss thy mouth, Jokanaan.[24]

To use a musical analogy, Wilde manipulates the scenes in his play by a repetition of dominant chords, that is, either Salome's or Jokanaan's ruling passions, in a polyphonic manner.

Obviously Wilde cultivates this mode of repetition to render the unity of self underlying Salome's obsession and Jokanaan's absolute dedication to his calling. Together they present a contrast to Herod's vacillations, the wanton dis-

---

[23] *Counter-Statement* (Chicago, 1957), p. 136. Actually, "climactic arrangement" exists on the content level of utterances. It fulfills a poetic function in that it "projects the principle of equivalence from the axis of selection into the axis of combination." See Roman Jakobson, "Linguistics and Poetics," *Style in Language*, ed., Thomas A. Sebeok (New York, 1960), p. 358.

[24] *Works*, pp. 544-45.

putes of the Jews and soldiers, the cautious and blunt manner of Herodias. Since repetition retards the development of the plot, Wilde charts the culmination of Salome's purpose in an accelerating pace. Salome's nature discloses itself in a line of climbing intensity. A marvellous simplicity of design radiates from her hieratic gestures and her incantations. Seduced by an imperious will, her personality becomes transparent. She exhibits a disengaged quality that separates Wilde's heroine from her prototypes in the Bible, in Moreau, Huysmans, and Flaubert.

The Salome legend, which is the basis of this play, actually begins with the bare Gospel narratives of St. Matthew (XIV, 3-16) and St. Mark (VI, 17-22). Both versions depict the episode, the raw material of the play, in bold strokes. By judicious selection Wilde takes only the central episode, Herod's feast and Salome's dance, for his pivotal incidents, simply drawing the background in retrospect by means of his chorus of soldiers and attendants.[25] Moreover, he frees Salome from her mother's sway and makes Herod command her death at the end. Following Heine's transformation of Salome into a satanic vampire who exults in disgusting *Liebeswahnsinn*—a trait absent in the Bible and in medieval lore generally—Wilde, with the suggestions of Moreau's visionary painting and Flaubert's tale, accentuates Salome's ill-omened narcissism and her convulsive depravities. There

[25] On the actual circumstances of Wilde's composition of *Salome*, the following are informative: Boris Brasol, *Oscar Wilde* (New York, 1938), pp. 216-25; Francis Winwar, *Oscar Wilde and the Yellow Nineties* (New York, 1940), pp. 205-10. On the question of the collective authorship of the French original, see Clyde De L. Ryals, "Oscar Wilde's 'Salome'," *Notes and Queries*, VI (January 1959), 56-57. For a treatment of the Salome legend and its literary tradition, the following have been consulted: Jacob N. Beam, "Richard Strauss' *Salome* and Heine's *Atta Troll*," *Modern Language Notes*, XXII (January 1907), 13-14; John S. White, *The Salome Motive* (New York, n.d.), Helen Grace Zagona, *The Legend of Salome and the Principle of Art for Art's Sake* (Geneva and Paris, 1960), pp. 121-28; Rafael Cansinos Assens, *Salome en la literatura* Madrid, 1919).

is much in Wilde's imagery of setting and speech that
matches Aubrey Beardsley's notorious drawings for the play,
his cloistral tableau of nudes and imps, his tortuous lines,
his macabre ornamentation.[26] Richard Strauss' opera
(1905), with the play as libretto, capitalizes on the sensational choreography of Salome for its appeal, deflating evil
sexuality into a "wild Hollywood belly dance," as one com-
mentator puts it.[27] Strauss, then, simply articulates the dominant features of *Salome*: Jokanaan is slain to the eerie sound
of a punched B flat on a double bass, and the dispute among
the Jews becomes a fugal quintet. When the opera was re-
vived in New York in 1949, it fittingly employed the setting
made by the surrealist Salvador Dali.

Salome's energy of imagination in the play never succumbs
to surrealistic distortions, however much her verbal arabesques multiply. Her consciousness works on sensory material; sensuous qualities possess her bodily and spiritually.
Her metaphoric flights represent the release of her libidinal
impulses. She gains an integration of self only by nourishing
and satisfying the will of the ego to dominate the world. She
seeks to invent a formula that would subsume a particular
intuition in a concrete object. By comparison she expands
a finite detail into an infinite panorama of possibilities—a
method that gives us also Herod's picturesque inventories
and the cosmic resonance of the prophet's allusions. Witness
the sustained parallelisms and balance of this passage:

> Thy mouth is redder than the feet of those who tread the
> wine in the wine-press. Thy mouth is redder than the feet
> of the doves who haunt the temples and are fed by the
> priests. It is redder than the feet of him who cometh from

[26] See Hugo Daffner, *Salome* (Munich, 1912); this is so far the
most comprehensive treatment of the Salome motif in art.

[27] *Kobbé's Complete Opera Book*, ed., Earl of Harewood (New
York, 1963), pp. 911-14. See also Joseph Kerman, *Opera as Drama*
(New York, 1956), pp. 259-61; Ernst Bendz, *Oscar Wilde* (Vienna,
1921), pp. 92-122.

a forest where he hath slain a lion, and seen gilded tigers. Thy mouth is like a branch of coral that fishers have found in the twilight of the sea, the coral that they keep for the kings . . . ! It is like the vermilion that the Moabites find in the wines of Moab, the vermilion that the kings take from them. It is like the bow of the King of the Persians, that is painted with vermilion, and is tipped with coral. There is nothing so red as thy mouth. . . .[28]

In the paroxysm of her desire, Salome binds together the numerous strands of association: the dark reverberations of the pit, blood, the ominous beating of wings, the lurid moon, and the overshadowing bird. She focuses also the cryptic warnings and forebodings that vibrate around her. Salome's poisonous malice and her careless cruel passion lie at the heart of Wilde's conception of her character. With a beauty "inhumanly immature," she acquires a quality of heroic firmness in her execution of the law of Eros that is within her. A feeling of inexorable fatality pulsates from her anguish as she confronts her death: "I hear nothing. Why does he not cry out, this man? Ah, if any man sought to kill me, I would cry out, I would struggle, I would not suffer. . . ."[29]

We can conceive of Salome's role as the symbol of an intention beautifully thrusting itself out on the plane of grotesque reality. Wanting to possess the body of Jokanaan, she evokes the presence of diabolic powers. She elicits awed response, obsessed in the pursuit of a sublime illusion. She chants her refrain, "I will kiss thy mouth . . . !" while the distracting voices around her insinuate agony and desperation. She looms as a force of destiny, or of nemesis, in her unflinching will to transcendence. She seeks to transcend her bodily desire by negating the limits of the human condition. She is apprehensive because she knows that the satisfaction of her erotic drives is beyond what the brief

[28] *Works*, p. 544.   [29] *Ibid.*, p. 558.

pleasures of earth can afford; her desire exceeds the finitude of the circumstances in which she is caught, as in a painful snare. Only death can exorcise the Eros within her and annihilate her guilt and the discords of existence. Jokanaan's body then becomes transfixed in the eternal realm of memory, represented by the past tense in "Thy body was a column of ivory set upon feet of silver," and so on. Just as she is about to be crushed, Salome affirms the singleness of purpose which endows her role with a purity of concentration that is her sublime radiance: "Ah! I have kissed thy mouth, Jokanaan. . . . They say that love hath a bitter taste. . . . But what of that? . . . I have kissed thy mouth."[30]

In contrast to Salome, Herod at first strives to achieve a compromise between lawless fancy and formal discipline, between social restraint and freedom of instinct. His saturnine temperament, however, compels him to self-indulgence. Although he counsels moderation—"It is not wise to find symbols in everything one sees. It makes life too full of terrors,"[31] he nonetheless yields to fantasy, to the splendor of his wealth and sovereignty, reminiscent of Dorian Gray's excesses: "It were better to say that stains of blood are lovely as rose petals. . . ." The world seems to obey Herod's bidding until Salome's wish shatters his optimism and his world suddenly becomes an alien place: "I will not look at things, I will not suffer things to look at me. . . . Let us hide ourselves in our palace, Herodias. I begin to be afraid." Herod tries to shield himself from mystery by artifice: "only in mirrors is it well to look, for mirrors do but show us masks."[32]

Initially forecast by Herod's superstitions, by Salome's nocturnal passions, and other ominous images, the "milieu" of the play adequately justifies the atmosphere of distortion and delirium. It prepares the setting and the mood for the

[30] *Ibid.*, p. 560.   [31] *Ibid.*, p. 553.   [32] *Ibid.*, p. 556.

irruption of the grotesque on the stage. Significantly, the grotesque in art represents "man's attempt to invoke and subdue the demonic aspects of the world."[33] Wilde introduces us to a grotesque world of a particular time and place in which the chaos of beliefs undermines any fixed standard of values —a state of affairs most conducive to hysteria.

Wilde evokes in us this particular quality of our impression by highlighting the historical circumstances of Salome's deed, such as Flaubert depicted with accuracy in his tale. I refer to that historical period involving the crisis of pagan cults and an emergent Christianity. At this crucial stage, nations intermingle and fight, with Rome's mercenary troops quite helpless in the background and unable to maintain Roman peace. To W. B. Yeats (see, for example, his play *Resurrection*), the figure of Salome symbolizes precisely that moment of cultural equilibrium that precedes the Christian dispensation and follows the full heroic life of Hellenism, the exaltation of the muscular flesh and civilized perfection.[34] One can make a persuasive argument that *Salome* is an allegory of a Spenglerian moment in European history. This idea, in fact, recurs as a theme in Victorian poetry as well as in *fin-de-siècle* philosophical reflections.

Henri Bergson's theory that crisis involves a change from a stable to an emergent world-view will illumine further Salome's mystic obedience to passion:

> The truth that these abnormal states (of the artist or mystic) have their resemblance to and sometimes also no doubt their participation in morbid states, will easily be understood if one considers the disturbance which is the passage from the static to the dynamic, from the closed to the open, from habitual life to the mystic life. When the obscure depths of the soul are agitated, what rises to the

[33] Wolfgang Kayser, *The Grotesque in Art and Literature*, tr., Ulrich Weisstein (Bloomington, Indiana, 1963), p. 188.
[34] Kermode, pp. 51ff.

surface and reaches consciousness, there takes on, if the intensity is sufficient, the form of an image or an emotion. The image is most often only a hallucination, just as the emotion is only futile agitation. But both indicate that the disturbance is a systematic arrangement looking toward a higher equilibrium: the image is then symbolic of what is being prepared, and the emotion is a concentration of the soul in the expectation of a transformation.[35]

Various images of kindred import, besides the central one of Salome's reaching out for Jokanaan's head, are conveyed to us in talk and scene. Following the Cappadocian's report that the gods "have hidden themselves. . . . I think they are dead," the Second Soldier informs us of the petty squabbles among the Jews regarding the existence of angels. Tigellinus gossips of wranglings among the Stoics. Amidst this collective anxiety, heightened by the prophet's shrieks of apocalypse, there emerges a world in which, as the Jews aver, "God hideth himself." Confusion of beliefs stems also from uncertainty of reference. Jokanaan's declarations demand constant explanation for their understanding, since the world of the play does not possess any authoritative code of meanings. Appearances no longer proclaim true identities. Over the identity of the prophet, the Jews, soldiers, and Nazarenes heatedly debate. Salome herself inquires about Jokanaan's origin. Both Herod and Herodias quarrel over the designation of "he" in the prophet's statement "He shall be eaten of worms." Herod's self-consoling "There is nothing in the world that can mar my happiness" is refused by the threats of Jokanaan. The Young Syrian projects in lyrical imagery his chaste love: "She is like a dove that has strayed. . . . She is like a narcissus trembling in the wind. . . . She

[35] *Les Deux Sources de la Morale et de la Religion* (Geneva, 1945), p. 220, quoted by Francis Fergusson, *The Idea of a Theater* (New York, 1949), pp. 82-83.

is like a silver flower." Awakened to Salome's carnal lust, he commits suicide.

Within the play itself, violent contrasts are juxtaposed by the momentum of events. After the Syrian's suicide, the Page of Herodias muses, "Ah, did he not say that some misfortune would happen?" As a fulfillment of the prophet's judgment of Herodias—"Let the captains of the hosts pierce her with their swords, let them crush her beneath their shields"—we have the last act, the visitation of punishment on Herodias' daughter: "The soldiers rush forward and crush beneath their shields Salome. . . ." Thus, each event appears carefully prefigured. Enigmas find their solutions after continual scrutiny of appearances. With "hardboiled" realism ("the moon is like the moon, that is all"), Herodias cynically disarms Herod's fancies; just as the soldiers, with their fidelity to observed phenomena, undercut Herod's beguiling rhetoric:

HEROD: Tonight I am happy, I am exceedingly happy. . . .
FIRST SOLDIER: The Tetrarch has a sombre look. Has he not a sombre look?
SECOND SOLDIER: Yes, he has a sombre look.[36]

Such a world of change and conflict affects the texture of the dialogue to the extent that the verbal medium and the situation it renders can be said to correspond with felicitous rightness. Salome's decadent trappings and her abnormal impulses dictate, at the same time as they emerge, the rhythm of lassitude and decay, the phantasmagoria, the bewildering abundance of wish-fulfillments. Spectacle and thought support each other in the weird landscape, a symbolic extension of moral perversities. Given this imbalance of relationships in which marital ties are broken and loyalties erratically shift, the absurd waywardness of the utterances is appro-

36 *Works*, pp. 552-53.

priate. The exchanges among the characters, sharing no common context, often hardly meet; a universal atmosphere of gratuitousness obtains.

We find the kernel of this situation in *La Sainte Courtisane*. The incident of that play occurs at a moment of history in which a world-outlook is gradually dying out and another is just struggling to be born. One will note the barren thorny desert, an accursed place, as a setting. The two men reflect on the vicissitudes of faiths; they reveal how Hellenic religion, with its centaurs and unicorns, is slowly collapsing before the assault of skepticism. Amid this anarchy, countless gods fight for survival. Superstition obscures the true sense of the holy; Honorius has no power to heal bodily afflictions; and Myrrhina predicts a new revelation. *Salome* presents a similar crisis in which extremes, paradoxes, and contraries revolve in a continuum of widespread disorder. The Fifth Jew summarizes this mood of alienation:

> No one can tell how God worketh. His ways are very mysterious. It may be that the things which we call evil are good, and that the things which we call good are evil. There is no knowledge of anything. We must needs submit to everything, for God is very strong. He breaketh in pieces the strong together with the weak, for he regardeth not any man.[37]

Seen in this perspective, the Gospel miracles assume an inevitability which is anticipated by Salome's overthrow of natural harmony. In a sense, her amorous celebration of the prophet's head already heralds the future crucifixion of Christ.

Salome, on the whole, presents a rapid and tightly knit sequence of intrigues and imagery in the pattern of a

[37] *Ibid.*, p. 548.

musical crescendo. With an adroitly conceived decor of moonlight, guards' talk, festival gaiety, and sinister shadows, Wilde provides the various possibilities of growth which would resolve the Tetrarch's passion, Jokanaan's wrath, and Salome's turbulence. The connotative details of the stage are animated by psychological motives whose directions can be roughly sketched in this self-explanatory diagram (the arrows indicate the several foci of interest):

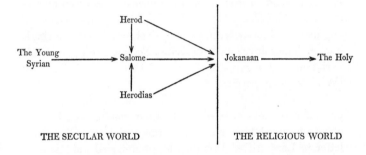

One will notice the differing objects of desire and intention. The central conflict of the play involves on the literal plane the corrupt, bejewelled paganism which statically repeats itself in the mesmerized voice of Salome, and the dynamic, forward-looking assertions of emergent Christianity represented by the inflammatory attacks of Jokanaan. While there exists between them an unrelenting tension, there is also a strange force of attraction that binds them together, as though complementary pairs, to constitute a whole. Salome represents the force of *cupiditas*, the erotic seeking of the good in material things; Jokanaan, the force of *agapé*, the upward reaching of the spirit to God.[38] Together they comprise a symmetrically structured whole.

[38] See Anders Nygren, *Agape and Eros* (Philadelphia, 1938), pp. 209-10, 471ff.

To image objectively the acceleration of plot and the changing dispositions of the characters, Wilde paints the mutations of the "cold and chaste" moon—an emblem of Salome's cruel virginity and Jokanaan's purity. As the play progresses, the moon's white beauty slowly becomes stark red, a signal for horror and impending doom. Colors evoke the developing complications, just as the frenzy of Salome's dance suggests the climax of the oppositions between Salome and Jokanaan, Herod and Herodias, the Jews and the Romans. Wilde, through manifold devices, has fused diverse elements—the scenic locale, the simple story, the feeling of anguished subjectivity, minor physical details—into a single image. James Joyce aptly describes *Salome* as "a polyphonic variation on the rapport of art and nature, a revelation of [Wilde's] own psyche."[39]

How did Wilde appraise his achievement in poetic drama? From his letters one can gather that he prized all the plays discussed here more than the social comedies. In a letter to Lord Alfred Douglas, he pronounced judgment on his art: "If I were asked of myself as a dramatist, I would say that my unique position was that I had taken the Drama, the most objective form known to art, and made it as personal a mode of expression as the Lyric or the Sonnet, while enriching the characterization of the stage, and en-larging—at any rate in the case of *Salome*—its artistic horizon."[40] These plays may then be looked at not only as "beautiful coloured, musical things," to quote Wilde's phrase, but also as examples of particular solutions invented for particular problems of dramatic expression. And even if they did not all succeed in providing new forms and modes, they at least posed the difficulties in a stronger, clearer

[39] "Oscar Wilde: Poet of Salome," *The Critical Writings of James Joyce*, p. 205. For the psychoanalytic view, see Edmund Bergler, "*Salome*, The Turning Point in the Life of Oscar Wilde," *The Psychoanalytic Review*, 43 (January 1956), 97-103.

[40] *Letters*, p. 589.

fashion. *The Duchess of Padua*, flawed by the excess of words over situation, stands on a firm, taut arrangement of plot. *A Florentine Tragedy* is a sustained dramatic action in which language and character are subordinated to the movement of plot and exemplification of theme. *La Sainte Courtisane* and *Salome* succeed primarily through their simple technique of dialogue and their unity of mood and subject matter.

What Wilde probably means by "a personal mode" is the particular concern of the theme of his plays, that is, the sudden recognition of the self's identity by virtue of its decisions at different points of crisis. Characterization becomes intensely psychological, since the pace of the plot depends almost always on the moods or sudden insights or whims of the characters. Wilde's feeling of having enlarged the drama's significance lies in his successful liberation of the Victorian theater from the tawdry conventions of naturalistic melodrama, French "well-made" entertainment pieces, and imitations of Shakespeare. The four plays look forward to Yeats and the Abbey theater, Pound's adaptations of the Japanese Noh, Strindberg's "dream plays," just as the comedies pave the way for Shaw. Wilde has done this by creating what Maeterlinck calls "the third character, enigmatic, invisible, . . . the sublime character"—the poet's idea of the universe.[41] Through symbol he has explored the depths of character, the profound complexities of the self and its manifestations. Wilde's limited but unique success should ultimately be measured according to the degree in which he was able to objectify in image and action the idea, "enveloping the whole work and creating the atmosphere proper to it," the idea—as Maeterlinck puts it—"which the poet forms of the unknown in which float about the beings and

[41] *European Theories of Drama*, ed., Barrett H. Clark (New York, 1945), p. 416.

things which he evokes, the mystery which dominates them, judges them, and presides over their destines."[42]

Salome was written a year before *Lady Windermere's Fan*. The mystery of the unknown, abruptly transferred to the drawing room and the boudoir, now becomes the presiding genius in Wilde's comedies of manners; all of his comedies won enormous financial success and critical acclaim— a warning blast, perhaps, of his coming downfall.

[42] *Ibid.*, p. 414.

V · The Action of the Comedies

Aside from the meaningful attempts at romantic drama in the late eighties, Wilde's dramatic achievement consists of the four social comedies which occupied him from 1892, when *Lady Windermere's Fan* appeared, to 1895, when *The Importance of Being Earnest* was staged with resounding success. During this period the "domestic" comedies of Henry Arthur Jones and the "problem plays" of Arthur Wing Pinero flourished; pieces like *The Second Mrs. Tanqueray* (1894) or *The Case of Rebellious Susan* (1894) confirmed certain fashions in playmaking.[1] To a great extent they helped establish the taste for the mannered gesture and the emphatic projection of social attitudes in the plays. Such trends, including analogous tendencies in dramatic acting, were ushered in when the audience, composed largely of the middle class, replaced the social "elite" as theatrical arbiters. What the middle class demanded, the playwrights and actors generally gave: melodramatic plots to excite the passions. Meanwhile, the actors attuned their methods to the unsophisticated mentality of the audience, heightening emotional virtuosity and dispensing altogether with the neoclassical stylized and formal manner of the preceding century.[2]

In the nineteenth century, Scribe and Sardou introduced the vogue of the "well-made" play on the European as well

[1] See Allardyce Nicoll, *British Drama* (New York, 1963), pp. 242-65. Curiously enough Shaw ranks Eugene Brieux, who adopts tactics similar to those of Scribe and Sardou, second to Molière and Ibsen. On Ibsen's influence on British playwrights of the later nineteenth century, see Harley Granville-Barker, "The Coming of Ibsen," *The Eighteen Eighties*, ed., Walter de la Mare (Cambridge, 1930), pp. 159-96.

[2] See Alfred S. Golding, "The Theory and Practice of Presentational Acting in the Serious Drama of France, England, and Germany during the Eighteenth and Nineteenth Centuries," *Dissertation Abstracts*, XXIII (1963), 745-46.

as on the English stage. The ingenious construction of their plots and the artificial techniques and devices they exploited to increase suspense easily appealed to the masses. For the sake of a sensational twist or a climactic scene, playwrights of this school subordinated character, dialogue, and all other elements to the aim of producing an immediate effect on the spectators. Wilde's comedies embody the melodramatic and farcical strains of the fashionable, "well-made" play—but with a difference. Commentators have noticed in his plays the disparity between speech and action, the disharmony between the conventional action and the unconventional characters and their speeches. For instance, while the aristocrats generally heed formal propriety, the radical sympathies of Lord Darlington or Lord Illingworth wreak havoc on propriety and every genteel orthodoxy. Within the framework of the conventional and credible plot, there exists a steady iconoclastic current of conversation. This yields intellectual farce which bears no reformatory purpose or ideal except the catharsis aroused by the dialectics of irony and sophistry. One can perceive in this kind of comedy a link between the "perverted grotesqueness" of the Savoy operas and the rational bourgeois-baiting of Shaw.[3]

The delightful make-believe that is the substance of Wilde's comedies draws strength chiefly from the effervescent wit and the mental alertness that inform the dialogue. This is conveyed by the easy, graceful prose. The idiom Wilde assigns to his characters, though often out of character, serves as a versatile instrument both for simple fun and serious mockery. Perhaps Wilde was just too clever and smart in the exercise of his histrionic power; he exhibits too

[3] Martin Ellenhauge, "The Initial Stages in the Development of the English Problem Play," *Englische Studien*, 66 (1932), 399ff. On melodrama, consult M. Willson Disher, *Melodrama* (London, 1954).

"wildly" his penchant for "posing."[4] How far has he really gone toward achieving a new dramatic form? One recalls that he began his career with imitations: *Vera* and *The Duchess of Padua*. There one notes the violent peripeteia, the "strong" curtains, and the sudden conversions or changes of heart of the leading characters. But in the witticisms of the villains these plays foreshadow the concentrated and ingenious paradoxes already marked in *A Florentine Tragedy* and in *Salome*, despite their emotionalism. This verbal wit culminates in the mathematical finesse with which maxims and epigrams are lined up in smooth sequence; witness the exchanges of the dandies in Lord Darlington's room in *Lady Windermere's Fan*.

With the comedies, Wilde modifies the "thesis" element of the "well-made" play by blending serious and trivial implications into a composite whole. Two temperaments or dispositions—one involving aggressive, worldly cynicism with its detached sensitivity and the other involving primitive emotionalism—clash in crucial scenes.[5] One observes how the dandies counteract the propensity to mawkishness which continually mars the plays of Augier and Dumas *fils*.[6] In *The Importance of Being Earnest*, serious meanings are conveyed by stylized language which, however, tends to slow down the movement of the plot. This feature has led many critics to formulate the notion of an inherent incongruity in the form of Wilde's comedies. For example, one reads the notion of a "divided self," a hypothesis that exists

[4] Hesketh Pearson, "Oscar Wilde and His Actors," *Theater Arts*, XLV (February 1961), 63-64; see Patrick Braybrooke, "Oscar Wilde: A Consideration," *Essays by Divers Hands*, XI (London, 1932), 21-40.

[5] Paul Custer Wadleigh, "Form in Oscar Wilde's Comedies: A Structural Analysis," *Dissertation Abstracts*, XXIII (1963), 2257; Norman James, "Oscar Wilde's Dramaturgy," *Dissertation Abstracts*, XX (1960), 3744.

[6] On the conjectured influence of Dumas *fils* on Wilde, see H. Stanley Schwarz, "The Influence of Dumas *fils* on Oscar Wilde," *The French Review*, VII (November 1933), 5-25.

only when the reader isolates certain contradictions apart from the other elements that constitute the play's total pattern of meaning.

Critics have remarked that between the sentimental plots of the comedies, where passion and seriousness predominate, and the dandiacal world of the villains, there exists an irreconcilable difference. Wilde's philistine self supposedly begs pardon from society for his excesses when we see, for example, Lord Illingworth pleading to Mrs. Arbuthnot on behalf of his illegitimate son. Meanwhile, his dandiacal self continues to defy that society and to proclaim absolute freedom so that he can express his own personal tastes and values. Torn between his contempt for empty social values and his desire to be accepted and praised by society, Wilde is supposed to have created plays in which the issues and problems are illogically posed and left unsolved or unresolved. For example, Arthur Ganz, in exploring this idea of Wilde's "divided self" (better, split sympathies), contends that Wilde "could not write as the ordinary satirist does for, where the satirist admires a social norm and ridicules deviations from it, the Wildean dandy is himself a deviation and ridicules the social norm."[7] The only form of a resolution in the plays can be found in the dandiacal joke, where external and formal manners triumph over internal moods and morals.

Censure has been levelled too against the dandy as an "idealized image"—a caricature or dummy. Other personages in the comedies impress the reader as being flat cardboard surfaces. But, Wilde himself retorts, is the dandy's image of lower value than the "round" lifelike creations of the realists? When a critic accused Ben Jonson's characters of being

[7] "The Dandiacal Drama: A Study of the Plays of Oscar Wilde," *Dissertation Abstracts*, XVIII (March 1958), 1429; see also his "The Divided Self in the Society Comedies of Oscar Wilde," *Modern Drama*, III (May 1960), 2-6.

masks and ready-made counters, Wilde countered by arguing that ready-made personages—like Iago or Sir Andrew
Aguecheek—are "not necessarily either mechanical or
wooden." He urges us, in other words, to accept the character of a particular person in the play as a *donnée* which
the play seeks to render in concrete terms. Jonson's comic
personages are not abstractions but types. The dramatist
can use, instead of psychological analysis, a more dramatic
and direct method, namely, "mere presentation." In any case
Wilde ascribes to Jonson the importance of having introduced "formal research" into the "laws of expression and
composition," embodying in himself "the most concentrated
realism with encyclopaedic erudition." His comedies inter-
mingled London slang and learned scholarship, his classical
lore giving "flesh and blood to his characters."[8] Hence
Jonson's "incongruity" Wilde finds congenial.

Now one fundamental premise of comedy is that man,
being finite, does not know all the situations that affect his
life. His knowledge, far from being complete, is wavering
and uncertain; he has many "blind spots." By reason of his
limitations in time and space, man is barred from knowing
many of the factors and forces that will affect his fate. This
is perhaps why a more or less rigid classification of characters exists in the comedies; for in man's tendency to justify
himself and his importance, he becomes obsessed with a certain quality or attitude. Eventually one can identify these obsessed figures with fixed patterns of action and response.[9]

We have in Wilde's comedies, for example, the woman
with the past: Mrs. Erlynne and Mrs. Arbuthnot. On the
other hand, Sir Robert Chiltern and Jack Worthing nourish
a past which later comes to affect their lives by some twist of

[8] *Reviews*, pp. 52-53.
[9] This is a common feature which theories of comedy, whether
that of Meredith or of Albert Cook, agree on; see the selections in
Theories of Comedy, ed., Paul Lauter (Anchor Books, New York,
1964), pp. 378-529.

circumstance, by some inscrutable concourse of events. Both sets of characters realize their true identity, in a sense, by sharing the knowledge of their past with other people. Counterposed to these "guilty" personages is the judicial role of the strict Puritan obsessed with categorical "good" and "evil": witness Lady Windermere, Hester Worsley, Lady Chiltern. Lady Bracknell, in this group, stands out by reason of her "dandiacal" or witty predilections. It will be seen that Lady Bracknell's spontaneous caprice of taste and judgment is closely related to the behavior of the dandies Jack and Algernon; the wit of these two "clowns" permeates the atmosphere of the play, and vitalizes the stratified and highly symmetrical society they live in. The vitalizing element stems from the almost animal exuberance with which they translate preposterous ideas into action; as when both of them engage in "Bunburying," sharing the disguise of "Ernest."[10]

Wilde's ironic wit has usually been regarded as antithetical to the moral questions and issues that he treats in the action of the play. Actually the total impression the comedies give is that of an integration of opposing viewpoints. It is as if a *discordia concors* has been attained in the structure of the plays. One example of this integration or combining of contraries is the reduction of manners to a game the moment the manners that form public conduct are subject to analysis. The comedies reveal the play-element at work in social affairs. They suggest that other forces, chiefly the instinctive and the irrational, exert a decisive influence on human behavior. Johan Huizinga's insight into the play-element in civilization is relevant here: "Play only becomes possible . . . when an influx of *mind* breaks down the absolute determinism of the cosmos. The very existence of play continually

[10] Arthur Ganz, "The Meaning of *The Importance of Being Earnest*," *Modern Drama*, VI (May 1963), 42ff.

confirms the supra-logical nature of the human situation."[11]
The impulse of "play" works also in the manipulation of the
dialogue. The dynamism of the verbal activity helps to
liberate obsessed minds from peculiarities that the laws
and taboos of customary intercourse have brought about.
Dialogue stirs thought, and thought opens up possibilities
of human growth.

Another aspect that one should bear in mind is the inter-
relation between character and situation in the comedies. In
Wilde's poetic dramas, the protagonists tend to acquire tragic
magnitude as the plot grows complicated to the point where
it challenges the protagonists to act in such a way that they
reveal the sublime forces working through them. The
heroic self looms large in *Salome*, where the action springs
from Salome's obsession, Salome being alternately drawn to,
and repelled by, Jokanaan. Wilde himself locates the
tragic quality in character, the comic in situation; thus the
comedies exploit "strong" curtains, build-up of suspense,
and radical transpositions of thought and impressions. The
manipulation of situations follows from the given premises
which the exposition of the first act makes clear, allowing
development only in certain directions. Often the action
falls within a schematic frame which approximates a game.
Accordingly *The Importance of Being Earnest* has been
described as "a reserved and stylized sybaritic dance."[12] One
critic has demonstrated the elaborate courtship dance in the
second half of Act II and the first scene of Act III, when the
couples unite and separate again. This systematic movement
forms part of the symmetry of situation and dialogue that

[11] *Homo Ludens* (Beacon edn., Boston, 1950), pp. 3-4.
[12] Harold E. Toliver, "Wilde and the Importance of 'Sincere and
Studied Triviality'," *Modern Drama*, v (February 1963), 389-399;
see also Werner Vortriede, "A Dramatic Device in *Faust* and *The
Importance of Being Earnest*," *Modern Language Notes*, LXX (December 1955), 584-85.

organizes the whole play. Not only does this visual chore-ography discipline the violence of farce by creating "aes-thetic distance," but it also protects the drama from the realistic judgment that it is, in the pejorative sense, "con-trived."[13]

Wilde's most significant achievement is that he success-fully combined the would-be serious subject, which often verges on sentimentality, with gay verbal wit and paradox. Situations that would otherwise be unreasonably pathetic— the comedies have strong affinities with popular extrava-ganza and melodrama—are sustained by the intellectual energy of the dialogue. Wilde exploits artificiality for jesting purposes, as in *The Importance of Being Earnest*; yet, amidst the absurdity of behavior, we hear the delicately pointed barbs of social criticism.[14] Disguised within seemingly irre-sponsible quips are seriously thought-out comments on a variety of subjects.

Most critics of Wilde's plays, concentrating more on the humorous context than on the particularities of speech and thought, have dismissed the continuities of sense in the individual epigrams. There need be no qualms in taking the aphorisms at their conceptual level, despite the hilarious joke that threatens to explode them. Although Wilde re-peatedly erects sensible propositions only to refute them, the propositions nonetheless remain valid reasoning. Just as Byron, in *Don Juan*, demonstrates to the full his talent for "nihilistic" humor, so Wilde does the same in the comedies. And just as Byron presents valid caricatures of vices and foibles of the Regency period, so Wilde articulates, in ironic modes, his condemnation of the follies of "decadent" society in the late nineteenth century.

I now aim to interpret in each play the witty utterances

[13] Otto Reinert, "The Courtship Dance in *The Importance of Be-ing Earnest*," pp. 256-57.
[14] See Nicoll, pp. 243-65.

and their ironic qualifications with the purpose of tracing the action, that is, the continuity of meaning and wholeness of thematic pattern. To apprehend the distinctive qualities of Wilde's satire, one must go beyond plot and character and attend also to the verbal texture and the correspondence of speech with character, plot, and theme.

The satire of the comedies does not so much lie in plot or character as in language, its imagery and its connotations, the dialogue being a "running accompaniment" to the visible physical performance. According to Eric Bentley, Wilde's "dialogue, which sustains the plot, or is sustained by it, is an unbroken stream of comment on all the themes of life which the plot is so far from broaching. . . . Wildean 'comment' is a pseudo-irresponsible jabbing at all the great problems, and we would be justified in removing the prefix 'pseudo' if the Wildean satire, for all its naughtiness, had not a cumulative effect and a paradoxical one. Flippances repeated, developed, and, so to say, elaborated almost into a system amount to something in the end—and thereby cease to be flippant. What begins as a prank ends as a criticism of life."[15]

Wilde's subtle and delicate witticisms, then, are not comic but "serious relief." Although he has no serious plot and no really credible character, Wilde achieves a peculiar effect in counterpointing agile criticism with the absurdities of action. Thus one can hardly catch his "philosophy" in order to approve or denounce it. The irony involves the contrast between "the elegance and savoir-faire of the actors and the absurdity of what they actually do."[16] This contrast, integral to the plays, is Wilde's efficient vantage point for ridiculing the aristocracy. The aristocrat's smooth, solid appearance reflecting inner emptiness, is matched by the inversions of standards so as to disclose what these standards really mean:

[15] *The Playwright as Thinker* (New York, 1957), p. 141.
[16] *Ibid.*, p. 144.

earnestness is equated with false seriousness, priggishness with hypocrisy, etc. With Congreve, Meredith, and Shaw, Wilde holds that the ironic attitude to life sees more than the deceptive, trivial surface that everyday reality confronts us with.

LADY WINDERMERE'S FAN

Wilde's first comedy *Lady Windermere's Fan* was written in 1891 and produced at the St. James' Theatre on February 20, 1892.[17] The difficulty Wilde experienced in its composition centers on the fact that he could not "get a grip of the play"; he confesses, "I can't get my people real." To dispel any wrong impression about the play's "form and spirit," Wilde himself delineates the action thus:

> The psychological idea that suggested to me the play is this. A woman who has had a child, but never known the passion of maternity (there are such women), suddenly sees the child she has abandoned falling over a precipice. There wakes in her the maternal feeling—the most terrible of all emotions—a thing that weak animals and little birds possess. She rushes to rescue, sacrifices herself, does follies—and the next day she feels "This passion is too terrible. It wrecks my life. I don't want to be a mother any more." And so the fourth act is to me the psychological act, the act that is newest, most true. For which reason, I suppose, the critics say "There is no necessity for Act IV." But the critics are of no importance. They lack instinct. They have not the sense of Art.[18]

Notice how Wilde isolates the maternal response of Mrs. Erlynne in Act III, when she pursues Lady Windermere to Lord Darlington's room and then anxiously but successfully

---

[17] These dates, and other matters surrounding the theatrical presentation of the plays, may be found in *Letters*.
[18] *Ibid.*, pp. 331-32.

persuades her daughter to return to her ⟨…⟩ risk
of being caught in a shameless act. Mrs. ⟨…⟩ led
by a natural instinct shared by "weak a⟨…⟩ a
sacrifice which requires utter selflessnes⟨…⟩ her
worldly ambitions; she affirms the truth ⟨…⟩ of
human affections. When she reflects on h⟨…⟩ begins to understand that all her life she has ⟨…⟩ for
that "climax," that crucible of her life. The ⟨…⟩ved
her innate love for her daughter, her instinc⟨…⟩ her
happiness.

When Lord Windermere inquires about ⟨…⟩ of
her visit in Act IV, Mrs. Erlynne replies with ⟨…⟩ice
and manner." Her voice has an accent suffused with "a note
of deep tragedy." For this moment "she reveals herself." She
intends no "pathetic scene" with her daughter. She reassures
him: "I have no ambition to play the part of a mother. Only
once in my life have I known a mother's feelings. That was
last night. They were terrible—they made me suffer—they
made me suffer too much. For twenty years, as you say, I
have lived childless—I want to live childless still."[19] But
though she might want "to live childless," she nonetheless
has proven herself a genuine mother in feeling. She has
shown at least that potency for losing herself, that selfless
love, dramatized in an episode which exactly reproduces what
she herself has done. This time she can predict the consequence: exactly what has happened to her. With full consciousness she directs her daughter's fate, as though she
had never abandoned her. She thus aborts the near "repetition" of her life; now the daughter can live with a memory
of this experience and hopefully be the wiser for it.

What Mrs. Erlynne doesn't know is that the passionate
impulse and energy that drove her to abandon her child and
husband for an illicit passion presuppose the same warmth
and impulsive selflessness that she exhibits in Lord Darling-

[19] *Works*, p. 410.

ton's room in trying to save her child from dishonor. She disregards the possibility that Lord Augustus might refuse her afterwards; her sole concern is for the untarnished reputation of her daughter. Had she been more egoistic and calculating, she could not have easily accepted the "scapegoat" function she assumed at the moment of crisis. But being an impetuous person whose emotion of love can truly possess her—it was not her fault that her lover deserted her, she claims—she acts in unconscious obedience to her real, maternal nature. Has she changed since her disgrace? Scarcely. She is as warm, alive, and—except for her shrewdness and firm, alert intelligence—as exuberant as before.

So Mrs. Erlynne declares she has no "ambition to play" the mother's part, having played it a while ago in Lord Darlington's room. The fact is that she no longer has any need to pose or play the role of mother to Lady Windermere; she has acted in consonance with her maternal nature, sincere and faithful to herself. She has revealed herself as a mother against her social instinct for mere pretense. She herself thought she was heartless—an illusion dispelled in Act IV when she cries out: "I thought I had no heart; I find I have, and a heart doesn't suit me. . . . Somehow it doesn't go with modern dress. It makes one look old. And it spoils one's career at critical moments."[20]

In the society of the Windermeres, to have a "heart" goes against the grain of characters like the Duchess of Berwick, Mr. Dumby, Mr. Cecil Graham, Lord Augustus Lorton, and their motley group. In society, fashion rules. Why, indeed, should men care for "purity and innocence," Cecil Graham remarks; "A carefully thought-out buttonhole is much more effective."[21] Appearance governs norms; Mrs.

[20] *Ibid.*, p. 51. For an extended structural analysis of *Lady Windermere's Fan*, see Cleanth Brooks and Robert B. Heilman, *Understanding Drama* (New York, 1945), pp. 43-45, 65-73.

[21] *Ibid.*, p. 402. The epigrams that the dandies shuffle off while lounging in Lord Darlington's room may be irrelevant to the plot.

Erlynne says: "Repentance is quite out of date. And besides, if a woman really repents, she has to go to a bad dressmaker, otherwise no one believes in her."[22] The portrait of herself in her youth shows her "dark hair" and her "innocent expression" supposed to be "in fashion" then. In the ballroom full of "palms, flowers, and brilliant lights," the names of guests serve as the tokens or counters of a game where empty frivolity occupies everyone. Lord Darlington refers to Lady Windermere as "the mask of his real life, the cloak to hide his secret,"[23] with respect to her husband's secret.

Wilde presents the question of true identity in all his comedies. Who am I?—that is, how define the network of social relations that condition and ultimately determine my public image? How articulate the stream of consciousness, impulses, feelings, and intuitions whose center I am? In Act I, the figure of Mrs. Erlynne denotes simply a woman of "more than doubtful character," casually mentioned by the gallants and dowagers; before the curtain falls, Lord Windermere exclaims, "I dare not tell her who this woman really is," after his wife's rebuke. We catch also the name of Mr. Hopper in an early scene, but Mr. Hopper is a puppet who offers a relief by contrast. While he is identified with "Australia" and "kangaroos," Mrs. Erlynne's presence begins to establish the profound emotional relationships in the play which are later to be clarified.

Quite obviously Mrs. Erlynne wears the trappings of a mysterious character. Lady Windermere, in Act III, disdainfully asks, "What have I to do with you?" to which she replies humbly, "Nothing." To Lord Windermere she is, in Act IV, "a divorced woman going about under an assumed

---

Actually, however, that episode provides a breathing spell from one crisis to another. If one strips the play of its verbal pyrotechnics, and such "mindless chatter" as that of the Duchess of Berwick, one gets the residue of cheap melodrama.

22 *Ibid.*, p. 410. 23 *Ibid.*, p. 388.

name, a bad woman preying upon life."[24] By the end of Act
IV, Mrs. Erlynne acquires the attributes of being "very
clever" and "very good." She progresses from anonymous
tormentor of the Windermeres to a congenial "matron" of
society. The development of the play as a whole involves
the gradual clarification of her identity. Bit by bit human
relations are particularized and objectified in action. If this
process depicts the complexities of human nature, it also
exposes the hollowness of social relations. As Lord Augustus, intrigued by Mrs. Erlynne's identity, puts it: "None of
us men do look what we really are. Demmed good thing,
too. What I want to know is this. Who is she? Where does
she come from? Why hasn't she got any demmed relations?
Demmed nuisance, relations! But they make one so demmed
respectable."[25] He expresses the point of the drama accurately in that human relationships give persons an identity,
even a distinctive "humor." Whereas Mrs. Erlynne, despite
the "curse" of her past, affirms the sanctity of the Windermeres' marriage and in fact condemns herself for violating
orthodox morality, the dandies affirm the value of their
anarchic views on marriage. To Lady Plymdale, Mrs. Erlynne and her ilk are aids to her flirtations:

> LADY PLYMDALE. . . . I assure you, women of that kind
> are most useful. They form the basis of other people's
> marriages.
> DUMBY. What a mystery you are!
> LADY PLYMDALE. (Looking at him) I wish you were!
> DUMBY. I am—to myself. I am the only person in the
> world I should like to know thoroughly. . . .[26]

The knowledge of self as well as of other people serves as
the focal interest here. It is the theme which underlies the
movement of the plot; complication, crisis, and resolution

[24] *Ibid.*, p. 408.   [25] *Ibid.*, p. 384.   [26] *Ibid.*, p. 388.

are all oriented toward revealing the actual personalities behind the masks of the *dramatis personae* who initiate the conflict, or comment on it.

The best way to explain how the matter of true identity and knowledge of self is concretely rendered in the play is to dwell on certain motifs that coalesce into what may properly be termed a symbolic cluster. In Act I we hear this dialogue:

> LADY WINDERMERE. Well, you kept paying me elaborate compliments the whole evening.
>
> LORD DARLINGTON. (*smiling*). Ah, now-a-days we are all of us so hard up, that the only pleasant things to pay *are* compliments. They're the only things we *can* pay.[27]

Lady Windermere accuses him of saying "a whole heap of things that he doesn't mean," to which he retorts: "Ah, but I did mean them."

Wilde deftly foregrounds the buried image in "paying," and puns on the "paying" of debts and compliments. We see Lady Windermere asserting her right as wife to peep into her husband's bank account. She observes that "now-a-days people seem to look on life as a speculation."[28] Lord Darlington says in this vein that most women "now-a-days, are rather mercenary."[29] Likewise Dumby remarks casually, "Awfully commercial women now-a-days."[30] All these allusions to "buying" and "selling" converge in Lady Windermere's accusation that Mrs. Erlynne belongs to that class who "are bought and sold."[31] This charge brings up the idea of Mrs. Erlynne's spiritual struggles: while she tries to "buy" her way into society, she is at the same time "paying" for it by blackmailing Lord Windermere. In effect she is capitalizing on that sordid past for which she has been ostracized. She says to her daughter, "One pays for one's sin, and then one pays again, and all one's life one pays."[32] Meanwhile the

---

27 *Ibid.*, p. 371. 28 *Ibid.*, p. 372. 29 *Ibid.*, p. 373.
30 *Ibid.*, p. 400. 31 *Ibid.*, p. 398. 32 *Ibid.*

Duchess of Berwick registers the impression that Mrs. Erlynne is a wealthy woman, whereas we know that she receives blackmail money from her son-in-law; Lord Windermere *pays* for the honor of his house.[33] The Duchess, on her part, knows the "value" of Mr. Hopper for the stupid Agatha.

But the most significant context in which the question of actual value occurs is in Act II, when Mrs. Erlynne urges Lord Windermere to bestow on her a "fictitious inheritance" so as to facilitate her marriage with Lord Augustus. She says to him: "It would be an additional attraction, wouldn't it? You have a delightful opportunity of paying me a compliment, Windermere. But you are not very clever at paying compliments. I am afraid Margaret doesn't encourage you in that excellent habit. It's a great mistake on her part. When men give up saying what is charming, they give up thinking what is charming.[34] Set against Lord Darlington's compliments, Lord Windermere's signify the price one pays for social acceptance. Mrs. Erlynne needs the money to get back into society's fold. When Lady Windermere, in the last act, decides to confess her folly to her husband, her mother dissuades her:

> MRS. ERLYNNE. . . . You say you owe me something?
> LADY WINDERMERE. I owe you everything.
> MRS. ERLYNNE. Then pay your debt by silence. That is the only way in which it can be paid.[35]

Mrs. Erlynne's investment "pays off" here. She has exercised her will on her daughter; she has shown "devotion, unselfishness, sacrifice." She has fulfilled what she felt before, when she was challenged by the situation: "What can I do? I feel a passion awakening within me that I never felt before. What can it mean? The daughter must not be like the mother—that would be terrible. How can I save her?"[36]

[33] *Ibid.*, p. 376. [34] *Ibid.*, p. 392. [35] *Ibid.*, p. 412.
[36] *Ibid.*, p. 394.

Fearing a repetition of the past, Mrs. Erlynne strives for dynamic growth and the enhancement of life. She embodies the comic force in action, guaranteeing man's unlimited possibilities for maturity and self-realization. To Lady Windermere's sentimental ideal of a "pure" mother, she opposes a critical awareness sharpened by the qualification of irony she gives to her daughter's illusions. Lady Windermere, however, still clings to her illusions despite the predicament she has undergone, despite her mother's belief: "ideals are dangerous things. Realities are better. They wound, but they are better."[37]

One perceives how Mrs. Erlynne "manipulates" most of the action, from the moment Lord Windermere invites her to her daughter's birthday party to the moment she clears up the complication for the sake of the incredibly naive Lord Augustus, whose rattling indictment of fashionable society— "Demmed clubs . . . demmed everything!"—climaxes Mrs. Erlynne's striving to enter society. The play ends like a fairy tale: Mrs. Erlynne and Lord Augustus depart from England, the Windermeres escape to the idyllic rose garden at Selby where "the roses are white and red"—not of mixed, equivocal hues.

Does Lady Windermere change at all? We meet her first as a stiff, narrow-minded Puritan who can tell exactly what is wrong and what is right. She tolerates no compromise between good and evil. Her forte is the mouthing of grandiose abstractions: life is "a sacrament. Its ideal is Love. Its purification is sacrifice."[38] If she is "good," she is unnaturally "hard": "If a woman really repents, she never wishes to return to the society that has made or seen her ruin."[39] She reviles her mother by calling her "vile." Happily Wilde always undercuts her excessive, forced casuistry with his deflating playfulness:

[37] *Ibid.*, p. 412.   [38] *Ibid.*, p. 372.   [39] *Ibid.*, p. 380.

LADY WINDERMERE. Because the husband is vile—should the wife be vile also?

LORD DARLINGTON. Vileness is a terrible word, Lady Windermere.

LADY WINDERMERE. It is a terrible thing, Lord Darlington.

LORD DARLINGTON. Do you know I am afraid that good people do a great deal of harm in this world. Certainly the greatest harm they do is that they make badness of such extraordinary importance. It is absurd to divide people into good and bad. People are either charming or tedious. I take the side of the charming, and you, Lady Windermere, can't help belonging to them.[40]

Ethical attitudes clash with "aesthetic" attitudes. Lady Windermere prides herself in declaring that "I will have no one in my house about whom there is any scandal," when almost all of her guests are either foppish or despicable shams.

Characteristically Lady Windermere is associated with roses and ideals. She boasts of her belief that "Windermere and I married for love." Wilde parodies her in the figure of Agatha, with her "mechanical" innocence and "pure tastes." But life, as Lord Darlington reminds her, is "too complex a thing to be settled by these hard and fast rules"; moreover, "life is far too important a thing ever to talk seriously about it."[41] By "seriously" is meant "dogmatically." Experience then—"the name everyone gives to their mistakes"—teaches by example; experience designates "instinct about life." Lord Darlington asserts further: "Love changes" men. Lady Windermere partly changes her attitude in the last act, after her escape from what would have been a compromising situation. She reflects thus: "How securely one thinks one lives— out of reach of temptation, sin, folly. And then suddenly—

[40] *Ibid.*, p. 373.   [41] *Ibid.*, p. 375.

oh! life is terrible. It rules us, we do not rule it."[42] Later on her absolutism relaxes. Meanwhile, Lord Windermere, in his ignorance, proceeds to condemn outright Mrs. Erlynne after the incident in the third act. He shifts his position from extreme tolerance to legalistic sternness. So his wife reproaches him with this bit of oratory:

> Arthur, Arthur, don't talk so bitterly about any woman. I don't think now that people can be divided into the good and the bad, as though they were two separate races or creations. What are called good women may have terrible things in them, mad moods of recklessness, assertion, jealousy, sin. Bad women, as they are termed, may have in them sorrow, repentance, pity, sacrifice. And I don't think Mrs. Erlynne a bad woman—I know she's not.[43]

Her knowledge has the confirmation of experience. Although she still sticks to her "ideals," she tones them down with a liberal generosity of temper: "There is the same world for all of us, and good and evil, sin and innocence, go through it hand in hand. To shut one's eyes to half of life that one may live securely is as though one blinded oneself that one might walk with more safety in a land of pit and precipice."[44]

Wilde modifies the "long-lost-child" pattern by not following it to its customary end: the expected dénouement of recognition between child and parent. What results is that Lady Windermere, even after the ordeal, remains essentially the same as she was before: an exponent of illusions. Although she has learned to question her judgments, she has not learned to question her moral standards—the traditional categories of good and evil. She has not earned "the right to the truth," her conscience goes on to feed on "white and red" roses. For in the idyllic world of the self-complacent rich, things are clear and simple: only by testing and recast-

[42] *Ibid.*, p. 405.   [43] *Ibid.*, p. 406.   [44] *Ibid.*, p. 414.

ing their categories can men prove equal to the complexity of his experience.[45]

Mrs. Erlynne, on the other hand, has preferred realities to ideals from the start. Lord Windermere's description that she is "a bad woman preying upon life" points to her "ferocity," which penetrates into social appearances and beyond them, into the realm of inward verities. Her spiritual encounters free her from the factitious and arbitrary rules of social existence. Lord Windermere suggests her inner suffering when he says: "Misfortunes one can endure—they come from outside, they are accidents. But to suffer for one's own faults—ah!—there is the sting of life."[46] After realizing a mother's devotion to her child, she has more or less lived in a single moment what she had until then failed to experience; one existential moment redeems her. She has lost her honor "by a moment's folly": she recovers it by a moment's selflessness. Losing herself, she gains identity. At the moment of deciding to "save" Lady Windermere, she feels "a passion awakening within." In contrast, Lady Windermere is the pale "coward" who, though now "of age," cannot choose what she really wants for herself. Lord Darlington challenges her: "It is wrong for a wife to remain with a man who so dishonours her. You said once you would make no compromise with things. Make none now. Be brave! Be yourself!"[47] Circumstances force her to decide; self-righteous indignation prods her to seek refuge in Lord Darlington's "friendship." Thus she forgets her mother's "past," compelled by the force of revulsion. Her birthday fan, which signifies her presumed "maturity," instead of being a weapon to strike her mother, becomes an instrument of escape. And so ultimately, her mother, her true origin, symbolized by the fan, saves her.

[45] Morse Peckham, "What Did Lady Windermere Learn?" *College English*, 18 (October 1956), 11-18.
[46] *Works*, p. 379.   [47] *Ibid.*, p. 389.

The recurrence of words like "save," "fall," "sin," "repent," "self-sacrifice," "know," and "understand," builds up the crucial scenes for spiritual commitment and renewal.[48] It amplifies the comic idea of self-knowledge through one's courage, initiative, and charity. Lady Windermere flees from her husband because he has, she says, never "understood" her. On the other hand, Mrs. Erlynne is a woman who "thoroughly understands" people.[49] Early in the play Lady Windermere evinces her crippling drawback when she refuses to know "details about" Mrs. Erlynne's life; she is responsible for her own dilemma. Lord Windermere speaks of Mrs. Erlynne's effort to "know" her daughter; on his part, he claims to "know" her thoroughly. In Act IV he believes her immorality to have been "found out." What the Windermeres lack is self-knowledge gained from self-detachment— an ideal which Dumby, by a form of understated boasting, exemplifies: "I am the only person in the world I should like to know thoroughly."[50]

The dandy, whose vocation is the dissection of motives, upholds self-knowledge as a virtue in action. Lord Darlington, for example, confesses his "little vanities" frankly. He can either display "verbal wit" or fabricate "extravagant silly things." He regards "marriage as a game." Although he exhibits "affectations of weakness," the "weakness" is only a matter of affectation. Lord Augustus' statement that "none of us men do look what we really are" is a serious confession and a public indictment.[51] Lord Darlington knows that sham and sincerity are relative: "If you pretend to be good, the world takes you very seriously. If you pretend to be

---

[48] See Northrop Frye, *Anatomy of Criticism* (Princeton, 1957), pp. 170-71: "Unlikely conversion, miraculous transformation, and providential assistance are inseparable from comedy. . . . Civilizations which stress the desirable rather than the real, and the religious as opposed to the scientific perspective, think of drama almost entirely in terms of comedy."

[49] *Works*, p. 400.   [50] *Ibid.*, p. 388.   [51] *Ibid.*, p. 372.

bad, it doesn't. Such is the astounding stupidity of optimism."[52] Bad or good, it's all a pretense. Lord Darlington may be an unscrupulous cad but his posture is more flexible and stimulating than that of the moralizing Windermeres. The play in effect proves the dandy's aphorism that "a man who moralizes is usually a hypocrite, and a woman who moralizes is invariably plain."[53] Misunderstandings cause divisions and "chasms"; Mrs. Erlynne warns her daughter of the "abyss" on whose brink, "the brink of a hideous precipice," she now stands; below is the "life of degradation." In contrast, the dandy accepts the state of things; but his realism comprehends the ideal:

> DUMBY. I don't think we are bad. I think we are all good except Tuppy.
> LORD DARLINGTON. No, we are all in the gutter, but some of us are looking at the stars.[54]

That last epigram, a memorable quip, stands out from the glib inanities of the drawing room talk.

Wilde's play presents a problem and, by the manipulation of events, solves it in a provisional fashion. The substance of the plot is composed largely of the conflict between men and women; the relationships of the sexes are constantly changing under pressure of criticism and argument. The Duchess of Berwick tells us that "all men are monsters."[55] Lord Darlington defines the relation in terms of attraction and repulsion: "Between men and women there is no friendship possible. There is passion, enmity, worship, love, but no friendship."[56] But these conflicts life resolves: Lord Windermere accepts the role of accidents. Accidents bring us misfortunes; chance may reconcile, as suggested by the coincidence of Lady Windermere's and Mrs. Erlynne's Christian

---

[52] *Ibid.*, p. 384. [53] *Ibid.*, p. 401. [54] *Ibid.*, p. 402.
[55] *Ibid.*, p. 377. [56] *Ibid.*, p. 389.

names: "What a wonderful chance our names being the same"—remarks Lady Windermere near the end.

Eventually Mrs. Erlynne "finds" herself by the felicitous interaction of circumstances. Because she desires to be accepted by society again, she manages to be "invited" to her daughter's party. The audience knows the situation; we know it too, and thereby a kind of reconciliation between the outcast and her past is effected. Mrs. Erlynne's effort is a quest for identity in a social setting; she has never really excluded herself from society because she has always acted in the light of the social condemnation of her past. Indeed, she testifies to the fact that nobody can be completely alone in the world. As Lady Windermere puts it to her husband: "You fancy because I have no father or mother that I am alone in the world and that you can treat me as you choose. I have friends, many friends."[57] One of her friends is Lord Darlington, who proves "annoying" in positive and negative ways.

The drama principally centers on the relationship between Mrs. Erlynne and Lady Windermere, between mother and daughter. Driven inwardly to her ego, the daughter becomes "cold and loveless"; whereas driven to her inmost passionate self Mrs. Erlynne is able to perform an act of self-sacrifice "spontaneously, recklessly, nobly"—as her daughter describes it.[58] Notice how the irony develops: Lord Windermere implores his wife to "save" Mrs. Erlynne; later, it turns out that Mrs. Erlynne has "saved" her daughter's honor, laboring under the fear that "the mask" of anonymity may be "stripped from one's face" by pathos and sentiment. The mother has no distinct "relations"; when Lady Windermere blurts out, "What have I to do with you?" she humbly responds: "Nothing." She adds later: "Our lives lie too far apart." She is known only as a woman with a past, but she

[57] *Ibid.*, p. 380.   [58] *Ibid.*, p. 405.

finds that nothing has altered in society; "there are just as many fools in society as there used to be."[59] Her act of love toward her daughter will always be kept a secret from the public. It was for the sake of preventing the repetition of her tragic life that she ignored her own interest when she rushed to Lord Darlington's room; but contrary to her belief that she is "lost," she has "found" herself—her mother-self. Finally explaining everything, as Lord Augustus testifies, Mrs. Erlynne "dances through life" with the poise that experience has given her.

A WOMAN OF NO IMPORTANCE

Wilde's second play, *A Woman of No Importance*, was written around September 1892 and produced at the Haymarket Theatre on April 19, 1893. The contemporary critic William Archer, on this occasion, pronounced Wilde's works "on the very highest plane of modern English drama."[60] But this particular work has generally been ignored as trivial, although the texture of the dialogue and the thematic complications somehow rescue the plot from banality.

The titular heroine Mrs. Arbuthnot, like Mrs. Erlynne, harbors a "tainted" past. She represents the "fallen woman," a literary type of the century which reflects in part the insidious effects of a double standard of morality, the ruthless indifference to feminine welfare, and the seduction of lower-class girls by "gentlemen" of the upper class.[61] But Mrs. Arbuthnot exists as a personality in her own right. She resolutely safeguards her past disgrace from oblivion; after twenty years, she still cannot forgive the villain Lord Illingworth, who now wants to take their son Gerald away from her. In the last act, Mrs. Arbuthnot inflates her glorious

---

[59] *Ibid.*, p. 391.   [60] *Letters*, p. 338n.
[61] See Bruce Alder Billingsley, "Take Her Up Tenderly: A Study of the Fallen Woman in the Nineteenth-Century English Novel," *Dissertation Abstracts*, XXIII (1963), 1681-82.

hardships for the sake of her son, in her speech beginning with "Men don't understand what mothers are."[62] Accepting "heavy punishments and great disgrace," she discovers that Gerald, the fruit of her sin, is her only wealth. She says that though her seducer dishonored her, yet he "left me richer, so that in the mire of my life I have found the pearl of price." Because of this she has never really repented; her son was worth more than innocence. She says:

> I would rather be your mother—oh! much rather!—than have been always pure. . . . It is my dishonour that has made you so dear to me. It is my disgrace that has bound you so closely to me. It is the price I paid for you—the price of soul and body—that makes me love you as I do.[63]

What Mrs. Arbuthnot expects from her acquiescence to fate and the painful humiliations she has suffered is that her son will "repay" her sooner or later. Mrs. Arbuthnot, like most women victimized by an illicit passion, seems to have become a degraded "promissory note," a property of the young Lord Illingworth. "Promissory note" is the phrase given by the flirtatious Mrs. Allonby to her husband.[64] For Lady Caroline, the Ideal Man "has to do nothing but pay bills and compliments"—a juxtaposition found also in *Lady Windermere's Fan*. We are once more involved in the measurement of human relationships not according to the "give-and-take" of affection but according to a calculus of advantage and disadvantage, investment and dividend. We are involved with the "mercantile" motive that initially animates Mrs. Erlynne's virtues in the preceding play, and that of Mrs. Cheveley in *An Ideal Husband*. In contrast with her counterparts, Mrs. Arbuthnot belongs to "the good, sweet, simple people"—to quote Lady Hunstanton—who live within

---

62 *Works*, pp. 459-60.   63 *Ibid.*, p. 460.
64 *Ibid.*, p. 430.

the "sensible system" and "artificial social barriers" of English society.[65]

Associated with this motif of "paying" and "repaying" is the idea of "saving" and "losing." Mrs. Arbuthnot, for instance, claims the "saving" of Lord Illingworth from the murderous rage of her son Gerald, who vowed to kill him after he dared to kiss Hester on a bet with Mrs. Allonby. Later she tells Lord Illingworth: "We are safe from you, and we are going away."[66] We find other connotations of "save," aside from "protecting," in this exchange in the last act:

> GERALD. . . . I would die to save you. But you don't tell me what to do now!
>
> HESTER. Have I not thanked you for saving me?[67]

She has been saved from a dandy's rudeness but not from her shallow attitude to life, which has not anticipated such a violent act coming from a person with an elegant, respectable façade. Gerald has saved Hester from Lord Illingworth's "joke," though the dandy's attempt on her virtue, like the Devil's on Eve's, is rather expected. Lady Caroline, one recalls, mentions America as "the Paradise of women," to which Lord Illingworth replies: "It is, Lady Caroline. That is why, like Eve, they are so extremely anxious to get out of it."[68] From what is Mrs. Arbuthnot safe? Certainly not from the good intentions of Lord Illingworth, who only wants to insure his son's stable future. To bring about his father's atonement, Gerald conceives of a "reparation": Lord Illingworth should marry his mother. But Mrs. Arbuthnot's mind is fixed: "What should I have done in honest households? My past was ever with me. . . ." Gerald, chivalric and prudent, seeks to vindicate his mother's honor and to realize justice within social norms; he urges his mother thus: "You must marry him. It is your duty."[69]

[65] *Ibid.*, p. 433.   [66] *Ibid.*, p. 463.   [67] *Ibid.*, p. 461.
[68] *Ibid.*, p. 421.   [69] *Ibid.*, p. 460.

Despite much preaching and sentimentalizing on her part Mrs. Arbuthnot, first uncertain in her decision, finally resolves to be firm in her refusal to forgive the erring dandy. This comes after the wealthy Hester proclaims her support of Mrs. Arbuthnot's stand. Both women then deliver grandiloquent speeches that seem out of proportion to the problem they face. Although twenty years have elapsed since her fatal passion; although Gerald now is already able to support himself, and Lord Illingworth prepared to "rehabilitate" her, Mrs. Arbuthnot still wants the past to prevail. She and Hester obfuscate the situation by their sentimental rhetoric:

> HESTER (running forward and embracing Mrs. Arbuthnot).... Leave him and come with me. There are other countries than England. . . . Oh! other countries over the sea, better, wiser, and less unjust lands. The world is very wide and very big.
>
> MRS. ARBUTHNOT. No, not for me. For me the world is shrivelled to a palm's breadth, and where I walk there are thorns.[70]

But their proposals are not solutions; in fact, they evade the problem. They are simply displays of mawkishness incited by floating abstractions. Wilde doesn't even justify Hester's radical change from dogmatic Puritan to charitable evangelist—unless Lord Illingworth's rudeness has quickly led her to identify herself with his former victim Mrs. Arbuthnot.

Set these exaggerations beside the dandy's metallic epigrams, and we grasp the central opposing forces in the play: feeling *versus* logic. Mrs. Allonby, in Act II, says that "there is something positively brutal about the good temper of most modern men"; Lady Stutfield replies: "Yes; men's good temper shows they are not so sensitive as we are, not so finely strung. It makes a great barrier often between hus-

[70] *Ibid.*, pp. 460-61.

band and wife, does it not?"[71] This opposition between reason and feeling, between the detached "dandy" and the sensitive woman, is conveyed to us in a straightforward manner:

> LADY CAROLINE. . . . It is much to be regretted that in our rank of life the wife should be so persistently frivolous, under the impression apparently that it is the proper thing to be. It is to that I attribute the unhappiness of so many marriages we all know of in society.
>
> MRS. ALLONBY. Do you know, Lady Caroline, I don't think the frivolity of the wife has ever anything to do with it. More marriages are ruined nowadays by the common sense of the husband than by anything else. How can a woman be expected to be happy with a man who insists on treating her as if she were a perfectly rational being?[72]

Lord Illingworth epitomizes the virtue of "common sense" in his offer of marriage with Mrs. Arbuthnot for the sake of their son's future. But she persists in her self-indulgent "humor"; she proves his opinion that "women are a fascinatingly wilful sex."[73] In Act III, Lord Illingworth tells Gerald: ". . . to the philosopher, women represent the triumph of mind over morals. . . . Nothing refines but the intellect."[74] When in Act II, he and Mrs. Arbuthnot first meet, he displays his calm in contrast to her nervousness:

> My dear Rachel, intellectual generalizations are always interesting, but generalities in morals mean absolutely nothing. As for saying I left our child to starve, that, of course, is untrue and silly. My mother offered you six hundred a year. But you wouldn't take anything. You simply disappeared, and carried the child away with you.

He gives the edge to his argument when he tries to dis-

[71] *Ibid.*, p. 430. [72] *Ibid.*, p. 431. [73] *Ibid.*, p. 445.
[74] *Ibid.*

sociate the mother's past from the son's future, scolding Mrs. Arbuthnot thus:

> What a typical woman you are! You talk sentimentally, and you are thoroughly selfish the whole time. But don't let us have a scene. Rachel, I want you to look at this matter from the common-sense point of view, from the point of view of what is best for our son, leaving you and me out of the question.[75]

Which is just precisely what Mrs. Arbuthnot cannot do. She cannot dispense with her possessive attitude toward her son ("my son"). She therefore refuses to compromise, rejoicing in her "tragic" burden, in her "sin." *She* does not think, she responds by impulse and sheer feminine intuition.

Earlier Lord Illingworth has expressed the idea that "all thought is immoral. It's the very essence of destruction. If you think of anything, you kill it. Nothing survives being thought of."[76] "We are all heart, all heart," Lady Hunstanton suggests, believing that all mothers are weak. Women— Mrs. Arbuthnot observes—are hard on each other, perhaps because they are all "heart" and lack detachment.[77] Take, for example, Hester's categorical judgments: "Let all women who have sinned be punished. . . ."[78] Lord Illingworth, in his ambiguous witticisms, recognizes the dualism of rational and instinctive qualities: "Nothing is serious except passion. The intellect is not a serious thing, and never has been. It is an instrument on which one plays, that is all."[79] On the intellect as an instrument Lord Illingworth plays craftily, to the discomfiture of Lady Hunstanton and her kind. The Lady herself remarks: "Personally I have very little to reproach myself with, on the score of thinking. I don't believe in women thinking too much."[80]

Hester Worsley embodies the rigid position that women

75 *Ibid.*, p. 441.   76 *Ibid.*, p. 449.   77 *Ibid.*, p. 457.
78 *Ibid.*, p. 434.   79 *Ibid.*, p. 423.   80 *Ibid.*, p. 449.

tend to take with respect to moral questions. She seems to conform to that prosaic image of the American woman Wilde describes in a review: "There is something fascinating in their funny exaggerated gestures and their petulant way of tossing the head. Their eyes have no magic nor mystery in them but they challenge us for combat; and when we engage we are always worsted."[81] Hester fits into the humorless category of women for whom "there is neither romance nor humility in her love." She is not only "painfully natural," as Lady Stutfield refers to her embarrassing candor; but she she is also pretentious in her righteousness. She declaims sanctimoniously amid the flippant chatter of dowagers. Lady Caroline's remark at the end of her speech, in its timely juxtaposition, deflates at once Hester's solemn rant:

> HESTER. It is right that they should be punished but don't let them be the only ones to suffer. If a man and woman have sinned, let them both go forth into the desert to love or loathe each other. Let them both be branded. Set a mark, if you wish, on each, but don't punish the one and let the other go free. Don't have one law for men and another for women. You are unjust to women in England. And till you count what is a shame in a woman to be an infamy in a man, you will always be unjust, and Right, that pillar of fire, and Wrong, that pillar of cloud, will be made dim to your eyes, or be not seen at all, or if seen, not regarded.
>
> LADY CAROLINE. Might I, dear Miss Worsley, as you are standing up, ask you for my cotton that is just behind you? Thank you.[82]

Wilde's fertile inventiveness provides a mode of fulfilling his impulse for exhibitionism, for the ostentatious show of his virtuosity. A variety of texture and tone in speech results.

[81] *A Critic in Pall Mall*, p. 82. [82] *Works*, p. 435.

Hester's flamboyance and pompous solemnity contrasts with the pithy epigrams of Lord Illingworth (e.g., "Nothing succeeds like excess"). The dry, elegant aphorisms of Wilde's dandies seem to infect the conversation of the other characters in the comedies. In the case of Lord Illingworth, his engaging wit redeems his callousness, his coarseness and vulgarity. On the other hand, there is something distasteful in Hester's stern pronouncements, which make her into an unlikely sage of eighteen. Mrs. Arbuthnot, like Hester, has a flair for flatulent oratory; she tends to convert pathos into a sticky fudge of verbiage. In between the thunderous curtains we listen to the pedestrian drivel of "the mindless boors" and "sycophantic cronies." A typical verbal trick of substitution occurs in the mannerisms of some of the "flat" characters, in Dr. Daubeny's repetitions, or in Lady Hunstanton's forgetfulness: "I was in hopes he would have married Lady Kelso. But I believe he said her family was too large. Or was it her feet?" Saying that Lady Belton had eloped with Lord Fethersdale, she adds, "Poor Lord Belton died three days afterwards of joy, or gout. I forget which. . . ."[83]

After Hester has observed and heard Mrs. Arbuthnot, she relaxes her obstinate casuistry a bit, confessing to her future mother-in-law: "When you came into the drawing-room this evening, somehow you brought with you a sense of what is good and pure in life. I had been foolish. There are things that are right to say, but that may be said at the wrong time and to the wrong people."[84] But though she may adjust herself to the situation, her corresponding attitudes remain fixed: "It is right that the sins of the parents should be visited on the children." Later she amends this "just" law. After Lord Illingworth's attempt to kiss her, and in her sympathy with the anguished Mrs. Arbuthnot, Hester now believes that "God's law is only Love."

[83] *Ibid.*, p. 419.   [84] *Ibid.*, p. 451.

Such a change in thinking springs from Hester's emotional susceptibility: she is either totally angry or totally sympathetic. Her moods and affections easily influence her judgments. Mrs. Arbuthnot, unlike Hester, alters her decisions in consonance with her attachment to her past. Reminded by her son, in Act II, that she is also in part guilty of her youthful "indiscretion," she yields to Gerald's wish; in Act III, however, she reverses her decision. While Gerald seeks to reconcile his parents in marriage, his mother, in righteous indignation, elects a double standard and affirms the inequality of fate between men and women: "It is the usual history of a man and a woman, as it usually happens, as it always happens. And the ending is the ordinary ending. The woman suffers. The man goes free."[85] This view prevents her from allowing for the imperfections of men and the absurdities of experience. Her judgments run on one track, permitting no possibility of growth or improvement in the process of life. She denies the possibility of an inward change in the character of Lord Illingworth: "It is not what Lord Illingworth believes, or what he does not believe, that makes him bad. It is what he is."[86] The recollection of the past seems to reduce her sensibility into a stasis of empty despair, which she rationalizes by her lachrymose portrayals of her suffering as a martyr of womankind. She is almost redundant in her reactions, which one can easily predict. In short, she can easily be "typed":

> GERALD. Is it fair to go back twenty years in any man's career? And what have you or I to do with Lord Illingworth's early life? What business is it of ours?
> MRS. ARBUTHNOT. What this man has been, he is now, and will be always.[87]

Evidently she is trying to liken him to herself in her stubborn clinging to her guilty past. Consequently she thinks of

[85] *Ibid.*, p. 458.   [86] *Ibid.*, p. 453.   [87] *Ibid.*

her "sin" as being visited on her innocent child. Nothing has changed for her in twenty years; one can even say that she has indulged in her role as victim. Whereas to Lord Illingworth "what is over is over," to Mrs. Arbuthnot the past lives on as a perpetual curse hovering in the air wherever she goes:

> MRS. ARBUTHNOT. . . . You don't realise what my past has been in suffering and in shame.
>
> LORD ILLINGWORTH. My dear Rachel, I must candidly say that I think Gerald's future considerably more important than your past.
>
> MRS. ARBUTHNOT. Gerald cannot separate his future from my past.[88]

Now Lord Illingworth, who corresponds to the conception of the Ideal Man because he is—as Lady Caroline says—"extremely realistic," is a man of compromise. His intelligence comprehends opposing views. It can turn platitudes topsy-turvy and still preserve its validity in application to life. His talent is directed toward refining the "art of living." To him modern life signifies being "fit for the best society. . . . Society is a necessary thing. No man has any real success in this world unless he has got women to back him, and women rule society."[89] Accepting the passage of time and its psychological impact, Lord Illingworth perceives with greater intensity the value of youth, youth having "a kingdom waiting for it." He declares, "saints have a past, sinners have a future."[90] He calls his looking glass "unkind" because "it merely shows my wrinkles." But his flexibility and generosity of temper could not influence the closed mind of Mrs. Arbuthnot. In the end he yields to a retrospective mood; all morality and prudence vanish, and he sees in Mrs. Arbuthnot only "the prettiest of playthings, the most fascinating of small romances. . . ."[91]

[88] *Ibid.*, p. 441. [89] *Ibid.*, p. 445. [90] *Ibid.*, p. 447.
[91] *Ibid.*, p. 465.

In general, comic characters are those whose attitudes and outlook in life are out of proportion to, and so falsify, the actualities of experience. They appear ridiculous in their exaggeration of certain ideas and sentiments without reference to the flux of circumstances. They adhere blindly to limited positions, heedless of time and the potencies for growth and inward change in man. Wilde thus criticizes Mrs. Arbuthnot's bondage to her past. Her past is indirectly diminished in importance by the fatuous forgetfulness of Lady Hunstanton, and by the infantile regression of Mrs. Daubeny, who recalls chiefly "the events of her childhood" after her last attack of illness. Wilde projects the idea of life's development in Gerald's grasping of "my one chance in life," his "wonderful piece of good luck." He entertains the prospect of being Lord Illingworth's secretary. Lord Illingworth is a man who commands great power and resources: "there is nothing he couldn't get if he chose to ask for it." To his pleas that Gerald and he be brought together, Mrs. Arbuthnot replies: "There can be nothing in common between you and my son."[92] But Gerald wants to be like his father, expressing the same temperament, cherishing similar ambitions. He likes Lord Illingworth's "cleverness, prosperity, and self-confidence." He asserts his freedom to choose and make "a position" for himself in the world.

In life as well as in comedy, time has a way of playing tricks that affect the destiny of individuals. Lord Illingworth says at one point that he has "found" his son. Words like "know," "mean," and the like, connote concealment and discovery. For example, Lord Illingworth says to Gerald, "I want you to know how to live."[93] Gerald says to his father: "I want you so much to know my mother."[94] Mrs. Allonby says of the "Ideal Man": "He should always say much more than he means, and always mean much more than he

[92] *Ibid.*, p. 439.   [93] *Ibid.*, p. 446.   [94] *Ibid.*, p. 438.

says. . . . "[95] Mrs. Arbuthnot maintains throughout that her meeting with Lord Illingworth "was a mere accident, a horrible accident." She cannot make the sacrifice of allowing her son to choose for himself, to *know* himself. In Act II Mrs. Arbuthnot comes in "unannounced" by way of the terrace; she is described as living too much "out of the world."[96] She is the outsider who penetrates "artificial social barriers." Lord Illingworth confesses to having concealed the truth from the world; from society's standpoint she is a "woman of no importance." Ultimately she refuses to abide by the dynamic rhythm of life in which accidents—such as Hester's casting her fortune with them—play a great role. To assume with her that "all love is terrible" and is a "tragedy" would be to condemn automatically Gerald's and Hester's alliance. In the end she succumbs to a self-engendered paralysis, dominating her son's will, and purging herself of warmth and kindness: "My heart is cold: something has broken it."

From another viewpoint Mrs. Arbuthnot appears to have grasped the opportunity presented by Hester's wealth. Paradoxically she resolves Gerald's problem by conforming to the social standard of wealth and material security. Her heart belongs to the "good, sweet, simple people" on whom the dandy's destructive energy feeds in its affirmation of life's capacity for change and development. Ultimately Lord Illingworth's vision reconciles life's discords in its recognition of incongruity: "the world has always laughed at its own tragedies, that being the only way in which it has been able to bear them. And that, consequently, whatever the world has treated seriously belongs to the comedy side of things."[97]

AN IDEAL HUSBAND

Wilde's least successful play on the stage and his third comedy, *An Ideal Husband*, was written between October

[95] *Ibid.*, p. 432.   [96] *Ibid.*, p. 435.   [97] *Ibid.*, p. 447.

1893 and March 1894. It was produced at the Haymarket Theatre on January 3, 1895. When Wilde in 1899 corrected the proofs of the play for publication, he said that it "reads rather well, and some of its passages seem prophetic of tragedy to come."[98] But Sir Robert Chiltern's predicament, though it bears a tenuous resemblance to Wilde's, has distinctive melodramatic overtones.

The play concerns itself primarily with Sir Robert Chiltern's past misdeed on which his fortune and eminent reputation now stands. The past, in the form of Mrs. Cheveley's immoral ends, revives in order to haunt and threaten him. Just as, in the three other plays, the past proves a force that motivates the thematic action, so here time seems to be the concept that governs the complication and resolution of the plot. The play deals with the problem of how well man, confronted with the alterable modes of his life, can adjust or adapt himself to the needs of changing situations. Where an absolute standard is obeyed despite the criticism of it by experience and actuality, there result irony, distortions, and absurdities that arouse ridicule and laughter.

Notice first how the scenes of the play shift from the "social" crowded atmosphere of the Octagon Room at Chiltern's house (Act I) to a "private" room (Act II), then to the secluded library of Lord Goring where the two letters —the fatal letter of Sir Robert Chiltern and Lady Chiltern's letter to Lord Goring—play decisive roles.[99] The scene finally returns to the setting of Act II, where social and private interests intersect; where all the rough, disturbing edges of the misunderstanding between husband and wife are smoothed off by obvious devices—by means of the diamond brooch that Lord Goring uses to restrain Mrs. Cheveley, and by Mrs. Cheveley's stupidity in not explaining to Chiltern the

[98] *Letters*, p. 787.

[99] This scene is analogous to Lord Darlington's room in *Lady Windermere's Fan*, where Lady Windermere and Mrs. Erlynne meet to dramatize the crisis of their lives.

nature of the letter his wife wrote to Lord Goring. Eventually
the play closes with a sense of new life for the Chilterns,
while Lord Goring and Mabel Chiltern entertain the prospect
of a happy marriage. The image of a stable society prevails
in the end, as the conventions of marriage, family life, and
public office are severally affirmed.

When Act I opens, Mrs. Marchmont and Lady Basildon,
"types of exquisite fragility," display their "affectations of
manner" which, however, do not make their remarks pointless:

> Mrs. Marchmont. Horribly tedious parties they give,
> don't they?
> Lady Basildon. Horribly tedious! Never know why I go.
> Never know why I go anywhere.[100]

Mabel Chiltern states in ironic terms the combination of
polished form and hollow insides that society presents: "Oh,
I love London society! I think it has immensely improved.
It is entirely composed now of beautiful idiots and brilliant
lunatics. Just what society should be."[101] Her indictment
gains pungent venom in Lord Caversham's opinion that
London society "has gone to the dogs, a lot of damned no-
bodies talking about nothing."[102]

Dress or fashion furnishes an index to social attitudes
and values. Lord Goring pronounces: "fashion is what one
wears oneself. What is unfashionable is what other people
wear."[103] When he offers to give Mrs. Cheveley "some good
advice," she replies: "Oh! pray don't. One should never give
a woman anything that she can't wear in the evening."[104] The
interest in appearance occupies the foreground in this exchange:

> Mrs. Cheveley (*languidly*). I have never read a Blue
> Book. I prefer books . . . in yellow covers.

[100] *Works*, p. 467. [101] *Ibid.*, p. 469. [102] *Ibid.*, p. 415.
[103] *Ibid.*, p. 507. [104] *Ibid.*, p. 516.

LADY MARKBY (*genially unconscious*). Yellow is a gayer
colour, is it not? I used to wear yellow a good deal in
my early days, and would do so now if Sir John was not
so painfully personal in his observations, and a man on
the question of dress is always ridiculous, is he not?[105]

Politics is a kind of "fashion," too, in its concern with
public appearance. Lady Basildon claims to talk politics
ceaselessly. Sir Robert Chiltern regards a political life as "a
noble career," though our knowledge of his past belies his
statement. But in the political or practical life, the criterion
of success reduces moral standards to the basic level of
pragmatic efficacy. As Lord Goring puts it, "in practical life
there is something about success, actual success, that is a
little unscrupulous, something about ambition that is unscrupulous always."[106]

In Act IV, Lady Chiltern believes that Sir Robert's ambition has led him astray in his early days. She says that
"power is nothing in itself. It is power to do good that is
fine."[107] Her husband admits to Lord Goring that he "bought
success at a great price."[108] And yet he is highly esteemed
for being a respectable, selfless "public servant," a model of
virtue, which is but a "front" or mask that he wears in conformity to social norms. After all, as Lord Goring remarks,
almost all private fortune in society has come from dubious
"speculation." On knowing her husband's guilt, Lady Chiltern hysterically complains not of his pretense but of his
inability to "lie" to her for the sake of "virtues" he has been
socially known for. Lady Chiltern cries out,

Don't touch me. I feel as if you had soiled me forever.
Oh! what a mask you have been wearing all these years!
A horrible, painted mask! You sold yourself for money.
Oh! a common thief were better. You put yourself up

[105] *Ibid.*, p. 502.　　[106] *Ibid.*, p. 496.　　[107] *Ibid.*, p. 486.
[108] *Ibid.*, p. 490.

for sale to the highest bidder! You were bought in the market. You lied to the whole world. And yet you will not lie to me![109]

This exposure means a stripping of costume, an "undressing," to disclose the authentic self. One recalls Lady Markby's experience, which prefigures Sir Robert's plight, when she describes the result of immersion in the crowd:

> The fact is, we all scramble and jostle so much nowadays that I wonder we have anything at all left on us at the end of an evening. I know myself that, when I am coming back from the Drawing Room, I always feel as if I hadn't a shred on me, except a small shred of decent reputation just enough to prevent the lower classes making painful observations through the windows of the carriage.[110]

Behind Sir Robert's open "goodness" lies a secret "truth," the as yet unacknowledged truth of human frailty. He has committed an immoral act in order to insure his social success.

Act I gives us the needed background information about the moral issue. Mrs. Cheveley remarks: "Nowadays, with our modern mania for morality, everyone has to pose as a paragon of purity, incorruptibility, and all the other seven deadly virtues." She threatens Sir Robert:

> Yours is a very nasty scandal. You couldn't survive it. If it were known that as a young man, secretary to a great and important minister, you sold a Cabinet secret for a large sum of money, and that was the origin of your wealth and career, you would be hounded out of public life, you would disappear completely. . . . You have a splendid position but it is your splendid position that makes you so vulnerable.

[109] *Ibid.*, p. 505.   [110] *Ibid.*, p. 500.

She elaborates on the punishment that the fallen victim is bound to receive from society:

> Suppose that when I leave this house I drive down to some newspaper office, and give them this scandal and the proofs of it! I think of their loathsome joy, of the delight they would have in dragging you down, of the mud and mire they would plunge you in. Think of the hypocrite with his greasy smile penning his leading article, and arranging the foulness of the public placard.[111]

Ironically Lady Chiltern thinks that her husband has no "secrets" from her.

Confronted with his "shameful" secret, Sir Robert Chiltern reflects on how most men have "worse secrets in their own lives." Lord Goring himself, in planning to thwart Mrs. Cheveley's designs, believes that "everyone has some weak point. There is some flaw in each one of us."[112] Aware of human limitations, he allows for imperfections in men. Observation, if not experience, has taught him that the "ideal husband" is a myth. He says to Lady Chiltern in Act II:

> I have sometimes thought that . . . perhaps you are a little hard in some of your views on life. I think that . . . often you don't make sufficient allowances. In every nature there are elements of weakness, or worse than weakness.[113]

Just as Sir Robert has a "past," so does his enemy Mrs. Cheveley. She ceases to be a mystery when Lady Chiltern recalls her as a schoolmate: "She was untruthful, dishonest, an evil influence on everyone whose trust or friendship she could win. . . . She stole things, she was a thief. She was sent

[111] *Ibid.*, pp. 480-81.   [112] *Ibid.*, p. 493.   [113] *Ibid.*, p. 496.

away for being a thief."[114] Lord Goring discovers later that she has stolen the diamond brooch he has given to a friend. Thus Mrs. Cheveley is not without her secret crime, of which Lord Goring accuses her later. Her image as an intriguing woman who "makes great demands on one's curiosity" is soon modified by the knowledge we get of her past life, her origin; she, who claims to possess integrity, turns out to be an embodiment of corruption.

It seems that the past, what is dead and forgotten, is always valuable for the perspective of the comic vision. The past qualifies man's pride; it gives an objective picture of any man's life. Whereas the past judges man in his finitude, the future gives him the freedom of choosing his possible, ideal selves. Mrs. Cheveley proves the most vulnerable character because, as she declares, her "memory is under admirable control."[115] The one real tragedy in a woman's life, she says, is the fact that "her past is always her lover, and her future invariably her husband."[116] Sir Robert, of course, is the "man" with a future, as Mabel Chiltern says; but his future rests on his past. When Mrs. Cheveley enters the scene, he starts reflecting on life:

> Is it fair that the folly, the sin of one's youth, if men choose to call it a sin, should wreck a life like mine, should place me in the pillory, should shatter all that I have worked for, all that I have built up? Is it fair, Arthur?[117]

Lord Goring replies: "Life is never fair, Robert. And perhaps it is a good thing for most of us that it is not."

What is the danger that life confronts us with? It is the danger of having an open mind, an equipoise within, a balance which comes from a just calculation of the factors that affect one's life. When Lord Goring suggests that Sir

114 *Ibid.*, p. 485.   115 *Ibid.*, p. 473.   116 *Ibid.*, p. 519.
117 *Ibid.*, p. 489.

Robert alter his wife's fixed views on life, Sir Robert replies: "All such experiments are terribly dangerous." Lord Goring, however, counters: "Everything is dangerous, my dear fellow. If it wasn't so, life wouldn't be worth living."[118] He entertains, in short, the surprises and novelties that organic life is ever producing. In Act IV, life puts Lady Chiltern's reputation in danger. We see how Sir Robert becomes desperate, then panicked: "I clutch at every chance. I feel like a man on a ship that is sinking."[119] The disaster being still on the level of conjecture, his interjections are maudlin: "My life seems to have crumbled about me. I am a ship without a rudder in a night without a star."[120] This radically qualifies the role of Sir Robert as a man with a "serious purpose in life," a "pattern husband." Lady Chiltern amplifies her husband's image:

> A man's life is of more value than a woman's. It has larger issues, wider scope, greater ambitions. Our lives revolve in curves of emotions. It is upon lines of intellect that a man's life progresses.[121]

"Lines of intellect" versus "curves of emotion"—this opposition involves society's failure to establish harmonious relations between men and women. It involves a milieu in which the accepted codes of behavior do not promote the sensibility of men to function integrally. Wilde's portrayal of his "ideal husband" sets directly the contrast between feeling and conscious thought, between perceived behavior and the groping, reckless inner self:

> The note of his manner is that of perfect distinction, with a slight touch of pride. One feels that he is conscious of the success he has made in life. A nervous temperament, with a tired look. The firmly chiselled mouth and chin con-

[118] *Ibid.*   [119] *Ibid.*, p. 494.   [120] *Ibid.*, p. 514.
[121] *Ibid.*, p. 533.

trast strikingly with the romantic expression in the deep-set eyes. The variance is suggestive of an almost complete separation of passion and intellect, as though thought and emotion were each isolated in its own sphere through some violence of will-power.[122]

Sir Robert Chiltern speaks in character when he insists on the idea of a compartmentalized life: ". . . public and private life are different things. They have different laws, and move on different lines."[123]

Elsewhere men are called "horribly selfish" and "grossly material."[124] Despite Sir Robert Chiltern's show of qualms and vacillation, Mrs. Cheveley is assured that he is "most susceptible to reason"—by which she means that he readily succumbs to fear of social disapproval. Women are gifted with "the moral sense." Lady Markby prefers anything other than "high intellectual pressure."[125] To Lord Caversham, "common sense is the privilege" of men; in his view, marriage is a matter not of affection but of common sense. Mrs. Cheveley herself separates "business" from "silver twilights or rose-pink dawns." She considers being "natural" the most difficult pose of all. She holds that there is a wide gap between the rational method of science and the irrational layer of experience:

MRS. CHEVELEY. Ah! the strength of women comes from the fact that psychology cannot explain us. Men can be analyzed, women . . . merely adored.

SIR ROBERT CHILTERN. You think science cannot grapple with the problem of women?

MRS. CHEVELEY. Science can never grapple with the irrational. That is why it has no future before it, in this world.

[122] *Ibid.*, p. 470.   [123] *Ibid.*, p. 485.   [124] *Ibid.*, p. 477.
[125] *Ibid.*, p. 482.

SIR ROBERT CHILTERN. And women represent the irrational.

MRS. CHEVELEY. Well-dressed women do.[126]

The double aspects of life seem to be focused in Mrs. Cheveley's mysterious identity. Lord Goring describes her as "a genius in the daytime and a beauty at night."[127] She plays with the attitudes of optimism and pessimism. What after all is the real self of a person? Lady Chiltern cannot believe her husband to be guilty of dreadful things which are "so unlike [his] real self." Her idealized image of him is that he has "brought into the political life of our time a nobler atmosphere, a finer attitude towards life, a freer air of purer aims and higher ideals."[128] But reality is never as simple and pure as Lady Chiltern would like to imagine it. Society has become "dreadfully mixed" for Mrs. Cheveley; Lady Markby, likewise, observes that " families are so mixed nowadays. Indeed, as a rule, everybody turns out to be somebody else."[129] Just as society is complex, so truth—as Sir Robert Chiltern believes—is a very complex thing.

To the unbending, puritanical Lady Chiltern, life however appears simple and fixed. She has always been noted for her stingy exclusiveness and conservatism. She has remained unaffected by changing circumstances:

MRS. CHEVELEY. I see that after all these years you have not changed a bit, Gertrude.

LADY CHILTERN. I never change.

MRS. CHEVELEY (elevating her eyebrows). Then life has taught you nothing?

LADY CHILTERN. It has taught me that a person who has once been guilty of a dishonest and dishonorable action may be guilty of it a second time, and should be shunned.

[126] *Ibid.*, p. 472.   [127] *Ibid.*, p. 474.   [128] *Ibid.*, p. 487.
[129] *Ibid.*, p. 471.

> MRS. CHEVELEY. Would you apply that rule to everyone?
> LADY CHILTERN. Yes, to everyone, without exception.[130]

We know of course that Sir Robert has changed. Mrs. Cheveley, though shrewder and more worldly-wise, has not reformed her ways. With firm logic Lady Chiltern holds to her conviction that human beings are what they are, past or present; that human nature is predestined, and is permanently fixed. She accuses Mrs. Cheveley of being dishonest on the basis of her past conduct:

> SIR ROBERT CHILTERN. Gertrude, what you tell me may be true, but it happened many years ago. It is best forgotten! Mrs. Cheveley may have changed since then. No one should be entirely judged by his past.
> LADY CHILTERN (sadly). One's past is what one is. It is the only way by which people should be judged.
> SIR ROBERT CHILTERN. That is a hard saying, Gertrude!
> LADY CHILTERN. It is a true saying, Robert. . . .[131]

Like her counterparts in the other plays, Lady Windermere and Hester Worsley, Lady Chiltern does not believe that the sinner can make amends or work for his redemption. Addicted to histrionics, she often forgets the harsh prosaic facts of experience which are necessary to obtain an adequate understanding of human nature.

In contrast with her tolerant husband, Lady Chiltern acts without regard for the variable situations of life. Sir Robert Chiltern, it must be stressed, conceives himself changed since his early indiscretion on the ground that "circumstances alter things." But his wife decrees otherwise: "Circumstances should never alter principles."[132] Nonetheless, life's circumstances play a joke on her: when Sir Robert, in Act I, asks Mrs. Cheveley what brought her into his life in order to destroy his reputation and family honor, she answers: "Cir-

---

[130] *Ibid.*, p. 504.   [131] *Ibid.*, p. 485.   [132] *Ibid.*, p. 486.

THE ACTION OF THE COMEDIES

cumstances." Accident makes Robert negligent to the extent that he leaves the incriminating letter in Baron Arnheim's possession. And the accident of circumstance makes Mrs. Cheveley drop her diamond brooch, thus giving Lord Goring a weapon to prove her guilty of theft. On the whole, life offers chances to qualify, change, or confirm the truths and beliefs men hold. Sir Robert, for instance, speaks of the "wonderful chance" the Baron gave him to enrich himself unscrupulously. Later, he would bank on the "chance" that some scandal might be found involving his blackmailer Mrs. Cheveley. Desperately he exclaims: "Oh! I live on hopes now. I clutch at every chance."[133]

We have noted previously the objective of success as a controlling force in Sir Robert's life. Early in his career he has been told that "luxury was nothing but background, a painted scene in a play"; what matters is power based on wealth.[134] To be sure, he has never truly regretted his youthful crime. But the opportunity to acquire wealth unscrupulously he denies to others. Success, the chief social criterion of value, is parodied in the humorous puns on "triumph"; for example, Mabel Chiltern mentions a tableau in which she and Lady Chiltern are participants:

> You remember, we are having a tableaux, don't you? The triumph of something, I don't know what! I hope it will be the triumph of me. Only triumph I am really interested in at present.[135]

Wilde describes the stage decoration in Act I: "Over the well of the staircase hangs a great chandelier with wax lights, which illumine a large eighteenth century French tapestry—representing the Triumph of Love, from a design by Boucher—that is stretched on the staircase wall." At the close of Act III, we see Mrs. Cheveley's face "illumined with

133 *Ibid.*, p. 494.   134 *Ibid.*, p. 490.   135 *Ibid.*, p. 498.

evil triumph."[136] What triumphs of course is the comic situation.

If the function of comedy is to reaffirm due proportion in life and restore "the golden mean," it is imperative that the "rules" for social existence be carefully defined. An attempt at this definition exists in Wilde's play. Sir Robert tries to expose Mrs. Cheveley's plan for a "swindle" instead of a "speculation": "let us call things by their proper names."[137] Eventually she turns the table over him:

> SIR ROBERT CHILTERN. It is infamous, what you pro-
> pose—infamous!
> MRS. CHEVELEY. Oh, no! This is the game of life as we
> all have to play it, Sir Robert, sooner or later.[138]

When he agrees on a bargain, with his support of her specu-lation in exchange for the incriminating letter, she says: "I intend to play quite fairly with you. One should always play fairly . . . when one has the winning cards."[139]

Both the "game of life" and blackmail suggest commercial exchange, bargaining, profit and loss. Allusions and meta-phors drawn from trade and finance are interwoven in the verbal fabric of the play. In Act I, Mrs. Cheveley appraises people according to their "price": "My dear Sir Robert, you are a man of the world, and you have your price, I suppose. Everybody has nowadays. The drawback is that most people are so dreadfully expensive."[140] Later she exhorts him: "Years ago you did a clever, unscrupulous thing; it turned out a great success. You owe it to your fortune and position. And now you have got to pay for it. Sooner or later we all have to pay for what we do. You have to pay now."[141] Offered a bribe, she refuses: "Even you are not rich enough, Sir Robert, to buy back your past. No man is." To Lady Chiltern, "money that comes from a tainted source is a degradation."

[136] *Ibid.*, p. 522.   [137] *Ibid.*, p. 478.   [138] *Ibid.*, p. 480.
[139] *Ibid.*, p. 481.   [140] *Ibid.*, p. 479.   [141] *Ibid.*, p. 481.

Sir Robert confesses that while he did not sell himself for money, he "bought success at a great price." Lord Goring thinks that he "paid a great price for it."[142] In his remorse, Sir Robert Chiltern vows that he has "paid conscience money many times" for his mistake. Mrs. Cheveley's transaction with Sir Robert, in Lord Goring's opinion, is a "loathsome commercial transaction of a loathsome commercial age." Mrs. Cheveley admits that much: "It is a commercial transaction. That is all. There is no good mixing up sentimentality in it. I offered to sell Robert Chiltern a certain thing. If he won't pay me my price, he will have to pay the world a greater price."[143]

So in the middle of the play Sir Robert Chiltern is threatened with scandal and ruin because of what he did in the past. He declares that he has fought the century with its own weapon, wealth. He has shown the courage, cunning, and strength to yield to temptations: "To stake all one's life on a single moment, to risk everything on one throw, whether the stake be power or pleasure, I care not—there is no weakness in that. There is a horrible, terrible courage."[144] Lord Goring's dandyism, his allowances for human vices and shortcomings, vindicate Sir Robert's resolution to defy Mrs. Cheveley. When Mrs. Cheveley boasts that she knows Sir Robert's "real character" by virtue of his letter, Lord Goring replies: "What you know about him is not his real character. It was an act of folly done in his youth, dishonourable, I admit, shameful, I admit, unworthy of him, I admit, and therefore . . . not his true character."[145] Of the Chilterns' intended withdrawal from public life despite his promotion to a Cabinet post, Lord Goring remarks: "We men and women are not made to accept such sacrifices from each other. We are not worthy of them."

142 *Ibid.*, p. 490.   143 *Ibid.*, p. 519.   144 *Ibid.*, p. 491.
145 *Ibid.*, pp. 518-19.

In the "flawless dandy" Lord Goring, we perceive the line-aments of "the ideal husband"—at least to Mabel Chiltern, in the future. He has a humaneness absent from his literary predecessors like Lord Henry Wotton, Lord Darlington, and Lord Illingworth. The dandy, in general, enacts the cult of the self not only in thought but also in the taste for dress and material elegance. He supports ceremony and social manners in principle. If he is anarchic, that is because he feels secure within the confines of society. Gestures and dress suggest the rhythm and harmony of a mind which depends on "the peculiar pleasure of astonishing and the proud satis-faction of never being astonished." Seriousness, or hypoc-risy, is the "unbecoming" cardinal vice. As a clown armed with trivialities, the dandy exemplifies the value of external form as the emblem of what is within the self; he dissolves any disparity between the moral and the physical aspects of life. Lord Goring, in particular, abhors all romantic ideals, just as the dandies of the other comedies do. Pursuing a "gentlemen's" routine, he exhibits "all the delicate fopperies of Fashion." Compared with Phipps the "ideal butler," the "mask with a manner," who represents "the dominance of form," Lord Goring has *élan vital*: "He plays with life, and is on perfectly good terms with the world. . . . One sees that he stands in immediate relation to modern life, makes it indeed, and so masters it."[146] Mabel Chiltern, whose good sense springs from a feeling for just proportion in matters of daily life, does not desire Lord Goring to be an "ideal husband." For she feels that "he can be what he chooses"; her only wish is to be "a real wife to him." The significance of the ad-jective "real" inheres in a flexibility of attitude to life, in the knowledge of human limitations—a knowledge of which the "ideal husband" must have a good share.

[146] *Ibid.*, p. 473.

THE IMPORTANCE OF BEING EARNEST

Wilde wrote his last and, it is commonly agreed, his most perfect play, *The Importance of Being Earnest*, in August-September 1894. It was produced at the St. James' Theatre on February 14, 1895. Wilde confessed that he found the "real charm of the play" in the dialogue. Although the "plot is slight" but "adequate," he liked the pure fun and amusing "trivial wit."[147] He cherished the play as a serious effort—"How I used to toy with that tiger Life!"—and even judged it with a certain wistful pride: "I like the play's irresponsibility and its *obiter dicta*, but it is essentially an acting play: it should have been a classic for the English Theatre, but alas! the author was struck by madness from the moon."[148]

There is no doubt that the unequalled farcical construction of this play, which has sustained the interest of the audience through the years, stems from premises that beg for no serious consideration. Perhaps it would be folly to analyze this masterpiece—most critics have simply contented themselves with fuzzy impressions. The play contains premises of make-believe material which are mathematically "demonstrated" in the formulas of stock situations: the motif of mistaken identity, the "twin" brothers, concealed information about birth and lineage, and so forth. Is there a plot in this piece of pure frivolity? Many discern none. Commentaries have frequently dwelt on the absurd *donnée* of characters obsessed with the name "Ernest." One sees at once the pun on the name, which Jack Worthing's serio-comic statement underlines:

> LADY BRACKNELL. My nephew, you seem to be displaying signs of triviality.
>
> JACK. On the contrary, Aunt Augusta, I've now realized for the first time in my life the vital Importance of Being Earnest.[149]

[147] *Letters*, p. 359. [148] *Ibid.*, pp. 778, 786. [149] *Works*, p. 369.

One will gradually perceive that the game played with the double meaning of words, such as "Ernest" and "earnest," controls not only the progression of the plot but also the minor details of dialogue. Miss Prism describes the fate of her novel: "The manuscript unfortunately was abandoned. I use the word in the sense of lost or mislaid."[150] Cecily says to Algernon whom she mistakes for the "wicked" Ernest: "I hope you have not been leading a double life, pretending to be wicked and being really good all the time."[151] These inversions and ambiguities fall under the general technique and concept of "Bunburying"—the adoption of two identities, of masks, so as to resolve in separate planes the needs of the energetic, vital, imaginative personality. At the center of this double life is the premise expressed by Algernon when Jack, in Act II, reminds him of the gentleman's duty to be sincere. Algernon answers: "My duty as a gentleman has never interfered with my pleasures in the smallest degree."[152] When Algernon meets his match, and Jack is recognized as Algernon's elder brother, the need and rationale for "Bunburying" disappears.

Despite the constant digressions and the fluent irrelevance of the dialogue—its enjoyable agility of pace conceals the skill with which it is composed—the sequence of the plot is simple. Jack Worthing, who desires to marry Gwendolen, can do so only if he satisfies Lady Bracknell's demands. Inspired by his discovery that Jack is doing some "Bunburying" of his own, Algernon, Gwendolen's cousin, goes to the Manor House at Woolton and there falls in love with Cecily Cardew. Gwendolen follows Jack (Ernest to her) to the Manor House; complications arise, until Lady Bracknell discovers Miss Prism, Cecily's governess, who clears up Jack's identity. Jack turns out to be the elder brother of Algernon and the nephew of Lady Bracknell. His new status

150 *Ibid.*, p. 339.   151 *Ibid.*, p. 341.   152 *Ibid.*, p. 346.

endorses his social importance, his "earnest" playing of the role of a fictitious "Ernest" paying up in the end; hence "the vital Importance of Being Earnest." The juggling with homonyms underscores the value of the imagination, symbolized by the assumption of the mask "Ernest," and the quality of "earnestness" which accompanies the disguise.

When both Jack and Algernon adopt the mask of "Ernest," the true lineage of Jack Worthing is eventually made clear:

> JACK (after a pause). Lady Bracknell, I hate to seem inquisitive, but would you kindly inform me who I am?
>
> LADY BRACKNELL. I am afraid that the news I have to give you will not altogether please you. You are the son of my poor sister, Mrs. Moncrieff, and consequently Algernon's elder brother.[153]

Soon, with the help of the military directory, he discovers that his pretense of being "Ernest" is needless, for he was actually christened "Ernest," after his father. He had then all along been "earnest" without realizing it; he says, "Gwendolen, it is a terrible thing for a man to find out suddenly that all his life he has been speaking nothing but the truth."[154] This is all obvious, perhaps, but the point suggested here is that the ability to assume roles and to adjust oneself to situations—that is to say, one's possession of an innate comic sense—is necessary sometimes to clear up confusions and resolve individual dilemmas. We find in the end the couples happily reunited after their separation as a result of misunderstandings. In the disclosure at the end, not only Jack's figure but also Miss Prism's gains substance as she is revealed to be the nurse employed by Lord Bracknell twenty-eight years ago. Miss Prism in effect provides the means whereby the complications of the plot may be re-

[153] *Ibid.*, p. 367.   [154] *Ibid.*, pp. 368-69.

solved; her character in fact represents the duplicity of things that pervades the whole play.

Miss Prism, at the start of Act II, appears as the perfect embodiment of the humorless governess, an example of "a redundant woman," whose policies revolve around such terms as "gravity of demeanour," "higher sense of duty and responsibility," and the like. What happened to her in the past directly contradicts her ethical posture. She hates "idle merriment and triviality"; she once wrote a "a three volume novel . . . of more than usually revolting sentimentality"— to quote Lady Bracknell—where "the good ended happily, and the bad unhappily." That is what "Fiction" means to her. Her opinions stamp her as a type with fixed patterns of thought and behavior; she declares, "I am not in favour of this modern mania for turning bad people into good people at a moment's notice. As a man sows so let him reap."[155] If memory, in her words, "is the diary that we all carry about with us," then she carries permanently within her the past that she is forced to divulge later. As she recounts the drab details of her mistake in the past, the figure of the mythical "Egeria" (as Canon Chasuble calls her once) and her discipline are at once deflated. Miss Prism relates the past incidents to the inquisitorial Lady Bracknell:

> The plain facts of the case are these. On the morning of the day you mention, a day that is forever branded on my memory, I prepared as usual to take the baby out in its perambulator. I had also with me a somewhat old but capacious hand-bag in which I had intended to place the manuscript of a work of fiction that I had written during my few unoccupied hours. In a moment of mental abstraction, for which I never can forgive myself, I deposited the manuscript in the bassinette, and placed the baby in the hand-bag.[156]

155 *Ibid.*, pp. 338-39.   156 *Ibid.*, p. 366.

Actually Miss Prism's memory proves as retentive as anyone else's; when asked to identify the handbag of black leather in Act III, she replies: "It seems to be mine. Yes, here is the injury it received through the upsetting of a Gower Street omnibus in younger and happier days. Here is the stain on the lining caused by the explosion of a temperance beverage, an incident that occurred at Leamington."[157] What makes her memorable is her absolute nonchalance in ignoring the gravity of the child's loss, in restoring immediate common sense to the tense situation: "The bag is undoubtedly mine. I am delighted to have it so unexpectedly restored to me. It has been a great inconvenience being without it all these years."[158] The crucial problem of loss and identity doesn't bother her a bit. As a comic character she subserves the general theme of presenting the truth that, to quote Miss Prism herself, "even these metallic problems have their melodramatic side."[159]

Throughout the play, one can observe the operation of Wilde's bifocal vision. It is implicit not only in the title but also in the resolution of the plot. This game of paradox and topsy-turvy characterizes also the individual speeches and the peculiar idiom of Jack, Algernon, Cecily, and Gwendolen. Cecily believes Uncle Jack "so serious that I think he cannot be quite well."[160] She also quips: "I have never met any really wicked person before. I feel rather frightened. I am so afraid he will look just like everyone else."[161] At one time Jack resigns himself to "a passionate celibacy."[162] And there is that felicitous logic of the dandy in Algernon's statement that "it is awfully hard work doing nothing. However, I don't mind hard work where there is no definite object of any kind."[163] The paradox has a peculiar way of fusing contradictory items. Wilde once wrote that the only valid meta-

<hr>

[157] *Ibid.*, p. 367. [158] *Ibid.* [159] *Ibid.*, p. 340.
[160] *Ibid.*, p. 338. [161] *Ibid.*, p. 340. [162] *Ibid.*, p. 364.
[163] *Ibid.*, p. 335.

physical truths are those whose contraries are also true. In the same way, Jack and Algernon, at first competitors for the name of Ernest, are discovered to be brothers; they are two sides of a coin. Wilde's use of names is also a way of transforming opposites into unities. For example, Chasuble's reference to Miss Prism as "Egeria" may be well-meant, but its connotations of public wisdom, of discipline and control, run against her real name, Laetitia meaning joy. "Prism" itself, presumably a fusion of "prison" and "prim," evokes the image of elegant surfaces and varnished appearance, concealing a vacuum within.[164]

The paradoxical epigrams, on the whole, illustrate verbally that double consciousness which pervades the whole play and makes it function as complex parody. Wilde thus attacks folly as it is represented in the typical roles of the opportunistic and cynical wits, the sour dowagers, the middle-aged spinsters like Miss Prism—all stock figures from the "moribund literature" of a progressive, yet decadent, milieu. Thus, as one critic puts it, Wilde satirizes, too, the society that sustains and produces it; "he has given us an oblique perspective on a society's shallowness through direct ridicule of the shadow act in which it sees its reflection."[165]

It is evident that most of the epigrams depend on the simple assertion of the opposite side of a platitude or a proverb. What this energetic play indicates, and affirms, is that vital comic outlook on life and the world which informs the double vision we saw in Miss Prism's formal and trivial aspects. It exists in the juggling of opposing terms, e.g., "passionate celibacy," or in the literal interpretation of metaphors, or in the figurative reading of literal expressions. For example, Lady Bracknell, hearing that Algernon's "Bunbury-

[164] See Arthur Nethercot, "Prunes and Miss Prism," *Modern Drama*, VI (September 1963), 112-16.
[165] Richard Foster, "Wilde as Parodist: A Second Look at *The Importance of Being Earnest*," *College English*, 18 (October 1956), 18-23.

ing" was "quite exploded," queries: "Was he the victim of a revolutionary outrage?" The comic orientation affords the constant undercutting of poses and hypocrisies. Chasuble, mourning the supposed death of Jack's brother Ernest, digresses in a matter-of-fact way:

> You would no doubt wish me to make some slight allusion to this tragic, domestic affliction next Sunday. (*Jack presses his hand convulsively.*) My sermon on the meaning of the manna in the wilderness can be adapted to almost any occasion, joyful, or, as in the present case, distressing. (*All sigh.*) I have preached it at harvest celebrations, christenings, confirmations, on days of humiliation and festal days. The last time I delivered it was in the Cathedral, as a charity sermon on behalf of the Society for the Prevention of Discontent among the Upper Orders. The Bishop, who was present, was much struck by some of the analogies I drew.[166]

Chasuble no doubt is a naïve and well-meaning person, but the stage directions intruded by Wilde convert his "sublime" candor into ridiculous self-exposure. He and Miss Prism, nonetheless, retain credibility even in absurd situations.

Underlying the burlesque of what would in reality be serious matters is the premise of a split between thought and feeling. In this particular setting, behavior and feeling seem two discordant things:

> LADY BRACKNELL. Good afternoon, dear Algernon, I hope you are behaving very well.
> ALGERNON. I'm feeling very well, Aunt Augusta.
> LADY BRACKNELL. That's not quite the same thing. In fact the two things rarely go together.[167]

Lady Bracknell also believes that "we live, I regret to say, in an age of surfaces."[168] She estimates Algernon as "an osten-

[166] *Works*, p. 343.   [167] *Ibid.*, p. 327.   [168] *Ibid.*, p. 362.

tatiously, eligible young man . . . has nothing, but he looks everything." At the beginning of Act I, Algernon already established the contrast between "accuracy" and "expression," between the impulse to rational correctness and emotional vigor.

Given this noticeable disparity of feeling and thought, the play tends to emphasize formal patterns of action. Algernon tells his manservant: "I don't play accurately—but I play with wonderful expression. As far as the piano is concerned, sentiment is my forte. I keep science for Life."[169] Propriety and etiquette distinguish a society that yet demands ceremony even when the circumstances do not warrant it. We see, for example, the absurdity of Miss Prism and Chasuble sympathizing with the supposed death of Jack's brother Ernest in Act II. In society, "good form" and respectable conduct require the strict observance of existing norms and customs. This observance is prescribed by those who behave in accordance not with their emotions but with their habits, which have been ingrained by social training and demand. Despite the danger of hypocrisy, custom conduces to a form of sincerity. At the play's opening, for instance, Algernon asks Lane why, in bachelor's establishments, the servants invariably drink the champagne; Lane's reply is an open acknowledgement that he has taken his share of his employer's abundance. "This charming and unimpassioned frankness is the main feature of the play in which there is no ill-temper, no pretence of offended dignity, no serious lying or deceit. . . . It is a tradition of service; and civilized people whether they be masters or men, do not quarrel about customs which have been made honorable by age."[170]

Society is represented here by Lady Bracknell who has impressed many as a "serious-minded fool." She recalls

169 *Ibid.*, p. 321.
170 St. John Ervine, *Oscar Wilde* (New York, 1951), p. 287.

for us the dandiacal and energetic wit of Wilde's dowagers: Lady Hunstanton, Lady Caroline, Mrs. Allonby, and the Duchess of Berwick. Her talent is for sententious comment; her delicious severities are delivered in a portentous manner, as when she addresses Jack kneeling before Gwendolen: "Rise, Sir, from this semi-recumbent posture. It is most indecorous." After inspecting Cecily's appearance before permitting her engagement with her nephew Algernon, Lady Bracknell comments:

> There are distinct social possibilities in your profile. The two weak points in our age are its want of principle and its want of profile. The chin a little higher, dear. Style largely depends on the way the chin is worn. They are worn very high, just at present.[171]

Gwendolen supports her aunt's attitude when she asserts: "In matters of grave importance, style, not sincerity, is the vital thing."[172] In the same trend, Algernon says: "I hate people who are not serious about meals. It is so shallow of them."[173] We notice Algernon's praise for clever, "perfectly phrased" observations, his need for buttonholes; and though he is "occasionally a little over-dressed," he justifies this excess by "being always immensely over-educated."[174] He apologizes for not treating Jack with more respect because he is "out of practice."[175] Gwendolen says that "men often propose for practice."[176]

To illustrate further this conflict between formal conduct and feelingful response, Wilde makes Cecily and Gwendolen converse with bristling animus.[177] Cecily accuses Gwendolen of the susceptibility to wearing "the shallow mask of manners." But "the shallow mask of manners" can afford clues for us to be able to define the weaknesses of those who wear

---

171 *Works*, p. 362. 172 *Ibid.*, p. 359. 173 *Ibid.*, p. 327.
174 *Ibid.*, p. 346. 175 *Ibid.*, p. 368. 176 *Ibid.*, p. 330.
177 *Ibid.*, pp. 353-54.

them. One clue is the stereotyped reaction which betrays the ascendant "humor" in the person, as in Jonsonian comedy. It is easy to classify characters according to their obsessions, like the misanthrope or the miser. Certain devices, such as mistaken identity, the tell-tale object, and others, are associated with the fairly recognizable "mask of manners" that comic characters tend to assume.

It has often been suggested that this play forms a genre by itself. One notes in it the infinite variety of humor, inconsequentialities, and the ambiguity of ideas; these qualities provoke either questioning doubt, belief, or spontaneous jovial surprise. This is only to say that not all of the play can be dismissed as mere farcical entertainment. Amid the banter and sprightly sophistry we find indications of a certain loosening up of rigid conventions and fashionable manners, especially in the anarchic mood of Algernon's opinion: "it is absurd to have a hard-and-fast rule about what one should read and what one shouldn't. More than half of modern culture depends on what one shouldn't read."[178] Jack argues for some variety in human nature, as implied by his remark: "Some aunts are tall, some aunts are not tall. That is a matter that surely an aunt may be allowed to decide for herself. You seem to think that every aunt should be exactly like your aunt! That is absurd!"[179] Gwendolen, who is delightfully facetious, voices some ideas worth a second look. She believes that "most metaphysical speculations" have "very little reference at all to the actual facts of real life, as we know them."[180] Algernon says: "The truth is rarely pure and never simple." Wilde skillfully cloaks truisms beneath an appearance of casualness.

One main function of the comic vision is to provide a means by which man can encompass the extremes of a situation, to attain what Kenneth Burke calls "perspective by

[178] *Ibid.*, p. 324.   [179] *Ibid.*   [180] *Ibid.*, p. 329.

incongruity."[181] Wilde's devices for attaining that end are verbal puns and dramatic irony. For example:

> JACK. You're quite perfect, Miss Fairfax.
> GWENDOLEN. Oh! I hope I am not that. It would leave no room for developments, and I intend to develop in *many directions*.[182]

Or the play on "duties" by the shifting of context: Lady Bracknell says, "What between the duties expected of one during one's life-time, and the duties exacted from one after one's death, land has ceased to be either a profit or a pleasure."[183] The effort to bring about a coalescence of extreme attitudes in a single perspective takes the form of "Bunburying." Cecily asks Algernon, disguised as Ernest, whether or not he has been leading "a double life, pretending to be wicked and being really good all the time."[184]

Early in Act I, Jack explains to Algernon that "my name is Ernest in town and Jack in the country," to which Algernon replies by labeling him "a confirmed and secret Bunburyist."[185] By "Bunbury" Algernon refers to his "double" or his mask, which he has invented in order to enjoy a wider latitude of freedom than his public image affords. Algernon clarifies his application of the term "Bunburyist" to Jack:

> You have invented a very useful younger brother called Ernest, in order that you may be able to come up to town as often as you like. I have invented an invaluable permanent invalid called Bunbury, in order that I may be able to go down into the country whenever I choose. Bunbury is perfectly invaluable. If it wasn't for Bunbury's extraordinary bad health, for instance, I wouldn't

[181] *Terms for Order* (Bloomington, Indiana, 1964), pp. 84-88.
[182] *Works*, p. 327.   [183] *Ibid.*, p. 332.   [184] *Ibid.*, p. 341.
[185] *Ibid.*, p. 325.

be able to dine with you at Willis' tonight, for I have been really engaged to Aunt Augusta for more than a week.[186]

Bunbury, that "invalid" with an "absurd name," is one engaging form of "humor." It furnishes a good pretext for escaping responsibility in the guise of fulfilling one's responsibility to a fictitious, recurrently sick younger brother. Algernon further says, "One has a right to Bunbury anywhere one chooses."—a privilege shared by "very serious Bunburyists."[187] It may be that Algernon's perpetual hunger, psychoanalyzed, indicates an unconscious impulse or hidden anxiety that he could not satisfy. One can hazard the view that his constant eating is not just a comic device but also an instinctive release of impulses, a sublimation of the id, that run counter to the external forces of inhibition.

Wilde's technique of heuristic inversion may be illustrated in Algernon's elevation of Bunburyism, virtually a break of convention, to the level of a norm. In assuming a code of behavior ignored by the philistines, Algernon attends to that aspect of life which gives shading and rich texture to our ordinary habitual awareness. If Bunbury escapes from convention, he pays the price of being simply a pretense. But when the locale of the action moves from the town to the country and the respectable Miss Prism is revealed as a foolish fraud, the play proves the Bunburyists right in their general attitude, despite their inevitable exposure. Both conformists and Bunburyists are earnest in their several ways; but the Bunburyists know what is real and what is pretense, and they have the energy and earnestness to play the game. The comic vision includes both the serious and the nonserious; it points out man's limitations, and the ways he can transcend them or adjust to his finite condition. Ultimately, "Bunburying means to invent a fictitious character, who can

186 *Ibid.*, p. 326.   187 *Ibid.*, p. 356.

serve as a pretext for escaping a frustrating social routine, regulated by a repressive convention. The pretended reason for getting away is perfectly respectable, even commendable, according to convention. Bunburyism is simply the mechanism that sets in motion the preposterously elaborate plot of mistaken identities."[188]

Whatever the judgment of psychoanalysis may be in regard to Bunburyism, it is certain that the philosophy or outlook behind it depends to a large degree on the structure of social relationship or kinship in society. To have identity, even in the paradisal atmosphere of the Manor House in Woolton, is to have family relations. We sense the importance of kinship when Algernon justifies his interest in Gwendolen's affair because she is his first cousin. On the other hand, Jack must needs win Algernon's favor in his courtship of Gwendolen. Jack, for his part, acts as an uncle to Cecily Cardew whom Algernon wants to marry. Relationship thus plays a decisive part in the organization of the different interests involved here. Even "apoplexy" is emphasized as a "hereditary" affliction. The most explicit stress laid on "relations" can be found in Lady Bracknell's advice to Jack on the matter of eligibility. What she demands are credentials of lineage which would serve as an assured basis for a recognized position in good society. She says: "I would strongly advise you, Mr. Worthing, to try and acquire some relations as soon as possible, and to make a definite effort to produce at any rate one parent of either sex before the season is quite over."[189] Jack Worthing's worth—if I may pun here—depends on his origin. For certainly Lady Bracknell cannot dream of her only daughter marrying "into a cloak-room" or forming "an alliance with a parcel." Jack's origin is, as she puts it, a "Terminus" outside of society. Likewise, Cecily's

188 Otto Reinert, "Satiric Strategy in *The Importance of Being Earnest*," *College English*, 18 (October 1956), 17.
189 *Works*, p. 333.

father, that "charitable gentleman," is unknown outside the intimate sphere of his family.[190]

Now the value of relationships that comedy seeks to affirm lies primarily in its function of harmonizing conflicting interests and destroying illusory, or exaggerated, claims. Two persons, Jack and Algernon, compete in the adoption of the name "Ernest." "Ernest" itself symbolizes the comic drive toward stability and "the golden mean." Gwendolen testifies to the connotations of the name: "My ideal has always been to love some one of the name of Ernest. There is something in that name that inspires absolute confidence. . . . It is a divine name. It has a music of its own. It produces vibrations. . . . The only really safe name is Ernest."[191] Gwendolen depicts Ernest thus: "Ernest has a strong upright nature. He is the very soul of truth and honour. Disloyalty would be as impossible to him as deception."[192] "Ernest" actually signifies the world of floating fancy and idyllic, romantic sensations. It represents wish-fulfillment and indulgence in projecting ideals into the realm of daydreaming. Cecily echoes Gwendolen: "it had always been a girlish dream of mine to love some one whose name was Ernest. There is something in that name that seems to inspire absolute confidence."[193]

"Absolute confidence" appears as the key-phrase which both Algernon and Jack want to attach to their doubles. How can they reconcile themselves to actuality? It turns out in the end that the actual is the most ideal situation after all; they prove finally to be brothers. Before the discovery, however, they vie for the name "Ernest" and all its symbolic properties; but their Christian names are "insufferable barriers." Toward the end Jack and Algernon kill their "doubles." As early as Act I, Jack proposes to "kill" his brother if Gwendolen accepts him. They decide to be christened

190 *Ibid.*, p. 351.   191 *Ibid.*, p. 330.   192 *Ibid.*, p. 351.
193 *Ibid.*, p. 349.

again—which, to the dandies, seems a "terrible" and "fearful ordeal," an infinite "self-sacrifice."[194] Their wish to be "immersed" again in baptismal waters leads to the clearing up of identities—for, were it not for Chasuble's mention of Miss Prism, Lady Bracknell would not have solved the obscure circumstances surrounding Jack's "origin." His identity is really the obstacle to his winning Gwendolen's hand.

In Act II Canon Chasuble urges Miss Prism to practice "charity" in restraining herself from condemning people. He suggests that "what seem to us bitter trials at the moment are often blessings in disguise."[195] He informs us that he intends to perform a baptism of twins before christening Jack. His words look forward to the discovery of the fraternal tie which transforms Algernon's address of "Brother John" into a truth of nature. We have hints in Act I, when Algernon describes Jack: "You look as if your name was Ernest. You are the most earnest looking person I ever saw in my life. It is perfectly absurd your saying that your name isn't Ernest."[196] But time and events will soon refute him. The turnabout finally comes when the quarrelling dandies are recognized as brothers. This is foreshadowed in the equally radical turnabout in the relationship between Cecily and Gwendolen: from friendship to enmity, and back to friendship. Alienated from each other for a while by their passion for "Ernest," they reunite when they realize the deception foisted upon them by the two impostors who each claim to be "Ernest."[197]

In the first part of Act II, Cecily effects a temporary reconciliation between Algernon and Jack. Over this matter Chasuble remarks: "It's pleasant, is it not, to see so perfect a reconciliation? I think we might leave the two brothers together."[198] This foreshadows the "recognition" scene at the end, when the dandies are discovered to be true brothers.

[194] *Ibid.*, pp. 359-60.   [195] *Ibid.*, p. 344.   [196] *Ibid.*, pp. 324-25.
[197] *Ibid.*, p. 363.   [198] *Ibid.*, p. 345.

But Chasuble seems never to have realized that "Ernest" is a myth. If, as Algernon believes, "the very essence of romance is uncertainty," then "romance" becomes dispelled when the realistic facts of Jack's "origin" are laid bare. "A somewhat old but capacious hand-bag" serves as the key to the truth. Although Lady Bracknell says that "strange coincidences are not supposed to occur" in families of high position, the identifications are carried out: Ernest as Jack, Miss Prism as the nurse of Lord Bracknell's son, Lady Bracknell as the sister of Jack's mother and therefore his aunt. When, in "a moment of mental abstraction," Miss Prism fatefully substitutes the baby for the manuscript in the handbag, she commits an act that is the result of a disregard for the immediate and present actuality. When she is confronted with the old stained handbag, her memory is enlivened and she becomes more sensible. She identifies the bag: "And here, on the lock, are my initials. I had forgotten that in an extravagant mood I had them placed there."[199]

Miss Prism's "extravagant mood" may recur, but not again in the world of this comedy. For in the comic world, things are constantly being "found out" or revealed. In Act I, Algernon "finds" Jack's cigarette case, which in turn leads to the subject of "Ernest," the imagined owner of the case. Bunbury, in Act III, suffers the end of being "quite exploded," as Algernon puts it. Later, Algernon's "disgraceful deception" is exposed by Jack. Lady Bracknell says that long engagements "give people the opportunity of finding out each other's character."[200] To expose and elucidate situations with an eye to attributing just proportions of value to each factor—this is the aim of the comic genius. Wilde's "earnest" dandies, with their antic spirit and robust fancy, purge the "serious," hypocritical tendencies of men caught in a crisis, restoring to them the balance founded on the

[199] *Ibid.*, p. 367.   [200] *Ibid.*, p. 363.

acceptance of their limitations. Both Jack and Algernon could not possibly be "Ernest" all at once and together; yielding to facts and circumstance, they attain their coveted wishes. Their actions and words earn for them the quality of being "earnest" as they finally accept the overpowering decree of life's realities, of the past, and of the frequently renewed compromises on which society depends. Wilde's comic strategy revolves around two ideals which reflect the changing relationships and the necessary adjustments between man and his world:

> ALGERNON. This world is good enough for me, Cousin Cecily.
>
> CECILY. Yes, but are you good enough for it?[201]

THE COMEDIES IN PERSPECTIVE

Wilde's comedies present fairly definite patterns of meaning which arise from the verbal associations of the dialogue as seen in relation to character and plot. Verbal ingenuity connects the plays with high comedy, which, for Meredith, means the traditional comedy of manners that evokes "intellectual laughter."[202] Although the spectators laugh, they remain emotionally detached from the spectacle of human folly and incongruity.

Generally, comedy presents characters who undergo embarrassments or discomfitures. But these discomfitures are managed so that they amuse without stirring profound sympathy. In high comedy, however, the focal interest is usually on wit combats, such as one finds in the sophisticated repartee of Benedick and Beatrice in Shakespeare's *Much Ado About Nothing*, or of Millamant and Mirabell in Congreve's *Way of the World*. Opposed to low comedy or slapstick, which relies on physical grotesqueries, the comedy of wit

---

[201] *Ibid.*, p. 341.
[202] See Meredith's "An Essay on Comedy," in *Comedy*, ed., Wylie Sypher (New York, 1956), pp. 3-60.

and manners depends on reason, which is responsible for much of its iconoclastic satire. It is generally agreed that the Restoration dramatists—Etherege, Wycherley, Congreve— were not absolutely flippant and cynical. What these dramatists and Wilde mainly accomplished is the presentation of man's egoism, his institutions and ways, to the scrutiny of humane reason.

Satire in English comedy dates back notably to Ben Jonson's *The Alchemist* and his other "humor" comedies. In them violations of moral and social standards by rascally swindlers, and the greed and gullibility of their victims, are all ridiculed. Although there are elements of romantic comedy in Wilde's plays, where a love affair is either tangential (like that between Lord Darlington and Lady Windermere) or central (as among the youthful pairs in *The Importance of Being Earnest*), the dominant tendency is toward the criticism of manners. Usually the criticism dwells on the relations and intrigues of gentlemen and ladies in a gregarious milieu, and especially on the violations of decorum as exemplified by Mrs. Cheveley's "crooked" designs, or by the deceitful disguises of Jack and Algernon. But Wilde's sparkling dialogue is relatively mild, less jolting than the "indecent" innuendos so characteristic of Restoration drama. Wilde's plot and characters form part of the property of traditional high comedy, discernible in Gilbert's operas as well as in Congreve, Sheridan, and Shaw.[203]

The form of Wilde's comedies results mainly from a curious mixture of the comedy of manners and sentimental comedy. We have, for instance, the delightful "never-never" land of Woolton where Bunburyism thrives. Yet the broadly humorous situation does not properly belong to "romantic comedy"; rather, it belongs to farce. Apart from *The Im-*

[203] For the satirical strain in the comedies, see Rose Snider, *Satire in the Comedies of Congreve, Sheridan, Wilde, and Coward* (Orono, Maine, 1937), pp. 74-97; see also Archibald Henderson, *European Dramatists* (Cincinnati, 1913), pp. 300-14.

portance of Being Earnest, Wilde's three earlier comedies have less of the farcical than of critical and sentimental qualities. The satire on Lord Illingworth, or on Mrs. Cheveley, however, shows a bluntness which results from Wilde's ambivalent attitude toward his characters. On the whole, the dandies are sophisticated improvements of their prototypes among the pleasant rogues, scoundrels, or gulls who are cozened by circumstances.

Analysis of the plays reveals their affinities with situational comedy insofar as the "villains" of Wilde are functions of the dramatic situations. In situational comedy, the dramatist spins clever plots and effects peripeteia in which the absurdity of the characters is exposed. Usually, the eccentric Puritan is exposed in his or her misjudgments of situations and personalities. Unlike the eighteenth-century comedies of manners, however, Wilde's plays treat less of deviations and more of the incongruities between abstract ideas and the facts of experience. Nonetheless, one perceives the tendency of the plays toward the form of sentimental comedy; as when Mrs. Erlynne or Mrs. Arbuthnot, who typifies middle class morality, approximates the stature of "monumentally" noble heroes and heroines who utter sentiments of unimpeachable rectitude and then suffer tribulations the enormity of which arouses tearful response from the audience. It can be argued, too, that in the disposition of "strong" comic situations, the element of farce predominates: one-dimensional characters like Chasuble, Mrs. Allonby, the Duchess of Berwick, are cast in settings where the only organizing force is the continuity of the highly animated, digressive dialogue. Wilde's horseplay, however, has cerebral content and refined articulation.

On the whole, the four comedies follow the general movement from a problematic to a happy scene, although the unhappy scenes entertain rather than distract us. One can intrude here the view that comedy, like dreams, represents the "disguised fulfillment of repressed wishes." According to Freud: "Humor is not resigned; it is rebellious. It signifies the triumph not only of the ego, but also of the pleasure principle, which is strong enough to assert itself here in the face of the adverse real circumstances."[204] Wilde exploits verbal wit more than the laughable appearance and posture of his characters. His field of action is language, his forte is wit. By wit one comprehends fanciful "assemblage of ideas," quick and varied juxtaposition of conceits that are felicitously phrased, the perception of resemblances in disparate elements, good sense. Sometimes the witty expressions convey compressed and mocking observations which verge on clever, aggressive raillery.

In contrast to Restoration wit, Wilde's wit belongs to harmless comedy or humor rather than to "tendency wit." "Tendency wit" evokes laughter with undertones of malice and contempt; the derisive laughter serves as a weapon of satire, a technique to diminish the vanity of men. Harmless wit, on the other hand, arouses laughter because "a person is ridiculous but not because he is being ridiculed." Humor is genial, delighting in eccentricities, revelling in the perception of incongruities found in life's imbroglios.

Two species of humor can be found in Wilde's comedies. First, the laughter evoked by a "kind of sudden glory," to use Hobbes' famous phrase. In Act III of *An Ideal Husband*, Lord Goring has finally trapped Mrs. Cheveley into admitting theft. She cries out: "You brute! You coward!" He replies: "Oh! don't use big words, they mean so little."[205] Second, the laughter aroused by a change of a strained expectation into nothing, for example:

> CECILY. Do you suggest, Miss Fairfax, that I entrapped Ernest into an engagement? How dare you? This is no

---

204 "Humour," *Collected Papers*, ed., James Strachey (New York, 1959), V, p. 217. See also *Jokes and Their Relation to the Unconscious* (New York, 1960).
205 *Works*, pp. 520-21.

> time for wearing the shallow mask of manners. When I see a spade I call it a spade.
>
> GWENDOLEN (*satirically*). I am glad to say that I have never seen a spade. It is obvious that our social spheres have been widely different.[206]

Here the tension the dialogue generates in us as we anticipate a heated fight is abruptly released in the reduction of the cliché "to call a spade a spade" to the literal, nonsensical plane.

Now the catharsis brought about by witty dialogues and compact, humorous situations rids men of excesses and hardened whims. Susanne Langer says that the comic rhythm "expresses the elementary strains and resolutions of animate nature, the animal drives that persist even in human nature, the delight man takes in his special mental gifts that make him the lord of creation"; comedy is thus "an image of human vitality holding its own in the world amid the surprises of unplanned coincidence."[207] In general, the movement of comedy is from illusion to reality. "Illusion is whatever is fixed or definable, and reality is best understood as its negation: whatever reality is, it's not *that*. Hence the importance of the theme of creating and dispelling illusion in comedy: the illusions caused by disguise, obsession, hypocrisy, or unknown parentage."[208] In Wilde's comedies, the illusions all evaporate in the end—the illusions caused by Mrs. Erlynne's anonymity, by Mrs. Arbuthnot's obsession with her "martyrdom," by Sir Robert Chiltern's hypocrisy, by the unknown parentage of Jack Worthing.

In the comedies, the duality between what the characters show on the surface and what they really are inside produces conflict and moral disequilibrium, leading to disillusionment

---

[206] *Ibid.*, p. 353.
[207] *Feeling and Form* (New York, 1953), p. 331.
[208] Frye, *Anatomy of Criticism*, pp. 169-70.

and a more intense awareness of reality. In *An Ideal Husband*, we are not satisfied with the promotion of Sir Robert Chiltern after having known his youthful malfeasance. On the whole, we are uneasy about the happy endings of the comedies. Orthodoxy, though accepted, is seriously undermined. We feel uneasy about the moral position arrived at in the dénouement, which directly contrasts with the sympathies revealed in the dialogue; the intrigue tends to negate the happy outcome. Some readers have the impression that in the complication of the intrigues, the constant reference to tainted life and the need for purity is almost pathological. But few object to the "serious" people who exaggerate and twist ideas, who play with sentiments; to the immoralists who attack bombast with jolly ripostes which savagely disabuse the moralists.

What sustains the tension and lucidity of the comedies is mainly the paradoxical formulation of dramatic speech. The habit of conformity, the blind adherence to organization and authority, to Wilde, springs from the lack of imaginative sympathy. Absence of imagination prevents men from recognizing that life is fluid and forever changing. In paradox Wilde found the appropriate medium for the sense of life as dynamic. For what he wanted to do above all was to dramatize the conflict of ideas in which truth emerges gradually, by selection and omission and emphasis. The paradox exaggerates under the semblance of logical deduction; it stresses a half-truth which is more fecund than the platitude. Its pattern is simple: A implies B; A is not B but C—thus frustrating our normal expectation of a syllogism. The paradox breaks categories and common-sense opinion in an experimental fashion. Conventional values are upset, new aspects of actuality disclosed, truths arrived at by a provisional "lie" usually expressed in a formula with a piquant epigrammatic turn.

All the comedies rest on a single stock situation: the secret past life of one of the characters must be revealed, with ostracism or pardon as the consequence. The secrets involve Mrs. Erlynne's identity; Mrs. Arbuthnot's natural sin, a "sexual fault"; Sir Robert Chiltern's youthful misdeed; and Jack Worthing's origin and double life. The Puritans demand outright condemnation of the "sinners." Lady Chiltern, however, acts not on moral grounds but from the simple instinct of self-preservation. The matrons and dowagers, upholders of traditional prejudices, are often capricious and fatuous. For instance, the Duchess of Berwick, a tireless chatterbox, changes opinions for convenience; she mixes thoughts of horrid kangaroos and moral judgments with impervious sobriety. The *ingénues*—Hester Worsley, Mabel Chiltern, Gwendolen Fairfax, and Cecily Cardew— display a disconcerting innocence, as attractive as the naïveté of the "old infants," Lord Augustus and Lord Caversham. These personages often converse with the rhetorical pointedness of the dandies, whose unabated questioning of facts by allusion and pun lead to the exposure of frauds, the unveiling of true identities, and the clarification of appearances. Between the distortions of the intrigue and the smooth, happy endings lies the epigram, holding opposites in taut, suspended motion.

Individually, the plays show variety of treatment. *Lady Windermere's Fan* applies the elegant conversation of Congreve to nineteenth-century domestic drama. Despite the play-up of hackneyed emotions, Wilde manages to imbue his portrayal of the protagonist with sympathetic warmth: Mrs. Erlynne sacrifices herself by refusing to tarnish her daughter's reputation and resuming her role of adventuress after the crisis.

In *A Woman of No Importance*, the allegory of Gilded Vice routed by Conscience and Virtue is enlivened with impudent paradox and violent passions. Apart from the effective curtains of cleverly devised scenes, the tension of conflicting attitudes diverts us from the obvious discrepancy between sparkling dialogue and boisterous plot. It directs our attention to the sense of pathos, struggle, and anguish that genuinely moves the major characters of the play.

Constructed according to the general requirements of the *pièce bien faite* with its neat order of exposition, complication, "great scene," disentanglement, *An Ideal Husband* presents characters who manifest not only polemic vivacity but also the typical strengths and flaws of men. The blend of intellectual charm and quiet cynicism in Lord Goring, and the light parody of romantic love, evidence Wilde's innovations in melodrama. The calculated manipulation of Mrs. Cheveley's intrigue closely parallels Sheridan's resolution of *The School for Scandal* in the famous screen scene.

Obviously the climactic twist in *The Importance of Being Earnest* belongs to a formula of topsy-turvy situations and sprightly disclosures. But in addition to being merely "inspired nonsense," it presents dissolvent gaiety couched in verbal nuances, ingenious plotting, and robust theatrical characterization.

In these various modifications of conventional patterns Wilde proves himself a dramatist of singular importance. Whereas T. W. Robertson, for instance, gains fidelity to reality by way of naturalism in feeling and situation, Wilde achieves artistic consistency and persuasive immediacy by the ironic dramatization of crucial social problems. To be sure, all the plays, with minor qualifications, adhere to the artificial prescriptions of the problem play and the "well-made" play. But their verbal complexity saves them from being shallow or dull. Although they conform in most essentials to the conventional play, they deviate largely in manner of expression and follow the tradition of elegant, amusing ridicule of sentimentalisms found in Wilde's predecessors. The uproarious verbal "games" and the farcical burlesques of topical affairs enrich the province of mirth with the analysis of human motivations and values implicit in them. Wilde lends to caricature and satire a poise and dignity which offset the vulgar staginess of commonplace melodrama. At best Wilde renders the very rhythm of life.[209]

[209] The following discussions of Wilde's comedies may be of interest: St. John Hankin, "The Collected Plays of Oscar Wilde," *Fortnightly Review*, LXXXIX (January-June, 1908), 791-802; Henry Ten Eyck Perry, *Masters of Dramatic Comedy and Their Social Themes* (Cambridge, Mass., 1939), pp. 359-62. See especially the following: Allan Harris, "Oscar Wilde as Playwright: A Centenary Review," *The Adelphi*, 30 (Second Quarter, 1954), pp. 212-40; Tyrone Guthrie, Introduction to *Plays* by Oscar Wilde (New York, 1956), pp. 11-16; A. G. Woodward, "Oscar Wilde," *English Studies in Africa*, 2 (September 1959), 218-31.

VI · *The Ballad of Reading Gaol*
and the Image of the
Human Condition

The compelling urge to poetic composition that Wilde felt in exile springs from the thought that self-fulfillment for him depended solely on the assertion of his *métier*. His letters, including *De Profundis*, fully testify to this urge.[1] Knowing the chastening discipline of artistic creation, he devoted himself to it as a test of self-integrity. Accepting humiliation and ostracism, he affirmed, through his last poem, his commitment to man's fate.

In confessing that *Reading Gaol* "aims at eternity,"[2] he implicitly defined his task of giving what one can call a "sacramental" value to life. His work would be "a cry of Pain—a song of Marsyas." The poet would uphold Dionysian rapture despite the fact that life, which he loved excessively, has (as he puts it) "torn me like a Tiger."[3] Though avowing a lack of the will power that propels creative toil, Wilde gathered his energy for one final struggle to erect a world of intimacy and reconciliation.

Reading Gaol may aptly be viewed then as a mode of understanding the value of experience in the effort to realize one's identity. What Wilde experienced as a convict he distilled to a refined substance which concentrated feeling and thought in an "infinite moment."[4] His firm control of lan-

---

[1] See *Letters*, pp. 447-56, 470-71, especially pp. 621-22. *De Profundis*, originally Wilde's letter to Lord Alfred Douglas, occupies pp. 423-511. The text of our poem is in *Works*, pp. 822-39.

[2] *Ibid.*, p. 626.   [3] *Ibid.*, p. 715.

[4] Richard Butler Glaenzer, "The Story of 'The Ballad of Reading Gaol'," *The Bookman*, XXXIII (*June* 1911), 376. For a detailed ac-

guage, sometimes studied and sometimes willful, may be described as purposive insofar as it posits a world of human designs. Wilde's art renders meaningful even neutral, or negative, stuff. We should modify Arthur Symons' superficial view of the poem as "a sombre, angry uninterrupted reverie";[5] instead of being a reverie, *Reading Gaol* is nothing less than an accomplished incarnation of values. It affords the possibility of living in a universe whose existence, in its very nature a prison, denies any communion between human beings. This denial produces in turn puzzling distortions of subject and object. The poem offers an adjustment, if not a reunion, of geography and inhabitants.

Wilde attempts, in short, a scheme of transfiguring the criminal's camp into a humanized milieu. During its composition and after, he kept asserting his deep personal involvement with the poem's immediate subject. Wilde knew the danger of sentimentality. His material required the insistent drive for tough objective definition, as witnessed by his strictures: "the poem is too autobiographical . . . *real* experiences are alien things that should never influence one."[6] The sentiments of the poem's narrator, violently wrung with obsessive insistence, attain an intelligible shape only when the experience from which they arise is organized through an impersonal narrative medium. The thin story-line tends to restrain the swelling lyrical effusions that threaten to reduce the whole structure into mawkishness or paltry bathos.

The salient problem in the construction of *Reading Gaol*

---

count of Wilde's life in prison, consult H. Montgomery Hyde, *Oscar Wilde: The Aftermath*, pp. 1-128.

[5] *A Study of Oscar Wilde*, p. 27. For contemporary opinion, see Robert H. Sherard, *The Life of Oscar Wilde* (New York, 1906), pp. 413ff. For foreign appraisals, see Abraham Horodisch, *Oscar Wilde's 'Ballad of Reading Gaol'*, *A Bibliographical Study* (New York, 1954).

[6] *Letters*, p. 708.

centers on the basic question of the imaginative process itself.
I refer to the presumed conflict between strictly mimetic and
symbolic representation. To Wilde this conflict—"a divided
aim in style"—springs from the keenly felt disparity of
texture and form due to the mingling of "realistic" and
"romantic" elements. Indeed he was disturbed by the amal-
gamation of "poetry and propaganda," not knowing that he
had created a peculiar sort of poetic artifice. Wilde acknowl-
edges the function of words to resolve facts into meaning
when he sensibly justifies his frequent use of "dreadful" and
"fearful":

> A cell . . . may be described *psychologically*, with refer-
> ence to its effect on the soul: in itself it can only be
> described as "whitewashed" or "dimly-lit." It has no
> shape, no content. It does not exist from the point of view
> of form or colour.[7]

Exploring the difficulty of presenting objects "artistically,"
Wilde argues that compared with the factual relationship
between him and, say, a water-closet, "the horror of prison is
that everything is so simple and commonplace in itself, and
so degrading, and hideous and revolting in its effect."[8] The
diction of the poem conveys the tension between factual
stimuli and psychological responses:

> They hanged him as a beast is hanged;
> > They did not even toll
> A requiem that might have brought
> > Rest to his startled soul,
> But hurriedly they took him out,
> > And hid him in a hole.

---

[7] *Ibid.*, p. 655.

[8] Robert Merle, in *Oscar Wilde* (Paris, 1957), provides a penetrating analysis of the Aristotelian tragic pattern in *Reading Gaol*. His
existentialist discussion of the peripeteia (pp. 95-108) should supplement other *explication de texte* such as those by Helmut Hatzfeld,
Einfuhrung in die Interpretation englischen Texte (Munich, 1922),
pp. 83-86, and Guillermo Valencia, *El Vengador de Wilde* (Popayan,
1936).

> They stripped him of his canvas clothes,
>   And gave him to the flies;
> They mocked the swollen purple throat,
>   And the stark and staring eyes;
> And with laughter loud they heaped the shroud
>   In which their convict lies.   (511-22)

Wilde agonized over this dilemma concerning the inadequacy of words to capture the exact quality of "felt life" in his experience. His critical revisions of the text prove this.[9] To be sure, his case is not unique. Its significance today involves the amorphous, inchoate nature of private experience in a culture devoid of common standards of belief or traditional norms, and this provides the familiar keynote in the theme of twentieth-century "dissociation of sensibility." One finds, in late nineteenth-century poetry, the habit of introspection indulged to a degree of solipsism which often tended to isolate the mind from the practical everyday world.[10]

In this context, Wilde's poem represents a reaction. It adumbrates the need for flexibility, ironic masks, and spontaneous response. What faced Wilde first of all was the choice of either registering phenomena *per se* or of exploiting them to express his own vision. Unless phenomena are integrated with the feeling mind, they remain without significant shape. The poet serves the interest of discovering the underlying configuration, the inner shaping principle of things in nature:

> They think a murderer's heart would taint
>   Each simple seed they sow.
> It is not true! God's kindly earth
>   Is kindlier than men know,

9 Mason, *A Bibliography of the Poems*, pp. 76-80.
10 Josephine Miles, *The Continuity of Poetic Language* (Berkeley and Los Angeles, 1951), p. 371.

And the red rose would but blow more red,
    The white rose whiter blow.

Out of his mouth a red, red rose!
    Out of his heart a white!
For who can say by what strange way,
    Christ brings His will to light,
Since the barren staff the pilgrim bore
    Bloomed in the great Pope's sight?

But neither milk-white rose nor red
    May bloom in prison air—
The shard, the pebble, and the flint,
    Are what they give us there;
For flowers have been known to heal
    A common man's despair.   (475-92)

It would be an easy task simply to demonstrate how the murderer typifies man's fallible nature and the stoic recognition of his destiny. One can also suggest that Wilde strongly wanted to reform the dehumanizing prison system of England. This is implied in the contrast between man's maniacal brutality and Christ's compassion (523-28), culminating in the notion that only a last judgment can restore meaning to life (643-44). The remorse accompanying Christ's forgiveness results from considering heavenly justice as equivalent to earthly justice (171-74).[11] The substance of the poem, however, as verbally rendered, defies any simplified reduction. For poetic discourse does not assert any judgment of truth or falsehood.[12] We shall see how the "thesis" concerning the prisoners' appraisal of God's justice by human standards points to the existential core of the poem. The existential attitude lies in the poet's fidelity to the crisis of the human condition.

[11] Cf. Editors, "Wilde's 'The Ballad of Reading Gaol'," *The Explicator*, I (March 1943), item 41.
[12] On poetic discourse, see Frye, pp. 131-57.

To disentangle the poem's complicated network of motives, a summary of the argument seems useful. Section I, by straight third-person recounting, introduces the condemned from a distance, as though seen through a camera-eye approaching for a close-up (1-18). The speaker indicates the point of view, the community of suffering man. This community annihilates differences, merging narrator and objects of narration in an all-inclusive truth: "Yet each man kills the thing he loves" (37-54). Encompassing extremes of all kinds, the generalizations about a death-bearing love lead to severely understated, ironic qualifications of the victim's fate (55-96). Through this anticlimactic introduction, the speaker resolves his anguish at one stroke: he desensitizes himself by membership in a class of objects. The disjunctive characterizations, as well as the symmetries of action, confirm the schematic bent of the speaker's outlook.

From the start the speaker evokes the emotional transitions of attitude by the hypnotic effect of his utterance:

> But I never saw a man who looked
> So wistfully at the day.
>
> I never saw a man who looked
> With such a wistful eye. . . .   (11-14)

These anxious claims (11ff.) may be construed as reflexive because they impose the burden of proof on the "I" as authority. The repetitions invite the reader to sympathize with the speaker's attitude:

> He does not sit with silent men
> Who watch him night and day;
> Who watch him when he tries to weep,
> And when he tries to pray;
> Who watch him lest himself should rob
> The prison of its prey.   (61-66)

The emotional coloring of stark red "blood" and "wine" dominates the background; with the heavy fall of "dead," it provides an uncanny, sinister atmosphere:

> He did not wear his scarlet coat,
>   For blood and wine are red,
> And blood and wine were on his hands
>   When they found him with the dead,
> The poor dead woman whom he loved,
>   And murdered in her bed.   (1-6)

The definition of the deed by negations (with the anaphoristic tag "He does not. . . .") charges language with pervasive nihilism. The discordances of knowledge and actuality, appropriate to this milieu, reinforce the speaker's sense of chaos.

In an effort to penetrate to the obscure workings of consciousness, Wilde employs a compulsive repetition of key words occurring in cinematic montage (1-6). Thematic development, as in traditional ballads, proceeds through incremental repetition (e.g., 61-66). Wilde manipulates the episodic appearance of the condemned in a gradation of scenic exposures within a social landscape; the emotional impact of waiting is subdued yet intense.[13]

Despite its technical accuracy in factual presentation, the poem does not realize any creative spiritual power—except, perhaps, the prisoner's consciousness which ornaments the clouds in their will-less unravelling (17-18, 107-08). The plain linear registering of perceptions conceals rather than discloses the cause of the murder. Participating in a traumatic experience, the speaker displays innocent incomprehension at what "great or little thing" the man's crime could be, until he is shocked into awareness by the idiomatic

---

[13] See Gordon Hall Gerould, *The Ballad of Tradition* (Oxford, 1932), pp. 105-10; Louise Pound, *Poetic Origins and the Ballad* (New York, 1921), pp. 120-53.

pointedness of *"That fellow's got to swing."* His knowledge
radically alters consciousness: the "little tent of blue" (15)
becomes "a casque of scorching steel" (28). The speaker's
stable world collapses while the man's identity gradually
acquires flesh and motion. Though benumbed, the speaker
shows terror, and appeals "Dear Christ!" But his environment bears no sign of a transcendent redeeming force.
Meanwhile, the condemned man's behavior supports only
a semblance of normality.

At this point we feel the facile comic improvisations
("with nimble feet" to dance "on a seat of grace," 149-50,
139) slightly forced, overwhelmed too much by the direct
expressions of feeling. This appears more obvious if we compare A. E. Housman's deadpan humor on a similar subject
which keeps itself to the scale of a moderately witty, epigrammatic imbalance: "And dead on air will stand / Heels
that held up as straight a chap," and so on.[14] Nonetheless
the jesting colloquialisms of a man caught in straits obtain
decorum if taken as serio-comic conceits: a rhetorical device
for sublimation. Moreover, a positive notation of the killing
would naturally exert a pressure so painful that it could
only be diminished by deflating caricature.

Caricature is invariably the display of mechanical reflexes.
After all prison is "Humanity's machine." Turning now to
the coarse-mouthed Doctor and his automatic precision, we
perceive the scientific maneuver—a ritual game gone bank-
rupt—applied to man treated as animal specimen. Debunk-
ing humor exemplifies itself in domestic disguise which
cloaks the Absurd: "the hangman with his gardener's
gloves" chokes the throat "with three leathern thongs" (81-
84). In our age of concentration camps, few would still be

[14] See lines 17-24, IX, *A Shropshire Lad*, with notes by Carl J.
Weber (Waterville, Maine, 1946), p. 19. Frances Winwar, like preceding commentators, notes Housman's terse simplicity as a possible
influence; *Oscar Wilde and the Yellow Nineties*, p. 345; see also
Letters, p. 317n.

surprised at the figure of the expert-specialist in his banal "purity."

Section II contains a picture of the man's appearance, his gesture embodying the immediate accessibility of freedom: "With open mouth he drank the sun / As though it had been wine" (119-20). Yet this freedom is illusive. The image epitomizes the clash between man in virgin nature and man in a social system. It also crystallizes the idea of nature perverted by human designs: oak and elm fail to bear "spring-time shoot" when transformed into "the gallows tree / With its adder-bitten root" (133-38). Not only has the iniquity of institutional laws abolished purpose, but it has also undermined natural functions, spoiling nature's beneficence: "With bars they blur the gracious moon, / And blind the goodly sun" (553-54). With this violation of natural order by flawed human agency, confusion rules until paralyzing doubt and pain seize the inmates.

Amidst this chaos we meet the decorative impulse of the speaker in its calculated and undeviating intent to allegorize reality. This emblematic mode ("cave of Black Despair," "a changeling Hope," 111-12) may be construed as a "dandiacal" leap of the imagination, "dandiacal" because the speaker refuses to be tickled, irked, or awed by what he says.[15] On the other hand, the condemned vindicates the natural order; air grants him "healthful anodyne" (118). The prisoners lose bearing of their situation, stunned by his disarming pose. Everything quickly assumes an alienating mask; soon the prisoners "with gaze of dull amaze" disbelieve the legitimacy of their punishment, so tormented are they by lack of faith: "For none can tell to what red hell / His sightless soul may stray" (155-56).

A sense of solidarity issues forth (despite the depiction of the human encounter as the parallel movement of "two

[15] *Works*, pp. 131-57 *passim*. See Charles Baudelaire, *Oeuvres Complètes* (Paris, 1961), p. 951.

doomed ships") into a participation in a common lot: "the iron gin that waits for Sin / Had caught us in its snare" (173-74). Their synchronous destiny distinguishes their intimate bond; both move within the orbit of the social outcast. Such a communion, induced by cosmic irony, evolves the synthesis of "I" and "Thou" in a tragic "We."

Wilde uses a poignantly repetitive, circular pattern in meter and narration. Its center of authority is the "I," alternately the elegiac chorus and protagonist. The "I" acts as a variable persona: spokesman or typical figure. His personal impressions, conditioned by the prison, bear no individualizing trait (331-42). Escaping from phantasy, the speaker directs the progression of his feelings toward involvement with the victim's end (161-74).

The crucial stage of the relationship between the victim and his companions occurs in Section III, which abandons focus on the victim's movements and directs attention to the "We." This would not be possible unless the speaker imposed a gap between the victim and his onlookers. The casual reserved conduct which characterizes the victim ("He often said that he was glad / The hangman's hands were near," 197-98), so disconcerting to the wretched inmates, dissolves their kinship. The "We" appears unmitigatedly damned, confined to a labyrinth where evil endures, a force as sovereign as the good: "And what should human Pity do / Pent up in a Murderer's Hole?" (207-08). Later, in Section V, the prisoners, though besieged by "lean Hunger and green Thirst," suffer more from the spiritual than the physical injury that penal servitude inflicts. When the speaker transposes ugly or dreadful circumstances into internal states, the psychic effect, not the physical symptom, receives the stress: e.g., "With midnight always in one's heart," and so forth (589ff). Surrounded by pitiless watching eyes, the prisoners retreat "each into his separate Hell," forced to recoil into the self's deepest recesses. Afflicted by "the soul's strife" and immersed in absolute hopelessness, the accursed criminals suffer the pangs of a sin which, though imagined, are nevertheless bodily realized. They witness "the damned grotesques made arabesques" (299) with "mop and mow"—phantoms that are at once a projection of conscience and a token of demonic supremacy. Despite their appeal to the "wounds of Christ," the prisoners elect an obscure notion of fate instead of providential guidance, having initially lost trust in earthly justice.

We can aptly interpret the heightened concreteness of prison life here as a faithful mirroring of the human sensibilities given concrete form by the narrator. Thus, on the reliable testimony of the speaker, stones are hard, the sky leaden, and so forth. To Wilde, the sensibility exercises its creative function through a wide-ranging empathy.[16] To be indifferent or apathetic, like the warden compelled to "make his face a mask," is to disclose the total disintegration of one's spiritual world. This is presented by means of the staccato rhythm of "documentary" discourse:

> The governor was strong upon
> The Regulations Act;
> The doctor said that death was but
> A scientific fact:
> And twice a day the chaplain called,
> And left a little tract.   (187-92)

Such a humdrum report, marked by utter disaffection, bears no import of "felt thought" because its uniformity of syntax, otherwise a vehicle of a normal situation, merely derives

16 Wilde writes: "The difficulty is that the objects in prison have no shape or form. To take an example: the shed in which people are hanged is a little shed with a glass roof, like a photographer's studio on the sands at Margate. For eighteen months I thought it *was* the studio for photographing prisoners. There is no adjective to describe it. I call it 'hideous' because it became so to me after I knew its use. In itself it is a wooden oblong narrow shed with a glass roof"; *Letters*, p. 454.

from conditioned reflex and sordid routine: "We rubbed the doors, and scrubbed the floors," and so on (219ff). The speaker insinuates a satiric undercutting of religious sentiment: "We banged the tins, and bawled the hymns" (225).

Throughout the ballad we encounter motifs of obsession in such clusters as "Dead and Dread and Doom." These are not, however, mere residues of the poet's early decorative idiom. Juxtaposed with these concepts, the palpable images of the hangman "with his little bag . . . shuffling through the gloom" (243-44), the freakish wardens with "shoes of felt," and so forth, sharpen the drawing of caricature.[17] The instinct for sardonic distortion is in turn derived from the behavior parodied in the "merry masquerade." The dance releases a blight of demonic possession which impels even mud to shriek for blood (237).

In general the ballad develops in scenic sequence, that is, through abrupt flashes of rapid, sharply contrasting tableaux. The phosphorescent silhouettes of hangman and gibbet, prisoners and judge, stamp the mind with such persuasive images that, even in nervous expectation, the prisoners seem to have already lived through the dying of a single man. Imagination thus realizes what men hope, think, and remember in terms of feelings given vivid expression.

Wilde now prepares the macabre setting for a medieval dance of death, though without its religious overtones: a virtual pageant of lost souls. Unlike the spirits in "The Rime of the Ancient Mariner," who are properly agents of purification, these "crooked shapes of terror" suggest the anarchy of the prisoners' world. Their "delicate turn and twist" mordantly burlesques the plight of derelicts "held in gyves," captives akin to inert puppets. Images of webs and snares powerfully render this situation:

[17] Add the incongruity of the wardens dressed in "spic and span" Sunday suits on the day of burial (446-47); also, during the turbulent night of Section V, the condemned "lay as one who lies and dreams / In a pleasant meadow-land" (253-54).

> The morning wind began to moan,
>   But still the night went on;
> Through its giant loom the web of gloom
>   Crept till each thread was spun;
> And, as we prayed, we grew afraid
>   Of the Justice of the Sun.
>
> The moaning wind went wandering round
>   The weeping prison-wall;
> Till like a wheel of turning steel
>   We felt the minutes crawl.   (325-34)

Despite the crowing of cocks, dawn—with its associations of purgation, rebirth, and cyclical continuity—never comes. What arrives instead is Death:

> He did not pass in purple pomp,
>   Nor ride a moon-white steed.
> Three yards of cord and a sliding board
>   Are all the gallows' need;   (349-52)

The urge to forsake sophisticated methodicalness and return to the surd, the primordial facts of existence, may be viewed as a recoil from the specters' "formal pace and loathsome grace." Refusing the lure of effete formalism paradoxically sprung from lawless phantasy, the speaker strives for clarity of outline. Hence the literalness of such haunting chiaroscuro:

> At last I saw the shadowed bars,
>   Like a lattice wrought in lead,
> Move right across the whitewashed wall
>   That faced my three-plank bed,   (337-40)

The speaker repeatedly tries to evoke a correspondent scene for the prisoner's ordeal; he imagines "a fen of filthy darkness," so that the wail of impotent despair comes to resemble "the sound that frightened marshes hear / From some leper

in his lair" (383-84). In this search for a verbal container of
emotions and attitudes in flux, the poem gives rise to a
dialectic of dream and actuality generating further tension.
The paradox whose germ lies embedded in the speaker's
claim that he "lives more lives than one" receives tangible
proof in the confluence of data and sensibility. We perceive
raw data filter through an active sensibility:

> And as one sees most fearful things
>> In the crystal of a dream,
> We saw the greasy hempen rope
>> Hooked to the blackened beam,
> And heard the prayer the hangman's snare
>> Strangled into a scream.   (385-90)

(Contrast Thomas Hood's quite hopeful connection between
God and sinner in "The Dream of Eugene Aram": "And unknown facts of guilty acts / Are seen in dreams from
God.")[18] In the world of the prisoners, man's "grim Justice,"
lacking charity, confounds the limitations of its finitude. It
leads to an indiscriminate punishment of every man. Wilde
affirms that any absolute, whatever its prestige or sanction,
yields nothing but futile chaos.

With the execution of the condemned man occurs a suspension of the link between the profane and the sacred, the
human and the charismatic realms. The afflicted chaplain,
presenting a "wan face," postpones his ministry (397-401).
What prevails throughout, like the flood of peace after the
ravaging storm in the "Ancient Mariner," is the ineffability
of death, the taut implacable presence of the unnameable,
which grows to screaming pervasiveness only in that "something" which "none should look upon" (402).

[18] *The Complete Poetical Works of Thomas Hood*, ed., Walter
Jerrold (Oxford edn., 1906), p. 210. Compare lines 61-72, 212-15.
Although Wilde disclaims Hood's influence (*Letters*, p. 667), the
connection is still being made; e.g., Roditi, p. 182.

Disenchantment preludes the atomistic split of prison society introduced in Section IV: each man now inhabits "his separate hell" (408). Soon after the execution, a decisive change occurs: the prisoners, degraded in their isolation, adopt the demeanor of the hanged man. In "God's sweet air," the prisoners assume the dead man's wistful look. By sheer identification with the scapegoat, they perform the rite of purgative sacrifice. Ecstatic with the "Savour of Remorse," they bow down, portentously wailing: "Alas, it is a fearful thing / To feel another's guilt" (265-66). Their forbidding postures serve as eloquent proof of that inward agitation which, despite their stupor, elicits poetic virtue: they name the sky "that little tent of blue" (417).

Tension wears off after the recognition: the prisoners now collectively incarnate the man who died in their nightmare (389-90). Stupefied beyond recall, they suffer the knowledge of shirked responsibility. For they have killed a fellowman by not acknowledging their true culpability before society's tribunal.[19] In their cowardice they ratify the Judge's decree of death, thus becoming accomplices in the crime. The prisoners sin when they recognize their share of the universal guilt; they continue to writhe in agony until the communion with God, disrupted by the stasis of despair, restores innocence to all. This is prophesied through the mediation of nature: the corpse will bear flowers in the end.

Eventually the speaker, unable to sustain the spectacle of a bleeding "soul," shifts to a portrait of his companions' "monstrous garb." He suggests that the circular path of their promenade, signifying empty duration, proves precarious above "a slippery asphalt yard" (433-39). "Slippery," "crooked," "ape," "clown"—these terms still connote distortion, though one infused with human relevance. Man

[19] Merle (p. 105) speaks of the "theme de la culpabilité universelle" as "le centre ideologique du poème."

himself, therefore, invents the hell he lives in. This mood persists until it gradually declines to animism in an effort to grasp the unnameable and fix it in recognizable shape: the ego diffuses itself in its environment. Allegorical summation then recurs to forestall vagueness of sentiment:

> Silently we went round and round,
>   And through each hollow mind
> The Memory of dreadful things
>   Rushed like a dreadful wind,
> And Horror stalked before each man,
>   And Terror crept behind.   (439-44)

Personification, moving from massive particularities to animated wholes, distances feelings and subsumes them under general categories.

After succumbing to the lure of abstract counters, the speaker immediately reverts to particulars. Though the prisoners have been reduced to animal stature, they still retain the capacity to draw out meanings from what their senses record. They perceive the context of the "quicklime on the wardens' boots" (449-50). This form-giving apprehension of the external world also explains the speaker's outrage at the desecration of the grave. His protest foils the reduction of human life to sheer inert matter through an act of imaginative transformation: the corpse's pall, "a little heap of burning lime," becomes a "sheet of flame" (451-62). Beyond death the hanged convict seems a numinous presence, a witness to the ever-renewed acceptance by man of his tragic existence.

On the speaker's part this act is self-purgative insofar as the prime effort of the imagination is to redeem man from the chaos of sensations, to affirm his status as a being whose circumference (to use Blakean analogy) depends on the infinite variety and plenitude of his possibilities.[20] Since expression brings about empathy, so what the corpse undergoes when lime eats flesh and bone the prisoners also undergo just as painfully. They then assume the dead man's immortality in envisioning their lot as men (462-68).

Meanwhile the grave itself becomes the man's visible counterpart: it looks "upon the wondering sky / With unreproachful stare" (473-74). The speaker affirms that "God's kindly earth / Is kindlier than men know" (477-78), for he knows that the permanence of nature will soon resurrect the victim. Nature in turn anticipates the unpredictable visitation of the spirit: "For who can say by what strange way, / Christ brings His will to light" (483-84). Despite this assurance, Reading Gaol remains an embodiment of nothingness found at the nadir of self-centered man. Since prison air proves congenial only to "the shard, the pebble, and the flint" (489)—emblems of hardness and the unfeeling absolute—it will never breed the rose-petals whose withering will "tell the men who tramp the yard / That God's Son died for all" (497-98). Just as the condemned suffered like a beast, enjoyed no sacrament, his body "hid in a hole," so the prisoners under this regimen will never know, within the Christian dispensation, the redeeming power of Grace.

Only in a limited sense could we infer from the poem Wilde's repudiation of his art, his decadent aestheticism, and his inevitable "*Ruckkehr zur Natur.*"[21] The unnatural calamity that befalls the prisoners is vicious and mutilating; even souls wander in fettered agony. Human justice reduces man to a sum of disconnected features: "the swollen

[20] See A. E. Rodway, "The Last Phase," *From Dickens to Hardy*, Vol. 6 of *The Pelican Guide to English Literature*, ed., Boris Ford (7 vols., Baltimore, 1958), pp. 398-99; and also Jorge Luis Borges, *Other Inquisitions 1937-1952*, tr., Ruth L. C. Simms (Austin, 1964), pp. 79-81.

[21] See the sixth chapter of Fehr's *Studien zu Oscar Wildes Gedichten*, pp. 196-209.

purple throat," "the stark and staring eyes" (519-20, 619-20). The euphony, the tuneful alliteration, the Pre-Raphaelite preciosity—these imply Wilde's attempts, however clumsy and desperate, to recompose discrete perceptions into a significant whole. The note of resignation in "Yet all is well; he but passed / To Life's appointed bourne" (529-30) seems a feeble expression of the solace which human solidarity and intimate dialogue afford. Often the linguistic texture functions as an ironic commentary on the narrative.[22]

Confronting the prisoners' fate in Section V, the speaker, in a forward thrust of reflection, envisions "God's eternal laws" intervening in human affairs (551-57). Unless the callous heart, or any limiting enclosure, breaks, the spirit cannot descend and purify (606-18). Man must forego all self-interests, it seems, in order to heal his soul through humility gained from cruel suffering. So that all crimes may be understood and accepted, the ultimate transformation of history by a divine power is invoked. But within the secular sphere it is man himself who gives to his nihilism an intelligible dramatic incarnation. That is his supreme achievement. Here, through the mediation of a victim whom the speaker celebrates for his sacrifice, all trials and self-questionings climax in the illumination: "And the crimson stain that was of Cain / Became Christ's snow-white seal" (635-36). Though he lived in an epoch of revolutions, Wilde was acquainted only with the language of orthodoxy in which to express his vision of self-transcendence.

Toward the end of the poem a natural and transparent simplicity of language appears. The conflicts of law and feeling, man and nature, partly resolved by the projection

[22] Lacking the elegiac tolling of bells for the dead, the poet substitutes the jingling of the wardens' keys—a not altogether mock requiem.

of the psyche in the pattern of man's physical behavior, are seen as a stage of the ordeal to achieve purification. Writing of W. S. Blunt's prison sonnets *In Vinculis* in 1889, Wilde thought that "imprisonment converted a clever rhymer into an earnest and deep-thinking poet"; it also strengthened and deepened the poet's nature. He observes how metaphorically "the narrow confines of a prison cell" correspond to, and suggest, the "sonnet's scanty plot of ground." He could have been describing his own fate in 1895 and the subsequent years of exile and despair.

In the concluding section, the appeal to Christ's judgment recedes into the background. What confronts us now is the human predicament and the speaker's unqualified acceptance of it (631-34): the wretched man rests forever in "a pit of shame" (637-42). Man, finite yet able to project ideal modes of self-fulfillment, encounters the only possible understanding of himself through the ironies of feeling and deed. A particular inward truth acquires historical reality when each man, murdering the loved person, performs the act in his own unique way (649-54).

Reading Gaol, though it tells a story, goes beyond mere narration by the richness of its sound patterns and imagery. The connotative texture of the soliloquy conveys the "feel" of a personal drama, and defines a particular world of subjectivity. Statement and observation coalesce in the shocking analogies and juxtapositions:

> He does not rise in piteous haste
>   To put on convict-clothes,
> While some coarse-mouthed doctor gloats, and notes
>   Each new and nerve-twitched pose,
> Fingering a watch whose little ticks
>   Are like horrible hammer-blows.   (73-78)

The simplicity of the horrifying transfixes attention. Necessity and fate vibrate in the ominous prophetic tone, in the grotesque and macabre details of the setting.

The interest of the ballad at first centers on the character of the hanged man; but toward the end, the victim becomes a universal symbol of man's fate. The dramatic force of the poem inheres precisely in the speaker's awareness of impending doom. As witness of the drama, the prison connotes the threatening force of contingency that dooms all men. And yet, somehow, the prisoners triumph over fate. Their feelings, concentrated in sympathy with the condemned man, the "I," the victim, and the "We," merge in a collective participation in pity and terror.

The existential dimension of the poem can be discerned in Wilde's conception of the speaker's consciousness. This consciousness projects the metaphor of man flung into an arbitrary world, into a stage where chance and accidence rule. By his own fallible designs, man has broken the concord that existed previously in some mythical paradise between his desires and recalcitrant facts. Significantly, the divine or spiritual force in life fails to appear anywhere in the unfolding of the prisoners' situation.

Man, as chief protagonist in the poem, is shown unable to project any spiritual otherness except through his own expressive instruments: the wretched corpse acquires spiritual identity in being "eaten by teeth of flame."[23] To the speaker, ideas and doctrines are meaningless unless they are embodied in concrete human acts, thoughts, desires. Even time is regulated by the modulation of feelings (229-30, 539-40). Assertions like "the wall is strong," etc., validate them-

[23] Hoxie N. Fairchild mistakes theme for "moral" so that in evaluating straight pronouncements, he forgets the tensive, metaphoric qualities from which such pronouncements draw semantic life; *Religious Trends in English Poetry*, v, pp. 151-53. A similar judgment is found in Samuel Chew, "The Nineteenth Century and After," *A Literary History of England*, ed., A. C. Baugh (New York, 1948), p. 1481.

selves as personal impressions—the ultimate justification for poetic utterance. Instead of referring to verifiable states of affairs, poetic utterance—hypothetical "pseudo-statements," if you like—prove themselves on the pulses; that is, they are valid insofar as they are conceived by man.

"And all men kill the thing they love," the speaker proclaims at the end. If we assume that the act of murder, the release of murderous impulse, functions as a stage in the growth of character (as Wilde argued in *The Critic as Artist*, in *De Profundis*, in *Dorian Gray*), then each man is condemned to live with his own guilt. But man, accepting responsibility for his acts, cannot judge himself by other than his own standards (631-34). The physical death of love must finally be located beyond the frame of human sympathy, beyond civilization itself, for the last appeal is to the dark primordial core of Being.

In trying to give coherence to the chaotic situation of the poem, Wilde adopts the impersonal structure of the ballad. The poem's "stark realism," enthusiastically commended by W. B. Yeats, finds a rationale in the initial choice of genre.[24] Wilde modifies the ballad form by adding two more lines to the regular tight four-line stanza; these two lines act either as refrains or as stages of narrative movement. This change fits the "Longinian" strategy of the poem, which involves extensive phrasal and clausal iteration, with emphasis on nouns rather than verbs, on essences rather than relations.[25] Essentially an observational medium, the ballad assumes in Wilde's handling an oracular tone: e.g., "Out of his

[24] "Introduction," *Oxford Book of Modern Verse* (New York, 1936), p. vi. Cf. Rudolf Stamm, "W. B. Yeats und Oscar Wildes 'Ballad of Reading Gaol'," *Wiener Beitrage zur Englischen Philologie*, LXV (1957), pp. 210-19; Albert Friedman, *The Ballad Revival* (Chicago, 1961), p. 329.

[25] See Josephine Miles, *Eras and Modes in English Poetry* (Berkeley and Los Angeles, 1957), p. 229; the proportion of Wilde's diction, Adjective–10, Noun–17, Verb–7, may be compared with Yeats': 9–6–9.

mouth a red, red rose! / Out of his heart a white!" (481ff)
But this lyrical strain, while lending vigor and sublimity,
is enriched and qualified by dramatized attitudes, by the
compression and resonance of imagery and rhythm in the
poem. All the time the sound of the verse provides a firm
counterpart of continuity. Some readers may object to the
mixture of styles, of pathos and farcical humor; but such a
mixture conforms exactly to the ironic juxtapositions unit-
ing the formal elements into a significant whole.[26]

In *Reading Gaol*, Wilde molds a metrical convention into
an organic pattern which affords us a means of reconciling
the stark contradictions of actual life. Contradictions per-
meate the whole course of Wilde's life. In the early sonnet
"Hélas!" he imagines himself a "stringéd lute on which all
winds can play." He renounces the "austere control" of
"ancient wisdom," craving "to drift with every passion."
Seeking to tread "sunlit heights," he arrives only at the infernal depths of Reading Gaol. Affirming his artistic vocation
he vows to select "from life's dissonance . . . one clear chord
to reach the ears of God." But in touching "the honey of romance," he hesitates and asks: "must I lose a soul's inheritance?" Right from the start of Wilde's career, we perceive
conscience and passion warring in his consciousness. His
life proceeded from one *succès de scandale* to another, culminating in the trial and chastisement of the willful aesthetic
ego; he played with romance and reality, the victim and hero
of the legend he created, embodying the conflicts of his life
in his works.

While it may be granted that Wilde "perversely allowed
his disillusioned intellect to mock his aesthetic emotion,"[27] it
is necessary to bear in mind the fact that Wilde himself, as

[26] Wilde's last work may be aligned with stylistic "perspectivism"
as shown in modern literature; see Erich Auerbach, *Mimesis* (New
York, 1953), pp. 463-92.
[27] Jerome H. Buckley, *The Victorian Temper* (Cambridge, Mass.,
1951), p. 234.

imaginative force, comprehended both intellect and emotion and their eternal conflict in artistic form. He did not lack faith in his creations; he lacked faith in himself, in his passionate sensibility and intelligence as the moral center of his works. It may be that he failed to maintain the precarious balance between the artist's pursuit of detached intensity and the personality's refusal to willingly suspend disbelief. But the resulting ambiguity itself testifies to his conviction that the value of literature depends on its inculcation of a constant flexibility of attitude, perhaps a consciously cultivated ambivalence which enables us, in blessed moments, to hold justice and reality together in a single thought.

NOTE ON REFERENCES

The Works of Oscar Wilde, edited by G. F. Maine (London, 1948), has been used throughout as a convenient compact edition. It contains practically the same texts as those of Wilde's *Complete Works* (New York, 1921), ten volumes, edited by Robert Ross. Maine's edition is referred to as *Works*. *The Letters of Oscar Wilde*, edited by Rupert Hart-Davis (New York, 1962), is referred to as *Letters*.

Apart from the occasional critical comments in the volume of collected letters, Wilde's literary and art criticism may be found in three books: *Intentions* (1891) embodies the most important critical principles and their expositions; *A Critic in Pall Mall* (1919), a collection of articles chosen by E. V. Lucas, most of which is found also, together with Wilde's lectures in America, in the Methuen edition (1908) of *Miscellanies*; and *Decorative Art in America* (1906), a compilation of lectures, letters, and interviews, edited by R. B. Glaenzer.

Wilde's replies to the attacks on *The Picture of Dorian Gray* had previously been gathered by the indefatigable bibliographer of Wilde, Stuart Mason (the pseudonym of Christopher S. Millard), in *Oscar Wilde: Art and Morality* (1908). All the works cited above were published in London.

The critical work on Wilde's poetry has been ably reviewed by Lionel Stevenson in "The Later Victorian Poets," *The Victorian Poets, A Guide to Research*, edited by Frederic E. Faverty (Cambridge, Mass., 1956), pp. 250-51.

The authoritative bibliography of Wilde's writings is Stuart Mason, *Bibliography of Oscar Wilde* (London, 1914).

Index

(Works by Wilde are entered individually except for the titles of single poems which are grouped together under the entry, *Poems*.)

INDEX

INDEX

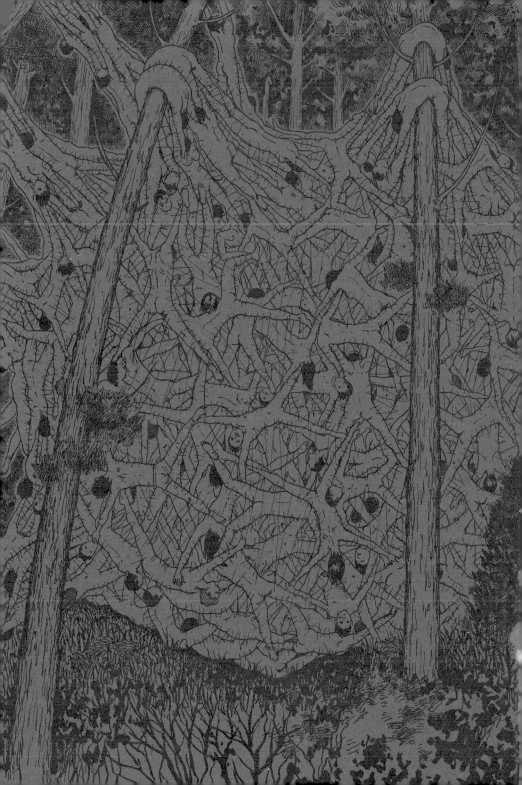

Frankenstein
in
Innsmouth

JUNJI ITO

VENUS IN THE BLIND SPOT

CONTENTS

BILLIONS ALONE

AAAAH!!

HM?

HUH? WHAT IS IT, SHIRO?

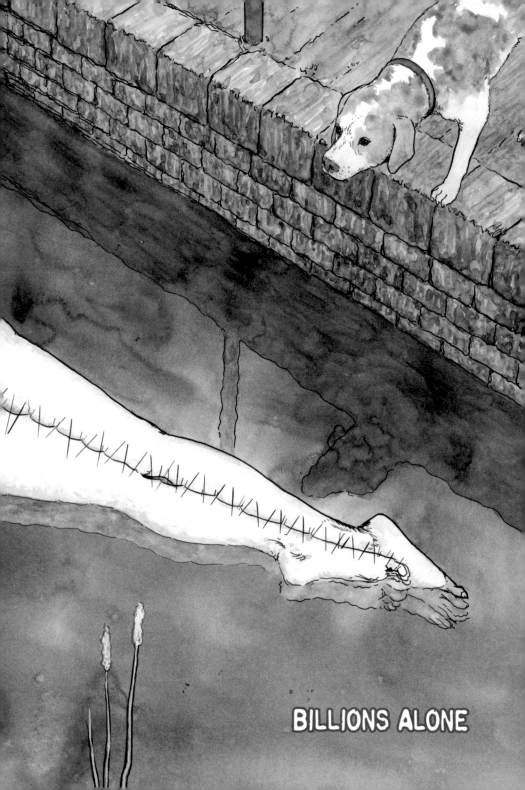

BILLIONS ALONE

THE BODIES WERE FIRMLY SEWN TOGETHER WITH WHAT APPEARS TO BE FISHING LINE.

THE TWO BODIES DISCOVERED IN A POND IN THE PARK EARLY THIS MORNING...

...HAVE BEEN IDENTIFIED AS A COUPLE WHO HAD RECENTLY GONE MISSING.

MICHIO?
MICHIO...
ARE YOU
AWAKE?

THE POLICE
STRONGLY
BELIEVE THIS
IS THE WORK
OF A DEVIANT
MIND.

LEAVE
ME
ALONE,
MOM.

SHUT
UP.

IT'D BE
A NICE
CHANGE
OF
PACE.

MICHIO?
HOW
ABOUT YOU
GO FOR
A WALK
SOME-
TIME?

I'LL JUST
LEAVE
LUNCH
HERE FOR
YOU.

I'LL
LEAVE
THEM
HERE
WITH
YOUR
LUNCH.

AND ALSO,
NOTICES FOR YOUR
COMING-OF-AGE
CEREMONY AND
CLASS REUNION
NEXT YEAR HAVE
COME ALREADY.

I SAID,
LEAVE ME
ALONE!

AND
YOU'LL
BE 20
NEXT
YEAR...

BUT, MICHIO,
YOU'VE BEEN
LOCKED UP
IN THAT ROOM
FOR SEVEN
YEARS NOW.

KWEEEEN

ZUN BAM
BAM BAM

I WONDER WHAT NATSUKO HORIE'S DOING THESE DAYS.

THAT REMINDS ME.

CLASS REUNION, HUH...

DUN DUN

ZUN BAM BAM

RSVP
will attend
will not attend

SHE WAS PROBABLY JUST TRYING TO BE NICE.

SHE WAS CUTE. AND CHEERFUL. AND POPULAR...

NATSUKO HORIE... SHE WAS THE ONLY ONE WHO STOOD UP FOR ME IN ELEMENTARY AND JUNIOR HIGH...

...WHEN NO ONE WOULD EVEN TALK TO ME.

TOSS

EVERYONE, COME TOGETHER...

COME TOGETHER... COME TOGETHER...

KWEEEEEEEN...

ZUN BAM BAM BAM

KWMMMM

BEING BY YOURSELF'S BORING...

BILLIONS ALONE... BILLIONS ALONE...

REACH OUT FROM THE HEART...

WE'RE ALL FRIENDS... ALL FRIENDS...

BEING BY YOURSELF'S BORING...

BEING BY YOURSELF'S THE ONLY WAY.

HMPH. TOTALLY STUPID. HOW EXACTLY ARE WE ALL FRIENDS?

LET'S ALL COME TOGETHER...

WE'RE ALL FRIENDS... ALL FRIENDS...

BILLIONS ALONE... BILLIONS ALONE...

REACH OUT FROM THE HEART...

LET'S ALL HOLD HANDS...

...WHAT IS THIS? THE RADIO?

I... MY NAME'S NATSUKO HORIE. I USED TO GO TO SCHOOL WITH MICHIO.

IS HE HOME?

WHO MIGHT YOU BE?

WHAT ?!

IT'S NATSUKO HORIE... WILL YOU COME TALK TO HER?

YOU HAVE A GUEST.

MICHIO !

MICHIO !

DID SHE SAY NATSUKO HORIE?

WHY WOULD SHE ...?

35 knots

...I'LL COME DOWN.

I...

OR SHOULD I SEND HER HOME?

MICHIO? HOW ABOUT IT?

SHE'S GOTTEN SO PRETTY.

I-IT REALLY IS NATSUKO.

BA-DMP

BA-DMP

Y-YEAH.

IT'S BEEN ABOUT SEVEN YEARS, I GUESS?

MICHIO! HOW ARE YOU?

IT'S AT THE SAME TIME AS THE COMING-OF-AGE CEREMONY. I'D LOVE IT IF YOU'D COME, MICHIO.

SO THE THING IS, I'M HELPING OUT WITH THE CLASS REUNION IN JANUARY.

YEAH... TOTALLY FINE.

AND I HEARD YOU DON'T GO OUT MUCH. ARE YOU ALL RIGHT?

EVERYONE'S WORRIED. YOU STOPPED COMING TO SCHOOL IN SEVENTH GRADE.

IT'LL BE FUN!

LET'S GO!

WHY DON'T YOU COME? THE GUYS'LL BE GLAD TO SEE YOU.

HUH? BUT...

ACTUALLY, A BUNCH OF US ARE PLANNING THE REUNION IN A CAFE AROUND THE CORNER.

I'M ON THE REUNION COMMITTEE.

REMEMBER ME? NORIYUKI SAKAI.

IT'S BEEN FOREVER, MICHIO.

AAH...

I REMEMBER YOU. ALL OF YOU.

I'M KEISUKE KASAGI. YOU DIDN'T FORGET, RIGHT?

HEY, KEISUKE. DON'T SAY IT LIKE THAT. IT'S RUDE.

YOU GOTTA COME! YOU CAN'T STAY LOCKED UP IN YOUR HOUSE FOREVER, Y'KNOW?

...

BUT WE'D LOVE IT IF YOU'D COME TO THE COMING-OF-AGE CEREMONY AND THE CLASS REUNION.

I THINK NATSUKO ALREADY TOLD YOU.

35 Knots

I'D MUCH RATHER SIT AND READ BY MYSELF THAN BE GROUND DOWN.

ONCE YOU'RE DONE WITH SCHOOL, YOU HAVE TO DEAL WITH BOSSES AND ANNOYING COWORKERS AND ALL THAT.

I MEAN...

I TOTALLY GET HOW YOU FEEL, MICHIO.

OH... RIGHT.

COOL IT, KEISUKE.

YEAH. NOT IN FRONT OF YOUR FUTURE WIFE.

C'MON, NORIYUKI, DON'T TALK LIKE THAT.

35 Knots

OKAY, I'M GONNA HEAD OUT.

UM...

IT'S KIND OF EMBAR-RASSING.

MICHIO, WE'RE ACTUALLY GETTING MARRIED NEXT YEAR.

CON-GRATS.

WOW... YOU ARE?

HEY, MICHIO! WAIT UP!

...

WHY DON'T YOU COME?

THERE'S THIS GROUP DATE, BUT WE'RE SHORT A GUY. AND I CAN'T EXACTLY ASK NORIYUKI.

DON'T GO RUNNING OUT ON US. YOU FREE TONIGHT?

BUT I'M JUST NOT IN THE MOOD FOR THAT.

NO. I APPRECIATE THE OFFER, KEISUKE.

...

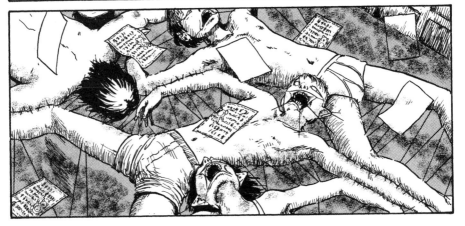

Michio

Anz>About the murder victims sewn together

Anz>Billions Alone. Lately what I've heard

Michio>What kind of rumor?

Anz>There's a weird rumor going around.

Michio>The thing on the radio, and then

...about that.

Anz>There's a weird rumor going around

Michio>The thing on the radio, and the

Anz>Oh, I know about that.

Michio>By the way, do you know about

Anz>Thanks.

Michio>Good luck.

the murder victims sewn together.

Alone. Lately what I've heard

22

I JUST WANTED TO ASK YOU SOMETHING.

MICHIO? SORRY TO CALL SO SUDDENLY.

HELLO?

WHAT?!

HUH?!

HE'S BEEN MISSING SINCE THAT NIGHT. ALONG WITH EVERYONE ELSE ON THE GROUP DATE.

IT'S ABOUT KEISUKE, ACTUALLY.

...WAS FOUND IN THE MOUNTAINS FAR FROM WHERE HE DISAPPEARED, HIS BODY SEWN TO THE OTHERS ON THE GROUP DATE.

A FEW DAYS LATER, KEISUKE KASAGI...

THE ENTIRE GROUP IS THEN LATER FOUND SEWN TOGETHER INTO A SINGLE CORPSE.

IN MANY CASES, PEOPLE SUDDENLY DISAPPEAR AFTER MEETING IN ONE PLACE AS A GROUP.

...ARE BEING DISCOVERED ONE AFTER ANOTHER AS PART OF "GROUP CORPSES."

MISSING PERSONS ALL OVER THE COUNTRY...

NEWS 9:00

TAK TAK TAK TAK

GIVEN THAT VICTIMS ARE BEING FOUND IN ALL REGIONS, THE PROBABILITY THAT THIS IS AN ORGANIZED CRIME...

THE FACTS EACH TIME ARE SIMILAR, SUCH AS THE TIGHT STITCHING WITH FISHING LINE.

PLACES WITH LOTS OF PEOPLE ARE DANGEROUS...

...

□ Anz>It's a rumor at best...

□ Anz>Basically, places with lots o

□ Anz>And everyone who comes togeth

□ Anz>Wherever people group, Billi

□ Anz>They'll be talking about it s

□ Michio>The media's not touching

places with lots of people

one who comes together

Wherever people group, Bil

talking about it soon enou

Sign up for free to get started.

24

NATSUKO? OH... HELLO?

BEEP BEEP

OH. ARE YOU COMING?

ACTUALLY, IT'S ABOUT THE REUNION.

GROUP CORPSE REMAINS

IT'S MICHIO.

OH, MICHIO? HI... WHAT'S WRONG?

SO IT MIGHT BE DANGEROUS TO HAVE A REUNION.

THERE'S A RUMOR THAT WHOEVER'S BEHIND ALL THESE DISAPPEARANCES AND MURDERS LATELY IS TARGETING GROUPS.

WHAT?! CANCEL?

NO, THAT'S NOT IT... IT MIGHT BE A GOOD IDEA TO CANCEL IT.

NO WAY! REALLY?! THAT'S...

LOOK. I REALLY WANT TO HAVE THIS REUNION, ALSO AS A MEMORIAL FOR KEISUKE NOW THAT HE'S GONE.

I WANT YOU TO COME, TOO, MICHIO.

I MEAN, IT'S NOT FOR SURE OR ANYTHING, BUT...

...

YEAH. I'LL THINK ABOUT IT.

OH. RIGHT. I GUESS... MAKES SENSE.

WE'RE UP IN THE LAST DAYS OF THE YEAR HERE, BUT TONIGHT AT LEAST IS CHRISTMAS EVE!

JINGLE BELLS! JINGLE BELLS!

AND MAYBE A FEW OF YOU ARE SPENDING THE EVENING ALONE, LONELY.

HOW ARE YOU SPENDING THE NIGHT THIS YEAR? WITH YOUR LOVER, JUST THE TWO OF YOU?

OR PARTYING WITH YOUR FRIENDS?

26

27

THIS GROUP HAS PREVIOUSLY DISTRIBUTED A LARGE NUMBER OF LEAFLETS VIA AIRPLANE AND REPEATEDLY HIJACKED THE AIRWAVES.

AND HERE WE SEE A PARTICULAR ORGANIZATION COMING TO THE FOREFRONT.

THEY CALL THEMSELVES THE "BILLIONS ALONE CLUB."

...WHO WENT MISSING ON CHRISTMAS EVE FROM VARIOUS AREAS OF THE COUNTRY WERE LATER FOUND AS GROUP CORPSES!

THE SITUATION IS EXTREMELY SERIOUS. THE MOSTLY YOUNG PEOPLE...

AT PRESENT, ALL WE CAN SAY IS THAT BILLIONS ALONE IS TARGETING GATHERINGS OF ANY KIND.

POLICE AND PUBLIC SECURITY HAVE BOTH SHOWN GREAT INTEREST AND STARTED TO INVESTIGATE, BUT THE TRUTH ABOUT THE GROUP REMAINS A MYSTERY.

IT'S ALSO CURIOUS THAT THE VICTIMS WERE NOT OBVIOUSLY INJURED, NOR DID THEY SHOW ANY SIGNS OF RESISTING.

IMPOSSIBLE TO THINK SO MANY COULD BE VICTIMIZED WITHOUT EVEN ONE OF THEM FIGHTING BACK.

...IS IT REALLY POSSIBLE TO CARRY OUT SUCH A LARGE-SCALE AND UNIQUE CRIME OVER SUCH A BROAD AREA WITHOUT DRAWING ANYONE'S ATTENTION?

BUT THAT SAID, NO MATTER HOW LARGE BILLIONS ALONE MIGHT BE...

BEING IN A GROUP IS DANGEROUS IN AND OF ITSELF NOW.

AT ANY RATE, WE'LL NEED TO PROCEED WITH CAUTION.

I BELIEVE BILLIONS ALONE IS IN FACT A UFO—THIS HAS TO BE THE WORK OF ALIENS, DOESN'T IT?

I FEEL AS THOUGH IT IS A POWER THAT SURPASSES HUMAN KNOWLEDGE.

...AND THE MAJORITY OF THE YOUNG PEOPLE BECOMING NEW ADULTS SPOKE OUT IN FAVOR OF THE CEREMONY HAPPENING.

THE CITY WAS CONFIDENT IN THE TIGHT GUARD SET UP...

...IN OUR CITY, THE CEREMONY ENDED UP TAKING PLACE.

WHILE MANY LOCAL GOVERNMENTS CALLED OFF EVENTS LIKE COMING-OF-AGE DAY...

THE CEREMONY WILL BEGIN SHORTLY, SO PLEASE MAKE YOUR WAY INSIDE.

HOW ARE YOU?

EEE! IT'S BEEN AGES!

YOU!

WHAT ARE YOU DOING THERE?!

WHERE'S NATSUKO?

I'M WORRIED.

NATSUKO!

OH!

WHAT'S GOING ON, MICHIO?

WHY ARE YOU STANDING OUT HERE INSTEAD OF GOING INSIDE?

WHAT? SO YOU REALLY *ARE* A NEW ADULT?

YES. HE WAS MY CLASSMATE IN JUNIOR HIGH.

DO YOU KNOW THIS MAN?

WELL THEN, GO INSIDE. THE CEREMONY'S STARTING.

IS THAT SO?

HE'S DEFINITELY NOTHING TO WORRY ABOUT.

HE'S NOT GOOD WITH CROWDS. HE WAS TRYING TO DECIDE WHETHER HE SHOULD GO OR NOT.

OFFICER, HE'S A VERY SHY PERSON.

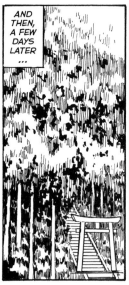

35

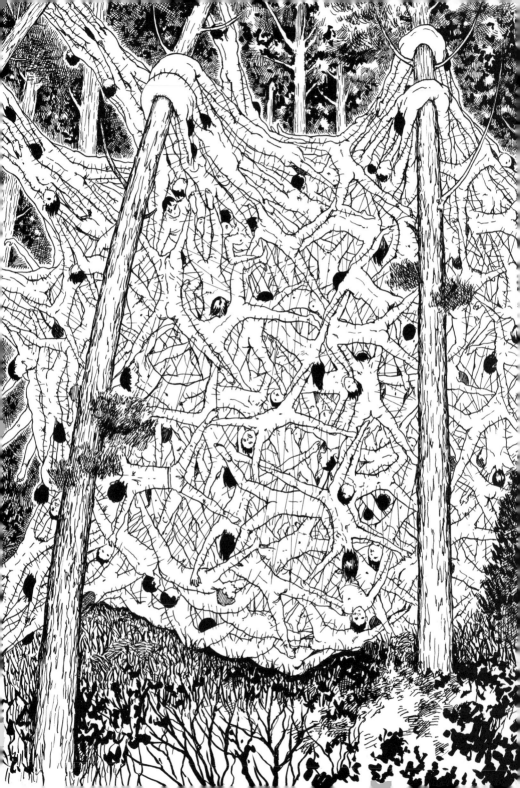

...AND MOTHERS WOULD SHUT THEIR WEEPING CHILDREN IN A DIFFERENT ROOM.

...AND ENDED UP HOLED UP IN ROOMS ALL BY THEMSELVES.

AFTER THAT, PEOPLE STARTED AVOIDING OTHER PEOPLE...

MARRIED COUPLES LOCKED THEMSELVES UP IN SEPARATE ROOMS ...

OH... HELLO?

...

NATSUKO?

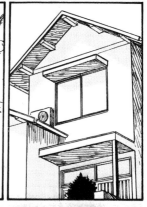

AND NORIYUKI'S GONE...

I'M A LITTLE BETTER. BUT I CAN'T MOTIVATE MYSELF TO DO ANYTHING.

Album

UM. EVERYTHING IN JAPAN'S A MESS RIGHT NOW, AND I DON'T KNOW WHEN THE PHONES'LL STOP WORKING.

I THOUGHT MAYBE YOU'D CALMED DOWN A BIT...

THANKS.

SO I THOUGHT I'D CALL NOW WHILE I CAN...

...IT WOULDN'T MATTER WHETHER HE WAS DEAD OR ALIVE.

AND IF THE PHONES AND EMAIL STOP WORKING...

EVEN IF HE WERE STILL ALIVE, I WOULDN'T BE ABLE TO SEE HIM.

...BUT IT'S WEIRD.

I'LL COME SEE YOU.

I THINK IT SHOULD BE OKAY IF IT'S FOR JUST A SHORT TIME.

N-NATSUKO. IF IT'S OKAY WITH YOU...

LOCKED UP IN A ROOM BY MYSELF, I'M SO LONELY... I WANT TO DIE.

BUT I... I'M LONELY.

IF I COULD SEE YOU, MICHIO... I'D LIKE THAT.

REALLY? JUST YOU SAYING THAT MAKES ME HAPPY.

OH? WELL, BE CAREFUL...

I'M GOING OUT FOR A BIT.

WHAT DO YOU WANT?

DON'T COME IN.

MOM...

MOM, YOU AWAKE?

TO BE HONEST...

I JUST WANTED TO SEE NATSUKO HORIE.

...I WOULDN'T HAVE MINDED BECOMING PART OF A GROUP CORPSE IF IT WAS WITH HER.

VRRRRRRK

THE CITY WAS SILENT.

WHRRRRRRR

THERE'S NO WAY THE GOVERNMENT WOULD JUST STAND BY AND WATCH!

RIGHT... NOTHING TO WORRY ABOUT!

THE GOVERNMENT'S STARTING TO TAKE REAL ACTION!

IT'S THE MILITARY! THE MILITARY'S SCRAMBLING AGAINST BILLIONS ALONE!

ONE MORE THING...

AND THEN... WHEN I SEE HER...

IT'S OKAY NOW!

I HAVE TO TELL HER!

43

THE HUMAN CHAIR
ORIGINAL STORY BY EDOGAWA RANPO

*Furniture Workshop Yorando

A FURNITURE WORK- SHOP...

...

47

A CHAIR HAS TO SUPPORT A BODY FOR A LONG TIME.

IF YOU CHOOSE THE WRONG ONE, IT CAN LEAD TO HEALTH PROBLEMS.

I SEE. A GOOD CHAIR REALLY IS KEY, *HM?*

YES. I KNOW OF A CASE LIKE THAT FROM A WHILE BACK.

GOOD-NESS. THEIR LIFE?

...A CHAIR CAN CHANGE A PERSON'S LIFE.

IN THE MOST EXTREME CASE...

...THERE'S SOME-THING I WANT TO SHOW YOU.

BUT FIRST...

IF YOU DON'T KNOW IT, MISS, I'D BE GLAD TO TELL YOU THIS MYSTERIOUS STORY.

IN THE TAISHO ERA, A CHAIR DID INDEED ALTER A CERTAIN PERSON'S DESTINY.

THIS WAY.

IT'S QUITE PRECIOUS, SO I KEEP IT IN THE BACK.

48

THIS OLD ARMCHAIR IS CONNECTED TO THE STORY I MENTIONED.

SHE'S BEEN COMPLETELY FORGOTTEN NOWADAYS. SHE WAS QUITE A POPULAR AUTHOR IN THE TAISHO DAYS.

WELL, IT'S NO WONDER YOU HAVEN'T.

NO...

MISS, HAVE YOU HEARD OF YOSHIKO TOGAWA?

AND THEN ONE DAY, A CURIOUS MANUSCRIPT WAS DELIVERED TO HER DOOR.

Mrs. Yoshiko Togawa

NEARLY EVERY DAY, UNKNOWN ADMIRERS WOULD SEND HER LETTERS AND MANU-SCRIPTS.

SHE WAS THE WIFE OF A SECRETARY AT THE MINISTRY OF FOREIGN AFFAIRS AND AN ACCOMPLISHED WRITER.

VIVID AND EARNEST... THE PAGES SPELLED OUT A MYSTERIOUS MONOLOGUE SOMEHOW NOT OF THIS WORLD.

THIS MANUSCRIPT HAD NO TITLE, NO AUTHOR NAME, AND IT BEGAN WITH THE ADDRESS "MADAME." ALMOST AS THOUGH SPEAKING TO HER DIRECTLY...

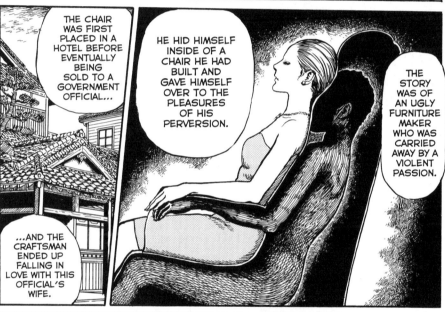

THE CHAIR WAS FIRST PLACED IN A HOTEL BEFORE EVENTUALLY BEING SOLD TO A GOVERNMENT OFFICIAL...

HE HID HIMSELF INSIDE OF A CHAIR HE HAD BUILT AND GAVE HIMSELF OVER TO THE PLEASURES OF HIS PERVERSION.

THE STORY WAS OF AN UGLY FURNITURE MAKER WHO WAS CARRIED AWAY BY A VIOLENT PASSION.

...AND THE CRAFTSMAN ENDED UP FALLING IN LOVE WITH THIS OFFICIAL'S WIFE.

SHE HEAVED A SIGH OF RELIEF.

BUT A LETTER ARRIVED SOON AFTER TO INFORM HER THAT THE MANUSCRIPT WAS FICTION.

Toshima-ku, Ikebukuro 3-chome 2

Mrs. Yoshiko Togawa

YOSHIKO TOGAWA ASSUMED IT WAS A LOVE LETTER TO HER OWN SELF, AND A SHIVER RAN UP HER SPINE.

AAH, HOW DISTURB-ING.

THE MANUSCRIPT TOOK THE FORM OF A LETTER FROM THE CRAFTSMAN CONFESSING HIS LOVE TO HER.

HOWEVER, THIS WAS NOTHING MORE THAN THE START OF...

...SOME-THING TRULY TER-RIFYING.

EVERYONE LOVED YOUR "BLOSSOM IN THE MOONLIGHT" IN LAST MONTH'S EDITION, TOO. IT WAS SECOND IN THE READER SURVEY.

GOOD-NESS. SECOND!

OH MY, I DOUBT THAT, MR. KAWA-GUCHI.

YOU'RE EVEN MORE ACTIVE THAN YOUR HUSBAND, AND HE'S A GOVERNMENT OFFICIAL.

THANK YOU AGAIN FOR THE MANUSCRIPT. YOU HAVE REALLY BROUGHT THE READERS TO OUR MAGAZINE *BITTER MEDICINE*, MRS. TOGAWA!

I WAS SURPRISED AS WELL. A NO-NAME NEWBIE JUMPING STRAIGHT TO NUMBER ONE!

INDEED. THE VERY MANUSCRIPT THAT WAS SENT TO YOU.

"THE HUMAN CHAIR"... THE STORY I SHOWED YOU?

"THE HUMAN CHAIR"?!

NO. NUMBER ONE WAS "THE HUMAN CHAIR."

WHO WAS NUMBER ONE THEN? MR. AOYAMA, I SUPPOSE.

51

THE AUTHOR IS JUST AWFUL, HOWEVER.

YES. THAT STORY ALSO STUNNED ME.

SUCH A BIZARRE IDEA, A MAN CLIMBING INTO A CHAIR.

BUT IT CERTAINLY IS A DISTINCTIVE WORK.

...IT APPEARS TO BE WRONG.

OH, THAT REMINDS ME! THE AUTHOR'S ADDRESS ON THAT LETTER...

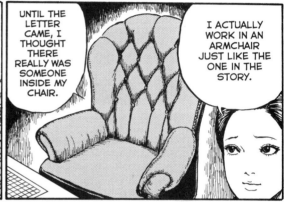

UNTIL THE LETTER CAME, I THOUGHT THERE REALLY WAS SOMEONE INSIDE MY CHAIR.

I ACTUALLY WORK IN AN ARMCHAIR JUST LIKE THE ONE IN THE STORY.

NO, NOT A WORD.

HAVE YOU HEARD FROM THE AUTHOR SINCE, MRS. TOGAWA?

THERE'S NO HOUSE AT THAT ADDRESS. SO WE STILL HAVEN'T BEEN ABLE TO GET IN TOUCH WITH THE AUTHOR. WE'RE AT WIT'S END.

LETTERS AND TELEGRAMS KEPT BEING SENT BACK, SO I WENT THERE MYSELF.

I WONDER WHAT COULD HAVE HAPPENED.

GOODNESS...

BUT WHERE DID YOU BUY THAT ARMCHAIR?

DARLING, I KNOW THIS IS A SUDDEN QUESTION.

OH... NO, IT'S NOTHING.

YOSHIKO? WHY DO YOU ASK?

...AT AN AUCTION?

WHAT? A FURNITURE SHOP...

HM? THIS? I GOT IT AT AN AUCTION AT A FURNITURE SHOP IN THE CITY OF Y.

YES, JUST A COINCIDENCE.

JUST AN UNPLEASANT COINCIDENCE.

THAT NIGHT.

54

KRIK KRIK KRIK

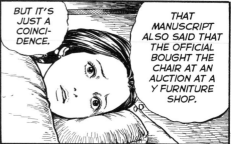

BUT IT'S JUST A COINCIDENCE.

THAT MANUSCRIPT ALSO SAID THAT THE OFFICIAL BOUGHT THE CHAIR AT AN AUCTION AT A Y FURNITURE SHOP.

...AT THIS HOUR?

KRIK

WHO COULD THAT BE...

PLAP PLAP

KRIK PLAP PLAP
KRIK KRIK

...MM.

KRIK KRIK

IT'S NOT. THE SERVANTS DON'T WALK LIKE THAT.

JUST A SERVANT?

MWAH, MYAH... WHAT?

SOMEONE'S WALKING AROUND THE HOUSE.

DARLING... DARLING, WAKE UP.

THAT... SOUNDED LIKE SOMEONE GOING INTO STUDY IN THE WEST WING.

FLAP FLAP FLAP FLAP

SLAM

KREEEE

A BUR-GLAR?

KRIK KRIK KRIK

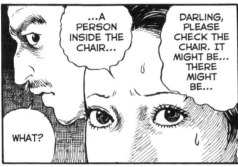

...A PERSON INSIDE THE CHAIR...

DARLING, PLEASE CHECK THE CHAIR. IT MIGHT BE... THERE MIGHT BE...

WHAT?

WHAT'S WRONG, YOSHIKO?

IT CAN'T BE.

IT CAN'T BE...

WATCH. I'LL CATCH HIM.

RUBBISH. THAT'S A BURGLAR DIGGING AROUND IN THE STUDY.

...I JUST FEEL LIKE THE MAN REALLY IS INSIDE THAT CHAIR.

AND NIGHT AFTER NIGHT, HE CLIMBS OUT...

REMEMBER? THAT MANUSCRIPT I GOT? "THE HUMAN CHAIR"... I THOUGHT IT WAS FICTION, BUT...

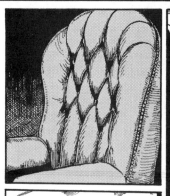

HEY!!

WHO'S IN HERE?!

AAAAH
!!

IT'S WRITHING!!

THE CHAIR... THE CHAIR'S MOVING!

YOSHIKO! WHAT'S WRONG?!

IT WAS... IT WAS REALLY WRITHING! A PERSON HAS CLIMBED INSIDE THE CHAIR!

IT IS *NOT* MOVING!

MASTER! MADAME!

WHAT ?!

WHAT'S GOING ON?!

PLEASE LOOK INSIDE THE CHAIR!

HURRY!

W-WHAT...?

59

WATCH!

IF YOU'RE SO WORRIED, I'LL JUST DO THIS.

DON'T BE RIDICULOUS! THIS CHAIR WAS EXPENSIVE!

IT'S CLEVERLY HIDDEN! PEEL OFF THE LEATHER AND LOOK!

MADAME, I CAN'T FIND ANYTHING RESEMBLING AN ENTRANCE ANYWHERE.

WHAP

WHAP

WHAP

WHAP

...

NO MATTER HOW I BEAT IT, IT DOESN'T SO MUCH AS TWITCH. THERE'S NO ONE INSIDE.

SO, YOSHI-KO?

HAAH.

WHAP

WHAP

THANK YOU.

MADAME, HERE IS THIS MORNING'S POST.

HAVE A SAFE TRIP, SIR.

A FEW DAYS LATER.

THIS HAND-WRITING...

Toshima-ku, Ikebukuro 3-chome Mrs. Yoshiko Togawa

AH!

Toshima-ku, Ikebukuro 3-chome Mrs. Yoshiko Togawa

Additionally, can you begin to understand, madame, how great was my suffering on a certain night when I received such poor treatment?

You haven't been sitting in my chair recently. I wonder if you have any idea how terribly sad this makes me.

RRRIP

61

I know that your work as a writer is more important to you than your husband. And also that the chair that I am is indispensible to your creation...

Madame, your husband is a terrible man. No, I say this not because he beat me. But rather, your husband is jealous of your work.

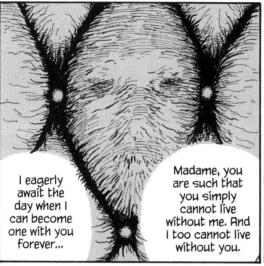

I eagerly await the day when I can become one with you forever...

Madame, you are such that you simply cannot live without me. And I too cannot live without you.

Otherwise, you cannot make full use of your true creative power. I know this as well.

You must sink down deep into me and be held gently by my body.

WHO DO YOU THINK I AM?!

RIDICULOUS. THE IDEA THAT I CAN'T WRITE WITHOUT THAT CHAIR...

CRUMPLE

62

WELCOME HOME, SIR.

DIDN'T WE AGREE YOU WOULD WRITE YOUR NOVELS IN THE STUDY DURING THE DAY WHEN I'M NOT HOME?

I'M SORRY. I'M STUCK ON THE NEXT INSTALLMENT OF MY SERIES. I JUST...

AHH...

YOSHIKO! WHY DIDN'T YOU COME OUT TO GREET ME?!

I REALLY AM SORRY.

OH, PLEASE...

YOU CAN STOP RIGHT NOW WITH BLAMING THE CHAIR IF YOU'RE UNABLE TO WRITE!

STOP MAKING EXCUSES ABOUT HOW THE CHAIR IS CREEPY.

I WAS WRONG. I'M JUST A LITTLE UPSET BECAUSE WRITING'S BEEN A STRUGGLE LATELY.

PLEASE ...

DARLING?

THUD

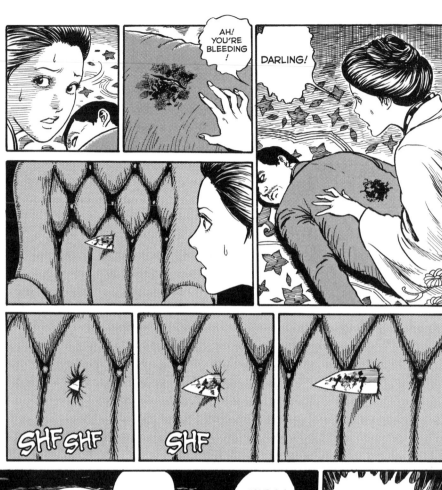

AH! YOU'RE BLEEDING!

DARLING!

SHF SHF SHF SHF

THE HIGH-RANKING OFFICIAL MR. TOGAWA'S BEEN MURDERED.

A MURDER, APPARENTLY.

WHAT ON EARTH'S HAPPENED?

CHATTER CHATTER CHATTER CHATTER CHATTER

AAAAAAAAH!!

66

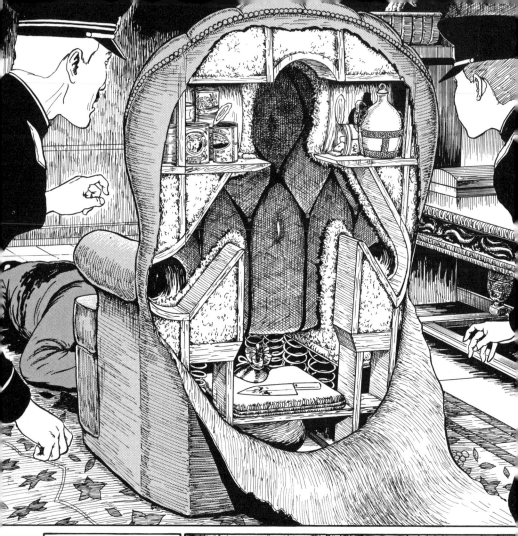

EEEAAAAH!

67

...TO THE WRITER YOSHIKO TOGAWA AFTER THAT?

SO THEN... WHAT HAPPENED...

AND INDEED, INSIDE THE CHAIR...

...WERE SIGNS OF A PERSON LIVING THERE.

HOWEVER, HER STRUGGLE TO WRITE ONLY GREW WORSE, UNTIL YOU COULD SAY SHE DEVELOPED A MENTAL ILLNESS.

THAT IS TO SAY, THEY DIDN'T BELIEVE IN THE HUMAN CHAIR.

THE POLICE ACCEPTED HER STATEMENT, BUT THE MEDIA SUSPECTED SHE HAD KILLED HER HUSBAND.

...HAVE BEEN AN ESSENTIAL PART OF HER CREATIVE PROCESS.

IN THE END... THAT CHAIR MIGHT REALLY...

EVENTUALLY, YOSHIKO TOGAWA WENT MISSING.

THEY SAY SHE WAS NEVER SEEN AGAIN AFTER THAT.

68

THIS? NO, THIS IS NOT THAT CHAIR.

THAT CHAIR WAS SEIZED BY THE POLICE, AND ITS WHEREABOUTS ARE NOW UNKNOWN.

...THE SAME ONE.

SO THEN... THIS CHAIR CAN'T POSSIBLY BE...

AH?!

RRK

TUG

PLEASE TAKE A LOOK.

BUT THIS CHAIR IS RELATED TO THIS STORY.

HAAH.

RRK

RRK

RRK

I ONLY SHOW THIS...

...TO PEOPLE I REALLY LIKE.

PLEASE HAVE A LOOK.

NOW.

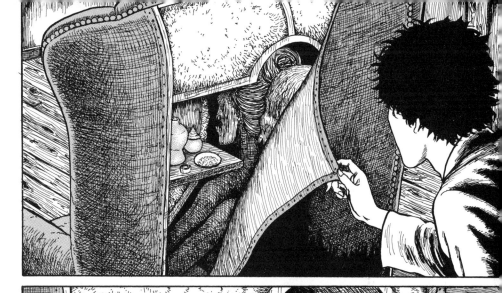

AAAAAH!

AFTER YOSHIKO'S DISAPPEARANCE, THEY LIVED AS A COUPLE IN THIS CHAIR UNTIL THE NATURAL END OF HER DAYS. I SUPPOSE IT WAS A STRANGE, SOMEWHAT BIZARRE MARRIED LIFE.

THE MAN'S FEELINGS WERE RECIP-ROCATED. AND SHE GAINED ETERNAL COMFORT.

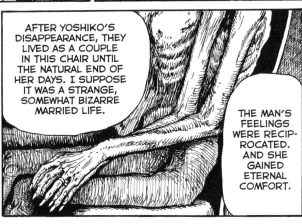

THIS IS THE FATE OF YOSHIKO TOGAWA... AND THE MAN WHO LOVED HER SO DEEPLY.

NO WAY.

...

WOULD YOU BELIEVE ME IF I SAID THAT *I* AM ONE OF THOSE DESCENDANTS?

MISS...

THIS CHAIR HAS BEEN CAREFULLY PRESERVED BY THE GENERATIONS OF THEIR DESCENDANTS.

OF COURSE, DURING THAT TIME, THEY WERE ALSO BLESSED WITH CHILDREN.

I LOVE YOUR WORK. I'VE READ IT ALL.

I REALIZED IT THE MOMENT WE MET.

WHAT?!

...YOU'RE THE WRITER YUZUHO HAYAMA, AREN'T YOU?

EXCUSE ME FOR ASKING, BUT...

YES... I GUARAN-TEE IT.

I'LL MAKE A CHAIR FOR YOU. YOU'LL DEFINITELY BE ABLE TO PULL OUT OF IT.

IS IT TRUE YOU HAVE WRITER'S BLOCK?

BUT I HEARD YOU'VE BEEN HAVING SOME TROUBLE LATELY.

THAT'S FINE... I...

N-NO...

PLEASE EXCUSE ME!

THE WRITER YOSHIKO TOGAWA REALLY EXISTED, AND THERE WERE ARTICLES ABOUT THE HUMAN CHAIR INCIDENT.

Yoshiko Togawa

Human Chair Murder

BUT I DID LOOK IT UP AND FOUND THAT THE FACTS CHECKED OUT ON THE STORY THE CRAFTSMAN TOLD ME.

...IT ALL A DREAM ...?

WAS ...

I'M TIRED OF RUNNING AND HIDING FROM MY EDITOR.

I CAN'T WRITE AT ALL.

IF WE COULD JUST GET YOUR SIGNA- TURE.

IT'S HEAVY, SO WE'LL BRING IT RIGHT INSIDE!

WE'VE GOT A DELIVERY !

HELLO !

MAYBE... THIS IS REALLY THE END.

DING DONG

AN UNEARTHLY LOVE
ORIGINAL STORY BY EDOGAWA RANPO

Edogawa Ranpo

1894—1965. Born in Nabari, Mie Prefecture, Japan he went on to graduate from the economics department of Waseda University. His real name was Taro Hirai. He took his pen name from the 19th century American writer Edgar Allan Poe. He published "The Two-Sen Copper Coin" in *Shin Seinen* in 1923, and created the foundations for the mystery genre in Japan. His most famous works include "The Human Chair," *Beast in the Shadows*, *The Golden Mask*, and the essay collection *The Phantom Castle*.

76

THEY WERE A FAMILY OF SOME RENOWN, SO I KNEW HIS FACE AT LEAST.

BUT I'D HEARD KADONO WAS RUMORED TO BE QUITE MOODY AND A HATER OF WOMEN.

I DO WONDER WHAT TWIST OF FATE LED TO ME MARRYING INTO THE KADONO HOUSE.

FWP

GLANCE

HE RATHER SEEMS MORE LIKE HE'D HAVE A BEAUTIFUL LOVER SECRETED AWAY...

SUCH A HANDSOME MAN AS THIS HATES WOMEN? HE COULDN'T POSSIBLY.

IN FACT, HE WAS KINDER THAN THE AVERAGE MAN AND HE TREATED ME RATHER GENTLY.

THEY SAY THAT IT IS WORSE TO WORRY THAN TO ACT. KADONO WAS NOT SO STRANGE A MAN AS RUMOR HAD IT.

DARLING KYOKO...

KYOKO ...

KYOKO.

KYOKO ...

OH, DARLING, I'M SO HAPPY.

I LOVE YOU. I TRULY DO...

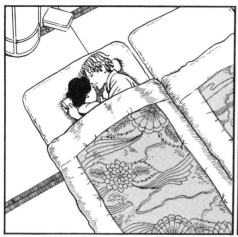

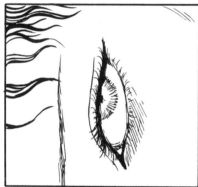

I WAS THINKING ABOUT HOW I CHERISH YOU.

KYOKO... ABOUT YOU.

WHAT ARE YOU THINKING ABOUT?

OH, YOU...

YOU'RE AWAKE?

DARLING
...

AH!

ARE YOU LISTENING TO ME?!

WHAT'S WRONG?

DARLING?

...

KYOKO?

I LOVE YOU.

83

SNAP

KLAKKA KLAKKA

...WHERE'S THE WOMAN?

KREEE

BUT I COULDN'T FIND SO MUCH AS A HOLE THROUGH WHICH A SINGLE MOUSE COULD ESCAPE.

I LOOKED IN EVERY NOOK AND CRANNY ON THE SECOND FLOOR.

WHERE IS SHE?

...

FROM THEN ON, I SLIPPED INTO THE STOREHOUSE IN THE MIDDLE OF THE NIGHT ANY NUMBER OF TIMES.

AND THE WHISPERED INTIMACIES OF MY HUSBAND AND HIS LOVER FILLED MY HEART WITH SUCH DESPAIR.

BUT I NEVER CAUGHT SO MUCH AS A GLIMPSE.

I TOOK ALL KINDS OF PAINS TO TRY AND SEE THE WOMAN.

DARLING...

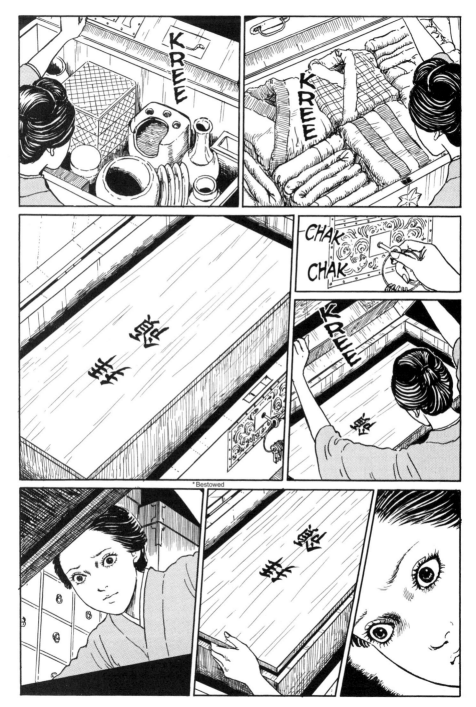

* Bestowed

IN THAT INSTANT, MY SUSPICIONS OF THE PREVIOUS DAYS WERE COMPLETELY UNDONE.

COULD SUCH A THING AS THIS BE CALLED A FLASH OF INSPIRATION?

...

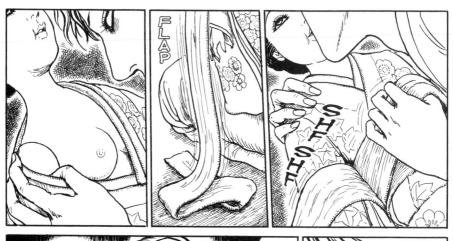

AAAH
...

I
LOVE
YOU...

I
TRULY
LOVE
YOU.

I
LOVE
YOU.

I WAITED AND WAITED, BUT MY HUSBAND DID NOT RETURN.

HOW LONG DID I SIT THERE THAT NIGHT?

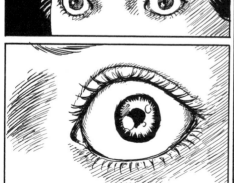

FLASH

AH!

FIZZLE

AH?!

IT DISAP-PEARED!

TOO BAD... I DIDN'T GET A PICTURE.

WHAT ARE YOU DOING THERE?

IF IT ISN'T IWATA!

...OH?

MY PRAYERS WERE ANSWERED.

BUT THAT'S THE FIRST ONE IN A WHILE.

HANG ON! I'LL COME DOWN.

YOU ALL SAW THE UFO, RIGHT?!

...

AND... KURATA! INOUE!

I'M HERE!

FWSH

...

MARIKO...

UH... UM.

UFOS COME FROM ANOTHER DIMENSION! I JUST KNOW IT! MAYBE MY PRAYERS WERE ANSWERED?!

HEY! YOU SAW THE UFO DISAPPEAR, RIGHT?

HUH? DID YOU MAYBE NOT SEE THE UFO?

BUT YOU'RE MEMBERS OF THE NANZAN UFO RESEARCH SOCIETY!

OH... SORRY.

HEY, IWATA, WHAT ARE YOU LOOKING AT? WHEN YOU'RE TALKING TO SOMEONE, YOU SHOULD LOOK AT THEM, YOU KNOW.

WHAT'S WRONG? YOU DON'T LOOK EXCITED AT ALL.

BYE!

I'LL SEE YOU GUYS AT THE NEXT MEETING.

OKAY.

WELL, WHATEVER. I HAVE TO GO PUT TOGETHER A WITNESS REPORT.

...

THEY COULDN'T SEE HER, EITHER...

GLANCE

I WONDER WHEN IT STARTED. WHEN DID MARIKO SHONO START DISAPPEARING FROM VIEW?

I CAN SEE HER FROM A DISTANCE, BUT SHE VANISHES THE INSTANT SHE GETS UP CLOSE.

BECAUSE WE LOVE HER TOO MUCH?

WHY, THOUGH?

EVERYONE EXCEPT ME AND A FEW MEN...

WEIRDLY, IT SEEMS LIKE OTHER PEOPLE CAN ACTUALLY SEE HER.

I CAN'T EVEN SEE THE PERSON I LOVE THE MOST UP CLOSE!

AAH, IT'S TOO CRUEL.

First Nanzan Municipal UFO Symposium

I FIRST SAW MARIKO AT A UFO SYMPOSIUM HELD BY THE CITY.

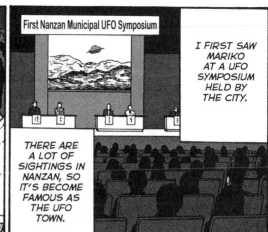

MARIKO SHONO WAS THERE WITH HER FATHER.

THERE ARE A LOT OF SIGHTINGS IN NANZAN, SO IT'S BECOME FAMOUS AS THE UFO TOWN.

COME JOIN THE NANZAN UFO RESEARCH SOCIETY!

...AND I SIGNED UP.

SOON AFTER CAME THE LAUNCH OF WHAT WOULD BECOME THE NANZAN UFO RESEARCH SOCIETY...

SHE STOLE MY HEART AT FIRST GLANCE.

SHE WAS STUNNING, WITH THIS AURA ABOUT HER.

NANZAN UFO RESEARCH SOCIETY LAUNCH PARTY

THE FOUNDER OF THE GROUP WAS NONE OTHER THAN ASAO SHONO— MARIKO'S FATHER!

A DOCTOR BY TRADE, HE WAS AN UNPARALLELED UFO OBSESSIVE, BUT HIS DAUGHTER MARIKO MANAGED TO HOLD HER OWN AGAINST HIM.

NOW THAT I THINK ABOUT IT, I WAS STILL ABLE TO SEE HER UP CLOSE BACK THEN.

DESPITE BEING OUR YOUNGEST MEMBER, SHE SPOKE MORE PASSIONATELY THAN ANYONE ELSE ABOUT UFOS.

THE MEETINGS WERE ALWAYS AT THE SHONO HOUSE.

OFTEN, MARIKO WOULD BE THE LEADER OF THE DISCUSSION, IN PLACE OF HER BUSY FATHER.

SHE WAS REMINISCENT OF THE BEAUTIFUL VENUSIAN THAT THE FAMOUS UFOLIGIST GEORGE ADAMSKI MET.

SEEING HER UP CLOSE... SURE!

...AND GET DRUNK ON THE DELICIOUS WINE SERVED AT THE SHONO HOUSE.

I'D LISTEN EAGERLY TO HER ENTHUSIASTIC TALK ABOUT UFOS...

THE MEN WOULD BE EVEN FURTHER INTOXICATED BY MARIKO'S BEAUTY.

AND IT LOOKED LIKE THE OTHER MEN ALSO FELL PREY TO THE SAME SYMPTOMS AROUND THE SAME TIME.

IT WAS AROUND THAT TIME THAT MARIKO STARTED TO DISAPPEAR FROM VIEW.

ALL RIGHT, I'D LIKE TO GET STARTED.

HA HA HA HA

IT'S A REAL SURPRISE HOW INCREDIBLY BEAUTIFUL CHAIRPERSON MARIKO IS, THOUGH.

HI, I'M SANO. I'M A TOTAL UFO FREAK. PLEASED TO MEET YOU!

THIS IS SANO.

BUT FIRST, LET ME INTRODUCE OUR NEWEST MEMBER.

I GUESS HE CAN SEE MARIKO...

CAN I HAVE A SECOND?

MARIKO.

...REPORTING ON THE UFO I WITNESSED THE OTHER DAY!

NOW THEN. I'D LIKE TO START BY...

WHAT IS IT?

YES, KURATA?

ALIEN ABDUCTION. SO YOU MEAN INCIDENTS WHERE ALIENS KIDNAP HUMAN BEINGS.

THERE IS? ALL RIGHT.

THERE'S SOMETHING THAT'S BEEN BOTHERING ME.

I KNOW WE USUALLY DISCUSS UFO SIGHTINGS, BUT CAN WE MAKE ALIEN ABDUCTIONS TONIGHT'S AGENDA?

THE TRUTH IS...

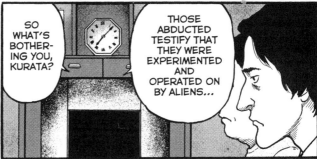

SO WHAT'S BOTHERING YOU, KURATA?

THOSE ABDUCTED TESTIFY THAT THEY WERE EXPERIMENTED AND OPERATED ON BY ALIENS...

WHAT ?!

THERE'S A PERIOD OF THE PAST... THAT I HAVE NO CLEAR MEMORIES OF.

...I MIGHT HAVE BEEN ABDUCTED BY ALIENS.

RIGHT AFTER MY MEMORY OF THE BRIGHT LIGHT!

MY FEELINGS KEPT GETTING STRONGER, AND JUST WHEN I COULDN'T TAKE IT ANYMORE... I STOPPED BEING ABLE TO SEE YOU!

MARIKO, I HAVE TO TELL YOU!

I'M IN LOVE WITH YOU!

PLEASE TAKE A LOOK!

AND I FOUND THIS.

SO I WENT LOOKING FOR PROOF!

I THINK THIS IS THE WORK OF ALIENS.

I FOUND A SMALL SCAR ON THE BACK OF MY HEAD.

!

I DO, TOO!

M-ME, TOO. I CAN'T SEE MARIKO, EITHER.

ME EITHER!

AH! I HAVE A SCAR, TOO?!

ME, TOO!

ALIENS EXPERIMENTED ON ME!

THIS IS PROOF OF AN ALIEN ABDUCTION.

BUT WHY?! WHY YOU OF ALL THINGS?!

THE RESULT OF THAT EXPERIMENT IS THAT I CAN'T SEE YOU ANYMORE.

AT LEAST HOLD MY HAND!

I-IT'S TOO MUCH. HELP ME, MARIKO... AT LEAST!

NO!!

AND YOU CAN'T SUDDENLY GO TELLING ME YOU LOVE ME!

W-WAIT. I DON'T UNDERSTAND AT ALL.

THAT'S ENOUGH!!

YOU DISGUSTING WORMS!

DON'T YOU EVER COME NEAR MY DAUGHTER AGAIN!

ALL OF YOU, GET OUT OF HERE NOW!!

AS OF TODAY, THE NANZAN UFO RESEARCH SOCIETY IS DISBANDED!

!

SOB SOB...

UNH...

UNH...

SOB SOB...

THANK YOU.

COME ON. HAVE ANOTHER GLASS.

SANO... WAS IT?

TONIGHT WAS A GOOD LESSON FOR YOU.

STOP CRYING ALREADY, MARIKO.

SOB SOB...

I'LL BE HER BODY-GUARD.

NO, NO. I WON'T STOP THERE.

YES, YOU DID A FINE JOB THERE.

I JUST FIGURED I HAD TO PROTECT MARIKO.

I HONESTLY DIDN'T KNOW WHAT WAS GOING ON.

SNRR SNRR

126

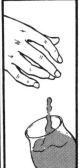

...SH'RILLY IS...

BUT MARIKO REALLY IS A BEAUTY...

SORRY TO BOTHER YOU AT NIGHT AGAIN. COME OVER RIGHT AWAY.

NISHI-MURA?

ZZZ

ZZZ

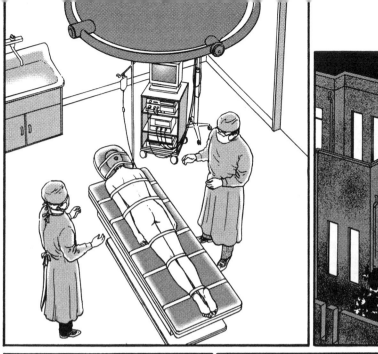

THEN MAKE A HOLE WITH A FINE DRILL RIGHT UP TO THE EDGE THERE.

FIRST, WE MAKE A SMALL INCISION IN THE BACK OF THE HEAD TO EXPOSE THE SKULL.

VWEEEN

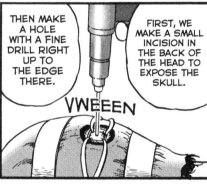

HOW MANY DOES THIS MAKE, I WONDER.

NOW THEN, WE'LL BEGIN THE SURGERY.

WE MUST FINISH THE OPERATION QUICKLY TO MINIMIZE THE PHYSICAL TRAUMA.

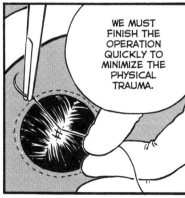

FINALLY, WE STICH THE SKIN BACK TOGETHER AND WE'RE DONE.

WE INSERT A SPECIAL MICRO CAPSULE AND THEN FILL THE HOLE WITH ADHESIVE.

128

WHEN THE MICRO CAPSULE IN THE SKULL RECEIVES THIS SIGNAL, IT AFFECTS THE VISUAL CORTEX IN THE OCCIPITAL LOBE.

...WE PUT A DEVICE THAT EMITS A PARTICULAR SIGNAL.

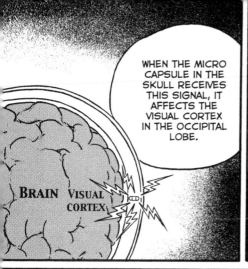

BRAIN

VISUAL CORTEX

MEANWHILE, IN THOSE EARRINGS THAT MARIKO NEVER FAILS TO WEAR, A KEEPSAKE FROM MY WIFE...

IN OTHER WORDS, IT'S ONLY MARIKO THEY CAN'T SEE.

REGARDLESS OF THE FACT THAT THE IMAGE IS PICKED UP BY THE EYES, THE BRAIN BECOMES UNABLE TO RECOGNIZE IT.

THE PERSON WEARING THE EARRINGS VANISHES WHEN THEY ENTER THAT BLIND SPOT.

THIS CAUSES A BLIND SPOT IN THE FIELD OF VIEW.

NOW, ONCE THE OPERATION IS OVER, WE ERASE THEIR MEMORIES OF THE LAST FEW DAYS WITH A SPECIAL DRUG AND AN ELECTRIC SHOCK, AND IT'S DONE.

I DEVELOPED THIS TECHNIQUE FROM MY HOBBY OF STUDYING UFOS.

BUT DOCTOR, THAT METHOD OF WIPING MEMORIES IS A FAIRLY DIFFICULT TECHNIQUE.

I DON'T BELIEVE UFOS ACTUALLY EXIST, BUT RATHER THAT THEY ARE A PRODUCT OF THE HUMAN BRAIN.

...AND I GOT A BAD FEELING, SO I RAN OVER TO THE SHONO HOUSE.

I HEARD THAT MARIKO'S FATHER, DR. ASAO SHONO, WAS BEING QUESTIONED BY THE POLICE THAT DAY...

THE GATE'S OPEN!

HAAH

HAAH

KSH KSH

AH?!

THE HOUSE-KEEPER!

NNGH
...

THIS WOMAN'S NOT HUMAN... SHE'S AN ALIEN! SHE'S A VENUSIAN WHO CAN MAKE HERSELF DISAPPEAR TO CONFUSE US!

WE CAUGHT MARIKO! SHE'S OURS!

STAY BACK, IWATA!

WHAT ARE YOU DOING?!

134

FROM TIME TO TIME, IT WOULD APPEAR LIKE A KALEIDOSCOPE, FILLING MY FIELD OF VIEW.

THEY APPEAR NOW AS AFTER-IMAGES.

EVEN THOUGH MY BRAIN HADN'T BEEN ABLE TO RECOGNIZE THEM, CLOSE-UPS OF MARIKO WERE BURNED INTO MY RETINAS.

THE NIGHT WAS...

...A LITTLE WARM, THE AIR HUMID.

HYOOO

HYOOO

HM?

THE BREEZE FEELS GROSS...

...

AAAH?!

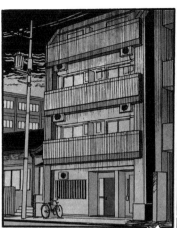

COME ON IN.

OKAY! I'M COOOOM-ING!

DING DONG

THAT HAS TO BE TSUYOSHI, PYON!

PANT PANT PANT

DING DONG

HUH? WHAT?!

...THIS WEIRD WOMAN LICKED MY FACE AND MY HAND.

YEAH... MIKU, IT'S NUTS. ON MY WAY HERE...

BARK BARK BARK

TSUYOSHI, WHAT'S WRONG? YOU'RE REALLY PALE.

141

CHAK

I'LL TURN THE LIGHT ON.

...IT STINGS. I CAN'T SLEEP...

WHAT'S THE MATTER, TSUYO-SHI?

AAH, SOME-THING'S WEIRD...

!

PYON ?!

FROTH FROTH

WHAT'S WRONG?!

TSUYO-SHI!!

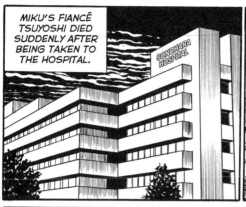

MIKU'S FIANCÉ TSUYOSHI DIED SUDDENLY AFTER BEING TAKEN TO THE HOSPITAL.

SONOHARA HOSPITAL

PLEASE! YOU HAVE TO CATCH HER!

PYON LICKED THAT WOMAN'S SALIVA.

THAT HAS TO BE WHY!

HE SAID A STRANGE WOMAN LICKED HIM.

...THE NIGHT WAS ONCE AGAIN WARM AND HUMID.

A FEW DAYS LATER...

TSUMURA SHOP

THEY'RE STILL INVESTIGATING, BUT WE KNOW IT'S AN ANIMAL POISON.

THEY DID FIND POISON IN THE BLOOD OF THE MAN AND THE DOG.

...

AROUND MIDNIGHT, A MAN IN THE CITY OF X WAS TAKEN TO HOSPITAL, COMPLAINING OF A SKIN ABNORMALITY. HE DIED EARLY THIS MORNING.

THE CAUSE OF DEATH IS THOUGHT TO BE POISON, AND THERE HAVE BEEN A SPATE OF SIMILAR INCIDENTS IN THIS AREA RECENTLY. THE VICTIMS ALL TESTIFY THAT A PASSING WOMAN ON THE STREET LICKED THEM, SO POLICE ARE...

OR MAYBE SHE WEARS A FILM COATED WITH POISON OVER HER TONGUE?

NO SUCH MONSTER EXISTS! MAYBE SHE WAS JUST BORN DIFFERENT?!

CAREFUL IF YOU'RE OUT AT NIGHT!

I GUESS THE WOMAN'S TONGUE IS POISONOUS!

WE HAVE TO FORM A WATCH GROUP AND CATCH THIS CRIMINAL!

BUT YOU'RE OKAY IF YOU GET LICKED AS LONG AS YOU WASH IT OFF RIGHT AWAY.

WHO ON EARTH IS SHE?!

SHE CAN'T BE HUMAN...

A MONSTER?!

TRUDGE TRUDGE TRUDGE TRUDGE TRUDGE

THAT'S WHY WE HAVE THE WATER. WE CAN WASH IT OFF RIGHT AWAY.

I DON'T WANT TO GET LICKED WHEN WE CATCH HER.

WHAT'S THIS LICKING WOMAN LOOK LIKE ANYWAY?

HURRY!

THAT WAS A WOMAN'S VOICE!

...ON WARM, HUMID NIGHTS LIKE THIS, WITH THE WIND BLOWING.

I HEARD THE LICKING WOMAN SHOWS UP A LOT...

AAAH!

147

148

...

TWIRL

EEEE!!

Y-YOU KILLED TSUYOSHI AND PYON... YOU'RE NOT GETTING AWAY WITH IT!

149

150

151

THERE'S NOTHING VISIBLE, BUT I FEEL LIKE I'LL LOSE MY MIND AT HOW IT ITCHES.

...EVEN STILL, MY SKIN FEELS WEIRD.

I WASHED OFF WITH WATER IMMEDIATELY, BUT...

NO, IT CAN'T BE... THAT WOMAN'S TONGUE WAS DEFINITELY POISONOUS.

...SO SHE WAS SENT TO A PSYCHIATRIC HOSPITAL, AND THAT WAS THE END OF THE INCIDENT.

...AND THE POLICE WERE UNABLE TO FIND ANY POISON THAT WOULD PROVE SHE WAS A MURDERER...

EVENTUALLY, THE PSYCHIATRIC EXAMINATION FOUND THE WOMAN TO BE UNSTABLE...

SHE SUFFERED EVEN AFTER HER SKIN HAD HEALED.

NATURALLY, MIKU WAS NO EXCEPTION.

HOWEVER, HER VICTIMS REMAINED PARALYZED WITH TERROR.

SOME PANICKED AT A DOG LICKING THEM, WHILE OTHERS COULD NO LONGER EVEN KISS THEIR PARTNERS.

AND THEN, SEVERAL YEARS LATER...

I... MY NAME'S NAGAOKA. NICE TO MEET YOU.

YOU JUST SEEMED LIKE ME SOMEHOW... SO YOU REALLY ARE, HUH?

WHAT? YOU ARE, TOO?

WHAT A COINCIDENCE. SO YOU'RE A VICTIM OF THE LICKING WOMAN, TOO?

COMPARED WITH THAT HATRED, THE FEAR IS NOTHING...

SHE MURDERED MY FIANCÉ AND MY DOG. THE HATRED I FEEL FOR THAT WOMAN WILL NEVER GO AWAY.

BUT LATELY, I'VE BEEN OKAY WHEN A DOG LICKS ME.

I GUESS A LOT OF US ARE STILL RECOVERING.

STUFF ABOUT HOW HER SYMPTOMS GOT BETTER AFTER HER TREATMENT.

IT WAS IN ONE OF THE WEEKLIES.

WHAT?!

WHAT'S... SO THE THING IS... DID YOU KNOW SHE GOT OUT OF THE HOSPITAL RECENTLY?

IF THEY SET HER FREE, SHE'LL ONLY DO THE SAME THING AGAIN.

SHE MUST HAVE POSED AS A REGULAR PERSON WHEN SHE WAS ARRESTED.

THAT WOMAN'S NOT HUMAN.

THAT'S RIDICULOUS.

WHAT?!

THE MAGAZINE SAID THAT AFTER SHE WAS DISCHARGED, THEY LOST TRACK OF HER, SO THE POLICE WERE FREAKING.

TRUE...

...I'LL KILL HER!

IF IT DOES HAPPEN AGAIN...

THE LICKING WOMAN POPPING UP IN PLACES...

MAYBE IT'LL REALLY HAPPEN ALL OVER AGAIN.

154

155

157

159

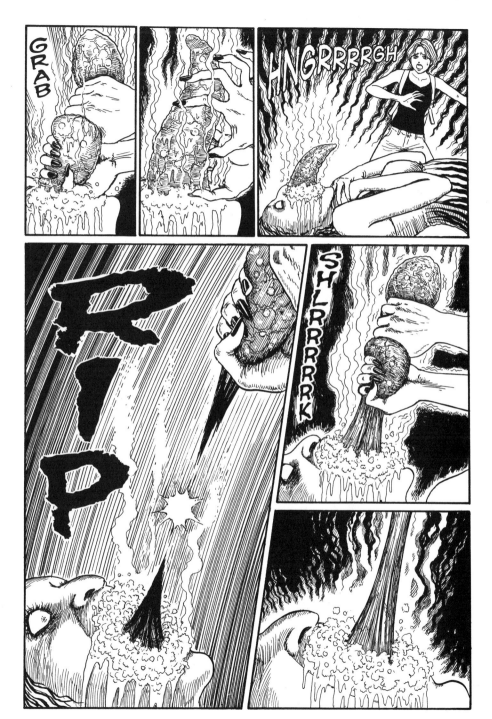

160

HAAH.

HAAH.

HAAH, HAAH.

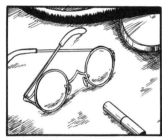

THIS WOMAN... SHE REALLY ISN'T HUMAN...

TO JUST RIP YOUR OWN TONGUE OUT LIKE THAT...

...

HAAH HAAH

!

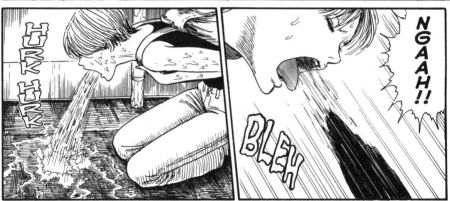

AAAAH!

...BOUNCED AROUND IN THE MOST DISTURBING WAY.

EVEN AFTER THAT, THE TONGUE COATED IN CYANIDE...

OMOTO

SPROING

THE POLICE ARE INVESTIGATING WHETHER THIS WAS HOMICIDE OR SUICIDE.

SHAKE SHAKE

THE CAUSE OF DEATH IS THOUGHT TO BE CYANIDE POISONING.

WE'RE HERE WITH YOUR FIRST NEWS OF THE DAY. AFTER MAKING THE RESIDENTS OF THE CITY OF X LIVE IN FEAR...

...THE LICKING WOMAN WAS FOUND DEAD ON THE ROAD LAST NIGHT.

THAT TONGUE... WHAT HAPPENED TO IT?

THE NEWS DIDN'T MENTION IT AT ALL.

NAGA-OKA?

OH!

...WAS SHE EXACTLY?

WHO...

MIKU SEARCHED FOR NAGAOKA, BUT THERE WAS NO TRACE OF HER.

SHE COULD FIND NO CLUES TO PROVE NAGAOKA EVER EXISTED.

THE NUMBER YOU HAVE REACHED IS NOT IN SERVICE.

THAT WOULD BASICALLY BE SUICIDE. THERE'S NO WAY!

NO... THAT'S RIDICULOUS?! IF SHE WAS THE LICKING WOMAN, THEN WHY GIVE ME THE CYANIDE?

IT—

IT COULDN'T BE.

I WONDER ...THE GLASSES IN THE LICKING WOMAN'S BAG...

THEY LOOKED A LOT LIKE NAGA-OKA'S.

...AND THE DAYS PASSED.

MIKU CONTINUED TO BE GRIPPED BY A POWERFUL FEAR...

IT ALMOST SEEMED AS IF THIS WAS EXACTLY WHAT THE LICKING WOMAN WANTED.

MIKU'S IMAGINATION AND CHAOTIC MENTAL STATE MAGNIFIED HER TERROR.

ARE YOU NOT GOOD WITH DOGS?

WHAT?

BARK BARK

BARK BARK

EVENTUALLY, THEY FELL IN LOVE.

YUKIO MADE MIKU FORGET HER MISERABLE PAST.

I...I LIKE DOGS...

?!

ME, TOO.

MIKU... I LOVE YOU.

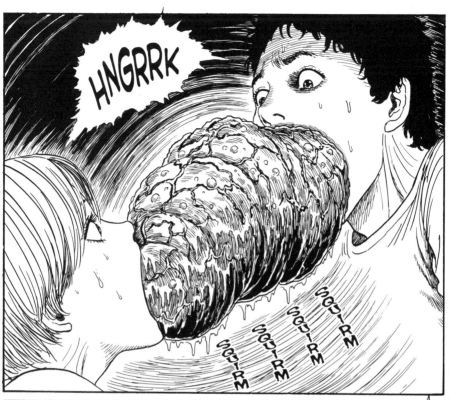

HNGAH

HNGAAH!

MIKU...

M—

HRRK
...

NNGH
...

SPROING

SPROING

WHUD

THE PERSON WHO
FOUND THEM
TESTIFIED THAT
THEY HAD SEEN
A GIANT TONGUE
JUMPING AROUND
BESIDE THE
BODIES, BUT THE
POLICE IGNORED
THIS INFORMATION.

SPROING

SPROING

AFTER THEIR
BODIES WERE
DISCOVERED,
POTASSIUM
CYANIDE WAS
DETECTED
IN THEIR
BLOOD.

168

MASTER UMEZZ AND ME

...Kazuo Umezz's *Sister Mummy.*

One of the books they had was...

Both of them loved scary manga.

I have two older sisters.

Akiko

Yoko

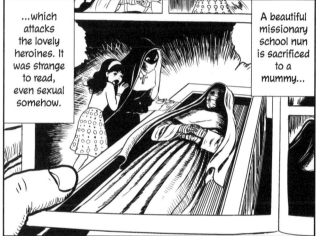

...which attacks the lovely heroines. It was strange to read, even sexual somehow.

A beautiful missionary school nun is sacrificed to a mummy...

I read it and was immediately enthralled.

...the book *The Cursed Mansion* (from *The Baby Girl*).

After that, for my birthday, my kind-hearted sisters got me....

The unsettling figure of Tamami, the basement of the Western building, the guillotine, the helmet and armor...

It all dictated an ideal of gothic horror to me.

I enjoyed the power of the art, but it wasn't until I was a little more grown-up that I understood the depth of the story.

The first volume of *Orochi*.

I decided to go buy a book myself with my allowance at the only bookstore in our small town.

THIS KINDA SHRIMP MONSTER CHOWS DOWN ON KIDS.

WHAT.

WHAT'S IT ABOUT?

JUN, THERE'S THIS AMAZING MANGA BY KAZUO UMEZZ IN *SHONEN SUNDAY*.

One day in grade three or four, my friend Ueda said...

When I finally stood and read *Sunday* at the bookstore, the bit about the shrimp monster had already ended.

I didn't usually read the magazines because I preferred the books, so I went without this manga for a long time.

I still had only seen a tiny part of *The Drifting Classroom*.

W-WHAT IS THIS MANGA ...?

Instead, a battle between students unfolded inside a smoky classroom.

WAAH!

WAAH!

GAAH!

THE AIR'S NO GOOD!

I CAN'T BREATHE!

DAMMIT!

How-ever...

OOH, THANKS.

HERE.

ALREADY NOTHING CUTE ABOUT ME

And the days passed. I finally got the book as a birthday present from my kind-hearted sister in sixth grade.

BUT I DON'T HAVE ENOUGH ALLOW-ANCE!

I WANNA READ IT ALL AT ONCE IN THE BOOK!

UNNNH. I GUESS. MAKES SENSE.

THAT'S ALL THEY HAD. WE LIVE IN THE MIDDLE OF NOWHERE, AFTER ALL.

IT'S THE LAST BOOK!!

TH-THIS IS VOLUME ELEVEN...

It was a long time before I managed to get ahold of all the books. And I was reluctant to say goodbye after I'd read them all, so I drew about ten pages on unlined report paper under the title *The Drifting Classroom volume 12*, but for some reason, it ended up being a total gag manga.

WHO'S THIS OLD GUY?!

I CAN TELL IT'S TOTALLY AMAZING HOW THEY'RE RECON-CILING HERE.

DYNA-MITE?!

THE DRIFTING CLASSROOM VOLUME 12

CHILDREN MUST PLAY CHILDREN'S GAMES!

I started reading *The Drifting Classroom* from the last volume. After being sent to the future, the children were already starving and half out of their minds as they headed like a surging wave towards the emotional big finish!

...was on the TV show *Kohaku Ten Best Songs*!

Incidentally, if my memory's correct, the first time I saw Master Umezz in motion...

It goes without saying that my sisters set a tape recorder in front of the TV and recorded it.

BICHIGUSO ROCK DE ICHI NICHI!!

Makoto-chan was a big hit at the time...

SO EXCITIIIIING!!

THAT'S THE REAL KAZUO UMEZZZZ!

...and Master Umezz gave a passionate rendition of "Bichiguso Rock" in costume as Ranmaru!!

...KYO MO BICHIBICHIIIIII!!

...someone (maybe my kindhearted sisters) brought me volume eight of *Makoto-chan*.

When I got appendicitis and peritonitis at the same time over the summer of ninth grade and I was in the hospital for a month...

Naturally, I loved *Makoto-chan*, too.

It's still a good memory even now.

OWWWWWWWW!!

It made me laugh so hard, even though I had a drain in my stomach.

I greatly admired Kazuo Umezz for not stopping at mere jokes, although I expected nothing less of him.

KAWHAM!

You could simply enjoy *Makoto-chan* as a gag manga, but for me, it was a scathing critique of humanity.

I think it was for chewing gum.

I'd only ever seen the character on a TV commercial when I was little.

By the way, I didn't know that *Cat Eyed Boy* was one of Master Umezz's works until I was in junior high.

The series hadn't been turned into a TV anime back then, so I wondered just who the characters were.

I remember it was animated. The characters later known as Cat Eyed Boy and Tsunami Summoners made an appearance.

DAMMIT!! WHAT AM I GONNA DO?!

WE DON'T GET TOKYO CHANNEL 12 OUT HERE IN THE BOONIES!!

FIRST GRADE DAYS

I think I found out it was Kazuo Umezz's *Cat Eyed Boy* because it was on Tokyo Channel 12 (now TV Tokyo) when I was in junior high.

Kazuo Umezz's Cat Eyed Boy set for TV broadcast!

Gifu TV broadcast a lot of Tokyo Channel 12 programs, and I spent day after day scouring the TV listings.

AAAAAH! I WANT TO WATCH IT! I HAVE TO!! THEY'RE NOT SHOWING IT ON GIFU TV?!

And then one day...

WHEN ARE THEY GOING TO SHOW IT?!

But no matter how much time went by, they didn't broadcast *Cat Eyed Boy*.

WHAAAAT ?!

THEY'RE GONNA SHOW *CAT EYED BOY*!!

JUN! I GOT GOOD NEWS!

My sister was wild with excitement in the living room.

HUH? WHAT?

178

When I was in high school, Asahi Sonorama put out the series *Kazuo Umezz Scary Books.*

They were large hardcover books, and in them I encountered many works I hadn't read before.

This was at the time a popular game in my kindhearted sister's class, apparently.

In the end, it wasn't until I was an adult that I got to watch *Ghost Story: Cat Eyed Boy.*

Discovering so many astounding stories with such a high artistic level like "Grave of the Butterfly" and "Fear"...

...made me realize all over again Master Umezz's genius.

I was meeting with my editor at *Spirits*.

I could never exhaustively list all my memories of Master Umezz's works, but I only have limited pages here, so I will have to jump ahead to more recent times.

WHAAAT?!

WOULD YOU LIKE TO ADAPT THE STORY OF THE FILM INTO A MANGA TO BE RELEASED AS A BOOK WHEN IT COMES OUT?

ITO-SAN, THE TRUTH IS, MASTER UMEZZ IS MAKING A MOVIE.

YOU'RE THE ONLY ONE WHO CAN TURN HIS SCRIPT INTO A MANGA, ITO-SAN!!

THAT'S EXACTLY IT!!

Y-YOU MEAN YOU WANT ME TO ADAPT MASTER UMEZZ'S FILM INTO A MANGA?

UNNH...

...BUT I WANT TO DO IT...

IT WOULD BE AN INCREDIBLE HONOR.

I SAY THAT...

ARE YOU SURE I'M THE RIGHT PERSON?

TH- THIS IS INCREDIBLE.

UNDERSTOOD.

WELL, I'LL SEND YOU THE SCRIPT LATER, SO PLEASE THINK ABOUT IT.

IT WOULD BE TOUGH.

AAH, BUT I'M ALREADY WORKING ON OTHER SERIES BEFORE THE FILM COMES OUT.

RIP

And then the script arrived.

EXPRESS

Mr. Junji Ito

SPIRITS

PROTAGONIST, KAZUO UMEZZ!!

MOTHER...

Mother (working title) Draft No. 4

Main Characters

Kazuo Umezz: Protagonist. Manga artist

Ichie Umezz: Kazuo Umezz's mother

Kimio Umezz: Kazuo Umezz's father

I started imagining what it would be like if it was drawn in picture form.

At the same time, it overturned stereotypes. I was blown away!

It was a frightening and sad story about Master Umezz and his mother.

AND THE KEY TO IT ALL, THE MONSTER... I'D WANT TO MAKE THIS IN THE STYLE OF UMEZZ!

AND THEN HIS MOTHER... RIGHT. I'M SURE I SAW A PICTURE OF MASTER UMEZZ AND HIS MOTHER IN A BOOK SOMEWHERE. I'LL HAVE TO LOOK FOR IT THE NEXT TIME I'M HOME.

...WOULD BE LIKE THIS!

FIRST, THE HERO KAZUO UMEZZ...

GWAEH

And then at last Kazuo Umezz's first work as a director, *Mother,* was complete!! I headed to the screening on June 20.

In the end, I had to abandon the idea of adapting the movie since my own schedule wouldn't allow it.

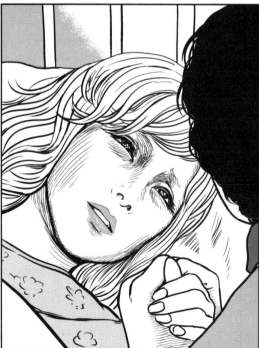

MOTHER.

As a fan, I'm eagerly awaiting new manga work, but I also can't wait to see what Master Kazuo Umezz does now that he's also got the medium of movies to work with!

I ended up visiting the Umezz home after that for this project! I never even dreamed I would have an opportunity like this!

HOW LOVE CAME TO PROFESSOR KIRIDA

BASED ON THE STORY "HOW LOVE
COME TO PROFESSOR GUILDEA"
BY ROBERT HICHENS

MY NAME IS YUZUHO HAYAMA. OCCUPATION: WRITER.

I'VE GOT TERRIBLE WRITER'S BLOCK, THOUGH, SO I'M CURRENTLY HIDING OUT AT MY PARENTS' HOUSE IN THE COUNTRY.

SO MANY OLD BOOKS...

HASN'T CHANGED AT ALL.

HOW MANY YEARS HAS IT BEEN SINCE I WAS IN THE STOREROOM?

THIS BOOK FELL OUT...

Sumiko Hayama
The Diary of a Parrot Woman

KLAK

JUMP

WHO'S THERE?!

190

MOM, THIS SUMIKO HAYAMA PERSON WANTED TO BE A WRITER IN TOKYO.

SUMIKO HAYAMA? NOW WHO'S THAT? ONE OF OUR ANCESTORS MAYBE.

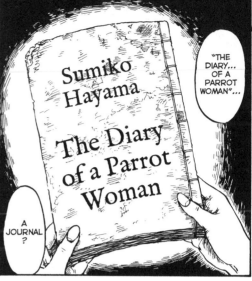

Sumiko Hayama

The Diary of a Parrot Woman

"THE DIARY... OF A PARROT WOMAN"...

A JOURNAL?

WOW... ENGAI KIRIDA? THE SAME ENGAI KIRIDA OF THAT PRIZE YOU WON?

PROFESSOR KIRIDA! THAT'S ENGAI KIRIDA!! THIS WOMAN MET ENGAI KIRIDA! AMAZING!

SHE WROTE ABOUT HAVING "STUDIED UNDER PROFESSOR KIRIDA AT XX UNIVERSITY"!

LOOK!

HMM. SO SHE IS A RELATIVE THEN.

KIRIDA WAS KNOWN TO BE AN EXTREME MISANTHROPE AND REMAINED SINGLE HIS ENTIRE LIFE UNTIL HIS MYSTERIOUS DEATH AT THE AGE OF 57.

SURPRISINGLY, THIS JOURNAL CONTAINED A RECORD OF THE PERIOD LEADING UP TO THAT DEATH. WHAT FOLLOWS ARE EXTRACTS FROM THE ENTRIES PERTAINING TO KIRIDA.

ENGAI KIRIDA.

HE WAS A SCHOLAR OF JAPANESE LITERATURE AND A LITERARY AUTHOR IN THE MEIJI ERA.

HIS LITERARY STYLE WAS AESTHETIC AND REFINED, MAKING HIM A UNIQUE PRESENCE IN THE HISTORY OF LITERATURE.

TOKYO...

THE TIME WAS THE LATE MEIJI ERA.

WELCOME. THE MASTER IS WAITING FOR YOU INSIDE.

APOLOGIES FOR HAVING YOU COME ALL THE WAY HERE. I NEED TO LEARN ABOUT CHRISTIANITY FOR THE NOVEL I'M WRITING.

SO YOU'RE FATHER MURCHISON?

193

194

THE PARROT HAS QUITE THOROUGHLY MEMORIZED THOSE CONVERSATIONS.

EACH TIME, I TELL HER MY HONEST OPINION.

SHE WISHES TO BE A WRITER WITH THE PASSION THAT ONLY *THAT* SORT CAN MUSTER. SHE COMES TO ME WITH THESE TERRIBLE STORIES.

THERE'S THIS DREADFUL WOMAN STUDENT AT MY UNIVERSITY.

I'M HAVING HER WAIT OUTSIDE UNTIL YOU AND I ARE FINISHED.

SHE'S ACTUALLY COME AGAIN FAITHFULLY TODAY.

DID YOU READ THE MANUSCRIPT I BROUGHT YESTERDAY?

PRO-FESSOR!

HOWEVER, THERE'S STILL MORE I WOULD HEAR. WILL YOU COME AGAIN, PERHAPS?

FATHER MURCHISON, YOU TOLD ME MANY THINGS TODAY WHICH WILL BE USEFUL.

YES, GLADLY.

YOUR WRITING IS NOTHING MORE THAN COMMON FIRST-PERSON NARRATIVE!

QUIT THIS NONSENSE AND STOP ROBBING ME OF MY PRECIOUS TIME.

HAYAMA? YOU'RE STILL HERE? ...YES, I READ IT.

WHERE DO YOU LIVE? I SHALL SEE YOU HOME.

MISS HAYAMA, PLEASE CHEER UP.

I WANT TO WRITE BEAUTIFUL, LOFTY NOVELS LIKE HIS.

AND THEN... MORE THAN ANYTHING, I WANT HIM TO APPROVE OF ME!

IT'S TRUE HE'S A MISANTHROPE, AND THERE ARE PLENTY OF PEOPLE WHO HATE HIM. BUT...

I... I RESPECT PROFESSOR KIRIDA FROM THE BOTTOM OF MY HEART.

I TRULY DO LIKE HIM AND THE BEAUTIFUL WORK HE CREATES.

196

NO. TO LOVE IS ONLY NATURAL.

W-WHY THAT'S— I MEAN, IN *LOVE* WITH HIM... A GREAT MAN LIKE THAT. AND HIS AGE...

...WHAT?!

MISS HAYAMA, ARE YOU IN LOVE WITH PROFESSOR KIRIDA?

...HE MIGHT SEE THE BEAUTY OF YOUR WORK.

IF YOU COULD LOVE HIM FROM THE BOTTOM OF YOUR HEART...

HE HAS LIVED THUS FAR WITHOUT BEING LOVED. WE OUGHT TO OFFER HIM OUR SYMPATHY.

I FELT THIS TODAY WHEN I MET WITH PROFESSOR KIRIDA. HE IS IN NEED OF LOVE.

FWOO

ALL RIGHT...

OH. I FELT A GUST OF HOT AIR JUST NOW...

WHAT'S THE MATTER, FATHER?

AH ?!

EARLIER, SHE BROUGHT ME ONE OF THOSE FRANK PSYCHOLOGICAL STORIES THAT ARE SO POPULAR RIGHT NOW.

WHAT ?!

FATHER MURCHISON. IT SEEMS YOU'VE BEEN WHISPERING IN HAYAMA'S EAR?

NATURALLY, I RIPPED IT UP AND TOSSED IT AWAY ON THE SPOT. AND THEN I TOLD HER SHE HAD NO TALENT FOR WRITING AND SHE SHOULD GO BACK TO HER HOMETOWN IMMEDIATELY.

SHE LEFT IN TEARS. I'VE FINALLY GOTTEN RID OF THAT IDIOT.

THANK YOU, FATHER MURCHI-SON.

AND IT WAS ANNOYINGLY A LOVE LETTER TO ME BORROWING THE FORM OF A STORY!

SPLSH

CHATTER CHATTER

CHATTER CHATTER

SPLSH

SUICIDE! IT'S A SUICIDE!

WHAT HAP-PENED ?

WE GOT A DROWNER !

AAH!

...

DEAR LORD...

OHHHH ...

199

IF I HADN'T SAID THAT TO HER...

LORD...

AAAH... WHAT SIN HAVE I COMMITTED...?

PLEASE SAVE SUMIKO HAYAMA.

LEAVE ME!

I-IT'S NOTHING.

NGH...

HNGH...

PROFESSOR? WHAT'S THE MATTER?

I WISHED TO SPEAK WITH THE PROFESSOR.

EXCUSE ME.

FATHER? YOU HAVE AN APPOINTMENT AT THIS HOUR?

201

SOMETHING IS DEFINITELY HERE WITH ME.

I AM OF SOUND MIND!

IT'S NOT... VISIBLE?

YES, THAT'S RIGHT! WHY DO YOU STARE AT ME SO?!

IT SEEKS LOVE FROM ME! EVEN THOUGH I'VE HAD QUITE ENOUGH OF THAT WITH SUMIKO HAYAMA!

IT CLEARLY HAS LUST FOR ME!

IT BREATHES ITS HOT BREATH ON MY NECK...

...IT CARESSES MY BODY!! AAH, SO DISGUSTING!

WHAT?!

...

SHE ATTEMPTED SUICIDE THIS AFTERNOON BY JUMPING IN THE RIVER.

PROFESSOR, ABOUT MISS HAYAMA...

Y-YOU—!!

...FOR THE LORD TO WATCH OVER MISS HAYAMA.

PROFESSOR, PLEASE PRAY WITH ME...

BUT SHE'S STILL UNCONSCIOUS, HOVERING BETWEEN LIFE AND DEATH...

NO. NOT AT THE MOMENT.

AND... IS SHE DEAD?

NO... THAT'S NOT WHAT I MEANT.

ARE YOU SAYING IT'S *MY* FAULT THAT HAYAMA TRIED TO KILL HERSELF?!

WHY SHOULD I PRAY?!

GET OUT...

AAH! DAMMIT!

GET OUT!

IF YOU CAN'T DO THAT, THEN GET OUT.

HMPH. PRAYER! YOU'RE A PREACHER. GET RID OF *THIS!*

IT COULDN'T BE ANYONE ELSE.

FATHER, *IT* IS IN FACT HAYAMA.

WHAT?

...SUMIKO HAYAMA...

Y-YOU SICKEN ME...

THAT HAYAMA... HOW FAR WILL SHE GO TO RIDICULE ME?!

BUT I'VE NO DOUBT THAT HAYAMA'S MIND SLIPPED OUT OF HER BODY AND CAME TO ME HERE.

I DO NOT WISH TO BELIEVE ANYTHING UNSCIENTIFIC.

IT APPEARED AT THE SAME TIME AS HER SUICIDE ATTEMPT.

I SUPPOSE YOU *CAN* ACCEPT THE LOVE OF ALL HUMANITY?

NO, YOU COULD NEVER UNDERSTAND. YOU AND YOUR LOVE...

YOU UNDERSTAND, DON'T YOU? HOW DISGUSTING IT IS FOR AN UNDESIRED PARTNER TO COME CLOSE, BE SWEET TO YOU, CARESS YOU IN THE MOST LEWD WAYS...

FATHER, I SUPPOSE YOU WOULD REPROACH ME. BUT A THING THAT IS HATEFUL IS SIMPLY HATEFUL!

I *DO* UNDERSTAND.

N-NO...

AND I TOO BECAME SUCH A TARGET ONCE.

IN MY NATIVE LAND, MEN OF THE CLOTH OCCASIONALLY BECOME TARGETS FOR LOVE.

I'VE ALSO HAD THIS EXPERIENCE.

I UNDERSTAND, PROFESSOR KIRIDA.

SHE LIVED IN CONSTANT FEAR OF ABANDONMENT.

IT WAS A SERIOUS WOMAN WHO DEVOTEDLY ATTENDED CHURCH REGULARLY. SHE SOUGHT ABSTINENCE. BUT IN TRUTH, A POWERFUL DEPENDENCE CONTROLLED HER SPIRIT.

AND HER FEELINGS CAME TO BE SOMETHING IMMORAL.

...BUT SHE WOULD NOT HEAR A WORD OF IT.

I LECTURED HER ON SELF-RELIANCE AND LOVE OF MAN...

HER FAITH EVENTUALLY DEVELOPED INTO A STRONG DEPENDENCE ON ME.

OF COURSE, FROM THE POSITION OF PASTOR...

BUT NOW I FEEL THAT I SHOULD HAVE BEEN MORE COMPASSIONATE WITH HER. I REGRET IT.

IT'S UNCOMFORTABLE TO REMEMBER IT.

SHE BEGAN TO AMBUSH ME AFTER EVENING PRAYERS.

SHE DID WHATEVER SHE COULD TO ATTRACT MY ATTENTION. YES, WHATEVER SHE COULD...

LOVE! HA HA HA!

PLEASE DO NOT MAKE ME LAUGH, SIR!

YOU SAY I SHOULD SHOW COMPASSION?! HOW?! SHOULD I HAVE ACCEPTED HAYAMA'S LOVE, LOVED HER BACK?!

PROFESSOR KIRIDA, IT'S THE SAME FOR YOU, WITH A POSITION SUCH AS YOURS.

NGH NGH NGH NGH NGH

AAAAAH!

SHF SHF

HAAAH

FWOOO

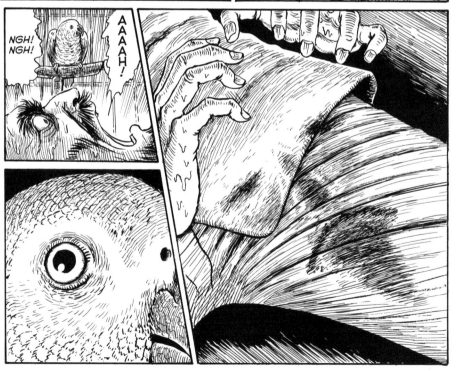

209

SOME-
THING IS
TOUCHING
THE PRO-
FESSOR...

HERE...
INDEED...
THERE'S
SOMETHING
HERE...

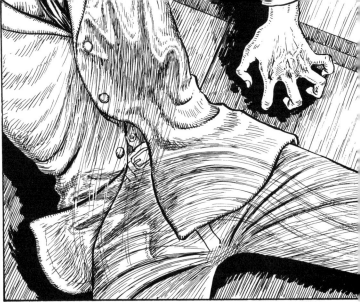

OHHHH!

OHHHH!

EEEEEE!

AAAAH!

AAAAAAH!!

OHHHHHHH!!

...MAYBE ONLY THE PARROT COULD SEE THE PASSION OF THE FURIOUS WOMAN.

IF THIS STORY IS TRUE...

THE PRIEST LEFT THIS WORLD WITHOUT TELLING ANYONE ELSE ABOUT ENGAI KIRIDA'S DEATH.

AFTER SHE REGAINED CONSCIOUSNESS, SUMIKO HAYAMA WROTE THE STORY FATHER MURCHISON TOLD HER IN HER JOURNAL.

FWOO

...I FELT A HOT BREATH JUST NOW...

I... I'M SURE...

AH ?!

214

THE ENIGMA OF AMIGARA FAULT

NOT TOO LONG AGO, THERE WAS A GREAT EARTHQUAKE IN H PREFECTURE.

SEVERAL TOWNS AND VILLAGES WERE DEVASTATED.

THE FAULT WAS DEEP AND SEVERAL KILO-METERS LONG.

FOLLOWING THE EARTHQUAKE, A LARGE FAULT WAS DISCOVERED NEAR THE EPICENTER...

...THE BEGINNING OF THIS STRANGE INCIDENT.

THIS SIG-NALED ...

...ON THE NORTH SLOPE OF THE AMIGARA MOUNTAIN.

BUT I
STILL
HAVEN'T
SEEN
ANY-
THING
...

AM I
STILL ON
AMIGARA
MOUNTAIN?
I'VE BEEN
CLIMBING
FOR A
WHILE...

HMM
...

217

HEY! HELLO OVER THERE!

I THOUGHT THAT MUST BE WHY YOU CAME HERE — I MEAN NO OFFENSE — A WOMAN HIKER, ALL ALONE.

SO ARE YOU LOOKING FOR THE FAULT, TOO?

I'M YOSHIDA.

I'M OWAKI... WHAT'S YOUR NAME?

REALLY? IT WAS THE SAME WITH ME.

IT'S A REAL MYSTERY, ISN'T IT?

I SAW IT ALL ON TV. IT KIND OF MADE ME RESTLESS...

...WHEN I SAW IT I KNEW I HAD TO GO.

DID YOU HEAR VOICES?

HM?

IT'S GOT THE ENTIRE COUNTRY— NO THE ENTIRE WORLD, TRANSFIXED.

IT'S A WONDER OF NATURE...

MUTTER

MUTTER

IT MUST BE THE OTHERS WHO'VE COME HERE.

LET'S HEAD THAT WAY! I'M SURE WE'RE NEAR THE FAULT.

!

HAAH HAAH...

IT'S JUST LIKE HOW IT WAS ON TV...

...BUT A LOT MORE POWERFUL.

IT MAKES YOU WONDER, HOW COULD IT HAPPEN...

SO BEFORE THE QUAKE, THEY WERE UNDERGROUND.

THOUSANDS OF HUMAN-SHAPED HOLES...

THEY'RE CHECKING OUT THE HOLES.

LOOK AT THAT... MAYBE THEY'RE UNIVERSITY RESEARCHERS.

...FOUND IN THE FAULT EXPOSED BY THE EARTHQUAKE.

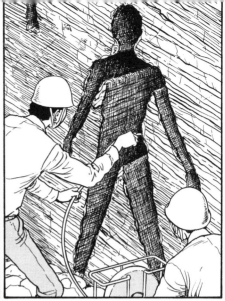

IN ANY CASE...

HMM... IT SEEMS TO CURVE OFF INSIDE THE MOUNTAIN.

HOW DEEP DO YOU THINK IT GOES, PROFESSOR?

EVEN THIS 30-METER FIBER SCOPE CAN'T FIND THE END.

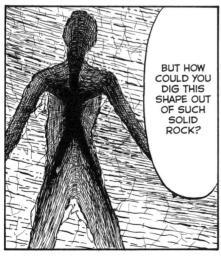

BUT HOW COULD YOU DIG THIS SHAPE OUT OF SUCH SOLID ROCK?

IT'S IMPOSSIBLE THAT THIS COULD BE A NATURAL FORMATION.

SOMEONE MUST HAVE DUG THEM OUT FROM INSIDE.

222

I THINK THE ENTRANCE WAS SEALED UP WITH THE ACCUMULATION OF SOIL OVER THE YEARS...

...THE SAME FORCES THAT COVERED UP THESE HOLES.

BESIDES, WOULDN'T THERE BE A TRACE OF AN ENTRANCE OF SOME KIND?

NO ONE'S FOUND ANYTHING LIKE THAT.

THEN THESE HOLES MUST BE ANCIENT. BUT IF THAT'S THE CASE, WHO HAD THE TECHNOLOGY TO MAKE THEM?

AND WHAT PURPOSE DID THEY SERVE ...?

CAREFUL, YOSHIDA.

IT'S STEEP.

GLANCE

GLANCE

GLANCE

...

223

WHAT'D YOU SEE?

WHAT ...

I SAW IT ON TV.

YOU LOOK LIKE YOU'RE LOOKING FOR SOMETHING.

WHAT ARE YOU DOING?

SO I CAME HERE TO MAKE SURE ABOUT IT.

I ONLY CAUGHT A GLIMPSE OF IT ON TV.

I KNOW I SAW IT... ONE OF THESE HOLES.

I...I SAW IT ON TV.

... WAS MY SHAPE.

IT...

SO WHAT'S SO SPECIAL ABOUT THIS HOLE?

BUT NOW THAT I'M HERE, THERE ARE SO MANY HOLES I HAVE NO IDEA WHERE IT IS...

IT WAS *BASED* ON ME. I SWEAR, I'M SERIOUS!

...THAT HOLE WAS MY SILHOU-ETTE!

IT WAS IDENTI-CAL... NO, IT WENT BEYOND THAT...

WHAT?

HOW COULD THEY HAVE BASED IT ON YOU? THAT'S KIND OF EGOTIS-TICAL, DON'T YOU THINK?

THESE HOLES ARE SUPPOSED TO BE THOUSANDS OF YEARS OLD.

WHAT ARE YOU SAYING?

SO, YOU TOO...

I KNEW IT WAS ME. IT DOESN'T HAVE TO MAKE SENSE!

I'M NOT JOKING! DON'T MAKE FUN OF ME!

MY NAME'S NAKAGAKI.

AND YOU'RE...

...I CAME HERE TO LOOK FOR MY HOLE.

I FELT THE SAME WAY. AFTER I SAW IT ON TV...

...I FINALLY FOUND MINE.

AND...

WE'RE ALL LOOKING FOR OUR HOLES.

IT'S AN UNBELIEVABLE PHENOMENON. MOST OF US CAME HERE FOR THE EXACT SAME REASON.

HMM? YOU LOOK LIKE YOU DON'T BELIEVE ME.

...SEE HOW PERFECTLY I FIT?

THIS IS IT...

WELL, I DON'T BLAME YOU.

I'LL PROVE THIS IS MY HOLE RIGHT NOW.

JUST WATCH ME!

HEY... WHAT?! HEY...

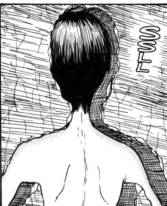
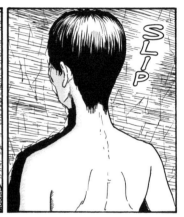

OH MY GOD! HEY! COME BACK!

HEY!

THAT'S DANGEROUS!!

HEY, COME BACK HERE!!

...

MUTTER MUTTER

I DON'T KNOW IF HE CAN GET OUT!

I CAN'T BELIEVE IT. THIS GUY JUST WENT INTO THE HOLE!

HMM...HE MUST BE FARTHER DOWN...

...BUT THERE'S NO TRACE OF HIM WITHIN 30 METERS!!

PROFESSOR, WE'VE BEEN SEARCHING FOR HIM WITH THE FIBER SCOPE...

A CROWD GATHERED AROUND THE HOLE, SHOUTING, BUT NAKAGAKI DID NOT COME OUT.

LET'S CALL IN THE RESCUE SQUAD!!

THIS IS AN EMERGENCY!

WE HAVE TO DO SOMETHING!

ONE OF THEIR MEMBERS, 5'2" TALL, IS TRYING TO GO IN...

A RESCUE SQUAD IS ATTEMPTING TO ENTER THE HOLE.

OVER THREE HOURS HAVE ELAPSED SINCE HIS DISAPPEARANCE.

WE NOW HAVE THIS UPDATE ON THE MAN WHO DISAPPEARED INTO ONE OF THE MYSTERIOUS HOLES...

HE MUST HAVE BEEN CRAZY TO GO IN THERE!

THE RESCUE SQUAD MEMBER HAD TO RETREAT AFTER GOING NO MORE THAN FIVE METERS INTO THE HOLE...

NIGHT HAS FALLEN AND THERE'S NO SIGN OF THE MAN WHO WENT INTO THE HOLE.

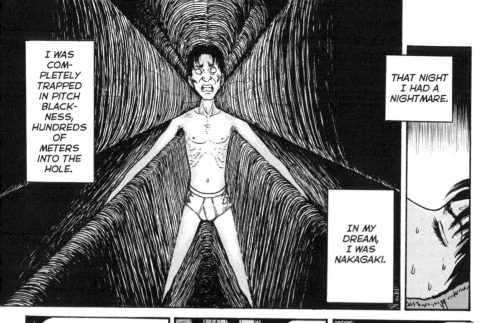

I WAS COMPLETELY TRAPPED IN PITCH BLACKNESS, HUNDREDS OF METERS INTO THE HOLE.

THAT NIGHT I HAD A NIGHTMARE.

IN MY DREAM, I WAS NAKAGAKI.

THE EARTHQUAKE. THE HOLE MUST HAVE BEEN DEFORMED BY THE EARTHQUAKE. SO I CAN'T MOVE...

I-I CAN'T MOVE...

I'M STUCK...

AGGH... GGH...

ANYONE! HELP ME!

S-SOMEONE!

...IT'S MORNING... IT WAS A NIGHTMARE...

HAAH HAAH...

AAGGH!

I'LL GO FIND OUT...

OR MAYBE HE GOT RESCUED...

IS HE STILL DOWN THERE, WRITHING NAKED IN THAT HOLE?

DO YOU KNOW WHAT HAPPENED TO NAKAGAKI?

YOU'RE UP ALREADY?

HE'S STILL GONE.

...

I FOUND MY HOLE.

I FOUND IT.

WHAT IS IT?

I NEED TO SHOW YOU SOME-THING.

NEVER MIND... OWAKI, CAN YOU COME WITH ME?

NO WONDER I COULDN'T FIND IT.

IT TURNED OUT IT WAS FARTHER DOWN AT THE FOOT OF THE FAULT.

WELL, IT DOES LOOK KIND OF LIKE YOU...

IT'S IDEN-TICAL TO ME.

THIS IS IT...

232

WHY ARE YOU SHAKING?

YOSHIDA, WHAT IS IT?

THIS IS MY TUNNEL... THEY DUG IT FOR ME...

I'M SCARED... I'M SO SCARED...

THIS IS MY TUNNEL!

NO...

IT JUST HAPPENS TO LOOK A LITTLE LIKE YOU!

IT'S JUST A COINCIDENCE!!

...I'LL BE TRAPPED IN THIS HOLE!

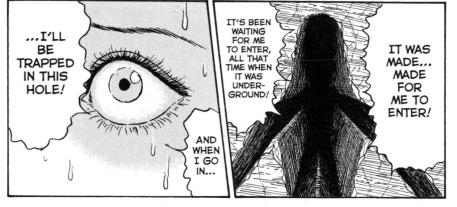

AND WHEN I GO IN...

IT'S BEEN WAITING FOR ME TO ENTER, ALL THAT TIME WHEN IT WAS UNDERGROUND!

IT WAS MADE... MADE FOR ME TO ENTER!

233

HEY...

...DISAPPEARED. HE HAS VANISHED WITHOUT A TRACE.

IT HAS BEEN A FULL DAY SINCE THE MAN WHO WALKED INTO THE HOLE...

HEY, WHAT ARE YOU DOING?! GET DOWN HERE BEFORE YOU HURT YOURSELF!!

WHAT'S THAT KID DOING?

LOOK OVER THERE!

IT WAS MADE FOR ME!

TH-THIS IS MY HOLE!

234

237

DON'T YOU HAVE TO GO BACK TO YOUR TENT?

...MY PARENTS DIDN'T CARE ABOUT ME... NEITHER DID MY FRIENDS...

I'VE ALWAYS BEEN ALONE... EVER SINCE I WAS A CHILD...

DON'T WORRY, I'M HERE WITH YOU.

I'M TOO SCARED TO BE ALONE.

NO...

REALLY?

YOU HAVE NOTHING TO WORRY ABOUT, THOUGH, NOW THAT I'M WITH YOU.

NOTHING COULD BE LONELIER THAN THAT HOLE.

DO YOU SEE, YOSHIDA? YOU'RE AFRAID OF THAT HOLE BECAUSE YOU'VE BEEN LONELY.

238

YES.

IT WAS ANOTHER TIME... I DON'T KNOW HOW LONG AGO.

I HAD COMMITTED A HORRIBLE CRIME, AND I WAS ABOUT TO BE PUNISHED.

SHNK

THAT NIGHT I HAD ANOTHER NIGHTMARE.

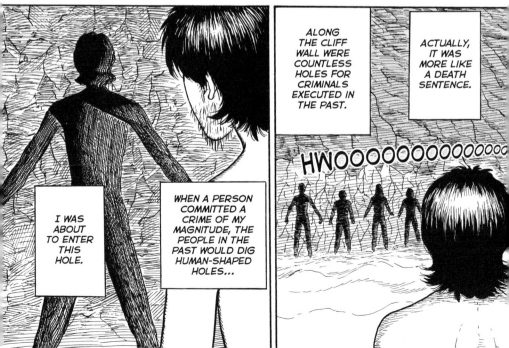

ALONG THE CLIFF WALL WERE COUNTLESS HOLES FOR CRIMINALS EXECUTED IN THE PAST.

ACTUALLY, IT WAS MORE LIKE A DEATH SENTENCE.

HWOOOOOOOOOOOOOOOOOOO

I WAS ABOUT TO ENTER THIS HOLE.

WHEN A PERSON COMMITTED A CRIME OF MY MAGNITUDE, THE PEOPLE IN THE PAST WOULD DIG HUMAN-SHAPED HOLES...

...I WAS SLIDING SLOWLY, SLOWLY DOWN... MOVING FORWARD WITH EACH MOVEMENT I MADE.

THE WALLS WERE CARVED IN A WAY THAT KEPT YOU FROM RETREAT-ING...

I HAD NO CHOICE BUT TO MOVE FORWARD, INTO THE CLAUSTRO-PHOBIA ALL AROUND.

I FELT THE COLD STONE ON ALL SIDES AROUND ME.

...STRETCHING IT UNTIL IT SHOULD HAVE TORN OFF.

TO MY HORROR, THE PART CORRE-SPONDING TO MY NECK ONLY GOT LONGER AND LONGER...

UNHH... UNHH ...!!

URR...

I FELT A TUG ON MY NECK.

AND WITH TIME ...

GYAAGHH!

SOME-ONE! ANY-ONE! HELP ME!

THE HOLE STRETCHED OUT INTO SEVERAL DIRECTIONS AT ONCE...!

NO...NOT JUST MY NECK... MY ARMS, LEGS AND TORSO...

HUH?!

ANOTHER NIGHT- MARE...

GASP... GASP...

AAAGH!

WHERE DID SHE GO?

N- NO...

SHE CAN'T HAVE GONE FAR IN THE DARK.

SHE TOOK THEM OUT!

THE ROCKS...

SHE WENT IN THE HOLE!!

AH...?!

...

COME BACK!!

HEY YOSHIDA!

WHY...

WHY'D YOU DO IT?!

DAMMIT...WHY...

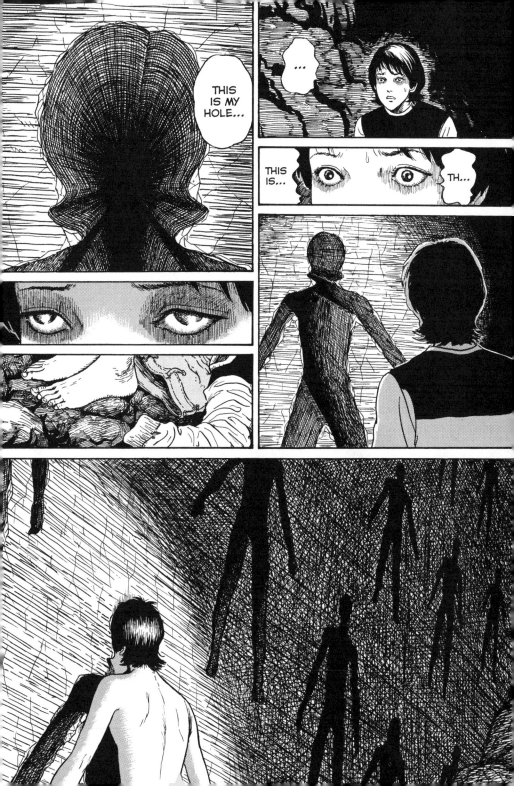

JUST AS THAT CLIMBER INFORMED US.

PROFESSOR... HERE IT IS!

SO THERE WAS A FAULT ON THE OTHER SIDE OF THE MOUNTAIN!!

SEVERAL MONTHS LATER...

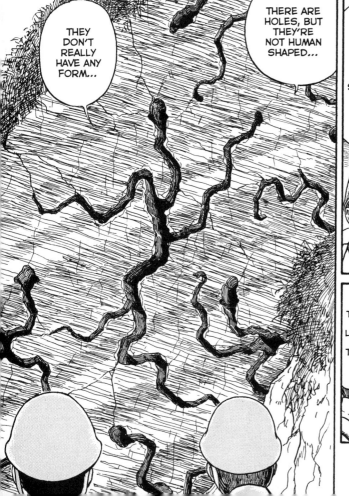

THEY DON'T REALLY HAVE ANY FORM...

THERE ARE HOLES, BUT THEY'RE NOT HUMAN SHAPED...

BUT UNLIKE THE ONE ON THE OTHER SIDE, THIS ONE'S QUITE SMALL.

HMM... I'M SURE THIS WAS FORMED BY THE EARTH-QUAKE AS WELL.

TAKE A LOOK AT THIS!

AHA!

THE SAD TALE OF THE PRINCIPAL POST

NGH ...

LOOKS LIKE I'M BEING CRUSHED BY THE POST...

D-DEAR... WHAT IN THE WORLD HAPPENED ?!

N-NO... WAIT...

THIS IS TERRIBLE... I'LL CALL THE CARPENTER!!

NGH... IT'S A LONG STORY...

B-BUT HOW?! HOW DID YOU GET UNDER THERE? THE WEIGHT OF THE WHOLE HOUSE IS ON TOP OF YOU!

THEN... WHAT ARE YOU SAYING WE SHOULD DO?!

IF YOU MOVE IT JUST TO RESCUE ME, THE ENTIRE HOUSE MIGHT FALL OVER.

I MEAN, WHAT A SHAME! OUR BRAND-NEW HOUSE !

TH-THIS LOOKS LIKE THE PRINCIPAL POST...

AS HIS WIFE, DAUGHTER AND FRIENDS WATCHED OVER HIM, HE PASSED AWAY LATER THAT EVENING.

I'M NOT GOING TO MAKE IT. I'LL DIE SUPPORTING THIS HOUSE.

W-WHAT?!

LEAVE ME HERE...

DEAR...

DADDY, NO!

...AND NOW NO ONE WILL EVER KNOW HOW HE ENDED UP GETTING UNDERNEATH IT.

HE STILL REMAINS UNDER THE PRINCIPAL POST...

BEEN ABOUT NINE MONTHS SINCE THE MADAME PASSED. QUITE SOMETHING HOW IT GREW IN THE BELLY OF HER CORPSE.

NOW THIS IS A SURPRISE... I'VE HEARD TALK OF THINGS LIKE THIS, BUT IT REALLY DOES HAPPEN.

THIS WOULD BE YOUR CHILD THEN?

YOUNG SIR.

SOMEONE MUST HAVE ABANDONED THE BABY IN THE GRAVE!

THIS IS IMPOS- SIBLE!

THAT'S RIDICU- LOUS...

TH—

IMPOSSIBLE... IM—

SEE? THE CORD'S STILL ATTACHED.

NO, THIS CHILD IS LEGITIMATE.

THEY ONLY JUST HAD A BABY OF THEIR OWN.

BUT WAIT A SECOND. THE YOUNG MASTER TOOK HIS MISTRESS AS HIS NEW WIFE.

IS THIS REALLY A HAPPY EVENT THEN, I WONDER?

THAT'S RIGHT. A KEEPSAKE FROM YOUR LATE WIFE.

AT ANY RATE, IT'S TO BE CELEBRATED, SIR...

WAAAH

WAAAH

APPEARANCES WENT OUT THE WINDOW WHEN TOYOJI TOOK HIS MISTRESS AS HIS WIFE.

BUT IT IS INDEED TOYOJI'S CHILD. WE MUST RAISE IT FOR APPEARANCES, IF NOTHING ELSE.

OH, IT'S SO DISTURBING. A BABY BORN OF A DEAD WOMAN...

WAAAH

WAAAH

I BARELY HAVE ENOUGH MILK FOR SHINNOSUKE!

WHAT ON EARTH DO YOU WANT? I'M NOT RAISING THAT CHILD!

I'LL HAVE THE MAID O-TANE TAKE CARE OF HIM.

WELL, I'LL GET A NURSE FOR THE CHILD. YOU NEEDN'T WORRY, O-MITSU.

YOU CAN'T BE SERIOUS.

NURSING THE BABY OF YOUR FIRST WIFE — AND BORN OF A CORPSE!

SO THEN WHY...?

BUT THE DEAD O-SUZU COULDN'T HAVE CHILDREN TO START WITH.

GAH

GAH

GOO

GOO

ISN'T YOUR MISTRESS IN THE FAMILY WAY?

DARLING.

THE PREVIOUS YEAR...

DO YOU INTEND TO MAKE THE CHILD YOUR HEIR?

YOU'VE GOT SOME NERVE JUST BECAUSE I CAN'T HAVE CHILDREN.

W-WHAT ARE YOU TALKING ABOUT, O-SUZU?

I KNOW EVERY-THING.

O-SUZU, HOW DO YOU...?

258

259

HEY.

SO? YOU'D DO IT IF YOU LOVED ME.

AND NO ONE CAN TELL THAT IT WAS POISON.

HE SAYS WHEN YOU ADMINISTER THIS POISON, THE PERSON GETS WEAKER AND WEAKER AND THEN DIES.

I KNOW SOMEONE WITH A POISON IMPORTED FROM EUROPE.

THUD

AH! MADAME!!

Y- YES...

I JUST TIRE SO EASILY OF LATE.

MADAME? ARE YOU FEELING POORLY?

A MONTH LATER...

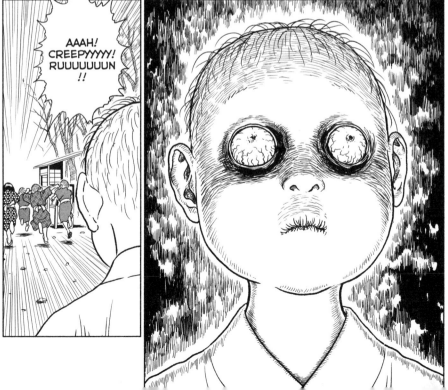

AAAH!
CREEPYYYYY!
RUUUUUUUN
!!

YOU'RE NOT DISCIPLINING HIM PROPERLY.

IT'S BECAUSE OF MANJURO THAT SHIN-NOSUKE'S SO TIMID.

I-I'M TERRIBLY SORRY.

WHO SAID YOU COULD UNTIE HIM?!

MADAME, I BEG YOUR FORGIVE-NESS...

COME!! I'LL DISCIPLINE YOU FIRST!

AH!

AAH, DISGUSTING! IF MY FATHER-IN-LAW DIDN'T GO ON AND ON ABOUT APPEARANCES, I WOULD HAVE CHASED YOU TWO OUT A LONG TIME AGO!!

SPLASH

HE WAS BORN FROM A CORPSE!!

SLAP

EEE!!

HIS VERY EXISTENCE IS HARMFUL!

MANJURO DOESN'T MEAN ANY HARM.

MADAME, I BEG YOU...

MADAME! I BEG YOU!

EEAH! OW!!

...HAVE A CHILD WITH YOUR WIFE WHEN SHE WAS DYING!

THIS IS ALL YOUR FAULT. TO THINK YOU WOULD TRY TO...

HEY, O-MITSU...

THAT'S ENOUGH ALREADY...

YOU'RE STILL DOING THIS?

266

ABOUT THE AUTHOR

Junji Ito made his professional manga debut in 1987 and since then has gone on to be recognized as one of the greatest contemporary artists working in the horror genre. His titles include *Tomie* and *Uzumaki*, which have been adapted into live-action films; *Gyo*, which was adapted into an animated film; and his short story collections *Fragments of Horror*, *Frankenstein*, *Shiver* and *Smashed*, all of which are available from VIZ Media.

Ito's influences include classic horror manga artists Kazuo Umezz and Hideshi Hino, as well as authors Yasutaka Tsutsui and H.P. Lovecraft.

His collection *Frankenstein* won the 2019 Eisner Award in the "Best Adaptation from Another Medium" category and his latest long-form manga, *No Longer Human*, has received critical acclaim.

VENUS IN THE BLIND SPOT

Story & Art by Junji Ito

ITO JUNJI TANPENSHU BEST OF BEST
by Junji ITO
© 2019 JI Inc.
All rights reserved.
Original Japanese edition published by SHOGAKUKAN.
English translation rights in the United States of America, Canada, the United
Kingdom, Ireland, Australia and New Zealand arranged with SHOGAKUKAN.

Original Cover Design / Keisuke MINOHARA

Translation for "The Enigma of Amigara Fault" and
"The Sad Tale of the Principal Post" / YUJI ONIKI

All Other Translation & Adaptation / JOCELYNE ALLEN

Touch-Up Art & Lettering / ERIC ERBES

Cover & Graphic Design / ADAM GRANO

Editor / MASUMI WASHINGTON

Printed in the U.S.A.

Published by VIZ Media, LLC
P.O. Box 77010
San Francisco, CA 94107

10 9 8 7 6 5 4 3 2 1
First printing, August 2020

viz.com   vizsignature.com